Richard Harvey is a psychotherapist and spiritual teacher. He is the founder of Sacred Attention Therapy, a radical, innovative, psycho-spiritual approach to human growth and development. For nearly forty years he has helped thousands of people find greater peace and fulfillment through his workshops, trainings, and private practice. He lives and works in the Sierra Nevada Mountains in Andalucía, Spain.

Visit him online at www.therapyandspirituality.com and www.centerforhumanawakening.com

To the children of the future… and to my lifelong friend
Ian "Lou" Lucraft

Richard Harvey

YOUR SACRED CALLING:
AWAKENING THE SOUL TO A SPIRITUAL LIFE IN THE 21ST CENTURY

AUSTIN MACAULEY
PUBLISHERS LTD.

Copyright © Richard Harvey (2017)

The right of Richard Harvey to be identified as author of this work has been asserted by him in accordance with section 77 and 78 of the Copyright, Designs and Patents Act 1988.

All rights reserved. No part of this publication may be reproduced, stored in a retrieval system, or transmitted in any form or by any means, electronic, mechanical, photocopying, recording, or otherwise, without the prior permission of the publishers.

Any person who commits any unauthorized act in relation to this publication may be liable to criminal prosecution and civil claims for damages.

A CIP catalogue record for this title is available from the British Library.

ISBN 9781786129031 (Paperback)
ISBN 9781786129048 (Hardback)
ISBN 9781786129055 (E-Book)
www.austinmacauley.com

First Published (2017)
Austin Macauley Publishers Ltd.
25 Canada Square
Canary Wharf
London
E14 5LQ

Unending gratitude to the masters, the great adepts, and avatars through whose presence the Golden Thread was wound, the music played, and the flame tended through their Sacred Calling. To all those friends, clients, students, and acquaintances who provided the material for the illustrative anecdotes. To Robert Meagher for infallible editing, support, and inspiration. To my wife Nicky for holding it all together and loving me in spite of my flaws. To all at Austin Macauley, in particular Vinh Tran and the production team, thank you.

When people come to know their real nature, their influence, however subtle, will prevail and the world's emotional atmosphere will sweeten up. A new golden age may come and last for a time and succumb to its own perfection. For ebb begins when the tide is at its highest.

Sri Nisargadatta Maharaj

Contents

PROLOGUE ....

    LOVE AND LIFE: CUSTODIANS OF THE FUTURE............................... 17
    WHAT THIS BOOK DOES 19
    ENCOURAGEMENT AND GUIDELINES FOR SPIRITUAL PRACTICE 21
    WHERE WE ARE GOING 23

INTRODUCTION ....

    A GLASS OF WATER 25
    HUMANITY AT A CROSSROADS.. 28
    THE ANCIENT THREAD OF AUTHENTICITY 31
    A TORNADO OF CHANGE: ONE DIVINE BODY 37
    IN SUMMARY 39

PART 1: THE MODERN CONTEXT ....

1. A LITTLE BACKGROUND ....

    SAVIORS AND CHARLATANS.. 44
    SELF-HELP GURUS AND DO-IT-YOURSELF SPIRITUAL TEACHING 46
    IN SUMMARY 49

2. SUFFERING IN A DARK TIME: THE AGE OF INDIVIDUALISM

    A PRICELESS FRESCO 51
    THE SHADOW AND THE ECLIPSE... 53
    THE MAGNIFICENT HUMAN... 56
    THE AGELESS PARADIGM... 58
    EXPERIENCES OF THE SACRED 63
    IN SUMMARY 68

PART 2: SOME GENTLE, COMPASSIONATE DEMOLITION ....

3. SLAUGHTERING SACRED COWS, SMASHING FALSE IDOLS..

The Dynamic Interplay of Creation 72
Death and Resurrection 74
Power and Fame... 76
Bringing It All Back Home 78
Spurious Themes of Contemporary "Spirituality" (and Psychology) 80
Transformation, Time, and Modern Nonsense..................... 98
In Summary 106

4. THE TEN TENETS (OR THE HERETICAL CREED)....................

Decimation and Tithing 109
In Summary 113

5. SPIRITUAL CELEBRITY OR SPIRITUAL TEACHER, AND THE CULT OF THE INDIVIDUAL ....

Specialness and the Spiritual Celebrity.............................. 114
An Individual Path to Spiritual Enlightenment? 117
Spirituality is Not Entertainment 121
Personality is Merely an Impression 126
In Summary 128

6. THE FORM OF NOTHINGNESS ....

The Advaita Answer—the Distress of Non-Duality 131
The Advaita Question—the Peerlessness of Non-Duality ... 134
In Summary 136

PART 3: PUTTING IT BACK TOGETHER AGAIN IN A NEW FORM ....

7. FIRST, FIX THE CAR—THEN, START THE JOURNEY ....

WHEN SHOULD I BEGIN INNER WORK? 139
THE INNER EYE 142
STAGES OF HEALING. MATURATION, AND *SADHANA* (WITH REFERENCE TO MASLOW AND JUNG) 157
THE THREE WORLDS: THE GREY, BRIGHT, AND BRILLIANT WORLDS 162
WHAT, IF ANYTHING, IS *ABSOLUTELY* REAL? 168
THE THREE "DS" —DISSATISFACTION, DISILLUSIONMENT, AND DESPAIR 171
GROUNDED SPIRITUALITY (AND THE LIFE OF COMPASSION) 174
THE FABLE OF THE FLOWER AND THE SUN 177
IN SUMMARY 179

8. THE LAST SPOT ON THE SUN: THE GUIDE MEETS THE SEEKER ....

THE RETURN OF THE WHOLE ENCHILADA 181
THE GOLDEN HALLS OF THE STARS 184
FEAR AND DESIRE CREATE ILLUSION 187
MEDITATION: THE JOY OF YOUR ETERNAL STATE 189
IN SUMMARY 192

9. A RESIDENT IN THE DIVINE REALMS: NUMINOUS "EXPERIENCES" ....

THE TRAVEL BROCHURE AND THE HOLIDAY 197
SACRED CALLING 201
AWAKENING IN THIS LIFETIME: INITIATORY EXPERIENCES 203
INTO LIFE'S MYSTERIES 215
IN SUMMARY 216

PART 4: REVOLUTION: THAT GLIMMER COULD BE THE DAWN LIGHT!

10. THE OCEAN OF CONSCIOUSNESS—THE FORM OF FORMLESSNESS

- TEACHER OR TEACHING? 221
- THE APPARENT DIFFERENCE BETWEEN SPIRITUAL TEACHINGS 222
- THE DYNAMICS OF TRUTH 225
- FIVE STAGES OF TRUTH 227
- IN SUMMARY 232

11. SINCERE THIRD-STAGE PRACTICE

- THE GATES OF THE SUN 234
- FOUR SIGNS THAT YOU HAVE FOUND YOUR SPIRITUAL TEACHER ... 235
- THE HEART OF ALL-EMBRACING LOVE 241
- RENUNCIATION OR CELEBRATION? 242
- THE THREE LEVELS OF LOSS 245
- BEHIND THE VEILS 250
- A LETTER TO EMMA 252
- IN SUMMARY 265

PART 5: A CRITICAL NEW INNOVATIVE PARADIGM

12. THE SPIRITUAL REVOLUTION: ASCENDING INTO THE HEART

- THE COMMITMENT TO LIVE FROM THE HEART 269
- HOW TO BE HAPPY: THE THREE PRINCIPLES OF HAPPINESS 272
- COMMUNITY—WHEN THE SOUL OF THE WORLD DANCES 277
- THE FOUNDATIONS OF SPIRITUAL LIFE 283
- IN SUMMARY 287

13. THE *PHILOZOVO*: THE CALL OF THE DIVINE

- DEFINING THE PHILOZOVO 289
- THE PASSIONATE RESPONSE TO THE CALL OF THE DIVINE 293
- LOOK UP AND SEE THAT EVERYTHING IS THE DIVINE 296
- IN SUMMARY 299

14. HOW ETERNITY LOOKS IN TIME

- COLLECTIVE RESISTANCE 301
- THE FREE INDIVIDUAL 303
- RIVER OF COMPASSION: WATERS OF LIFE 313

EPILOGUE

- THE END OF OUR JOURNEY TOGETHER 315
- REMEMBERING THAT WE ARE DIVINE 316
- GUIDANCE FOR THE SACRED JOURNEY 318
- THE FUTURE: A VISION OF THE NEW WORLD 319

APPENDICES

- THE SACRED SPACE MEDITATION 330
- THE CONSCIOUSNESS EXERCISE: A SPIRITUAL METHOD FOR THE 21ST CENTURY 333

BIBLIOGRAPHY 338

INDEX 340

PROLOGUE

Love and Life: Custodians of the Future

The topics in this book are vital for our survival, as a species, as evolving humanity. Not only is the material in this book vital for our physical survival, but also for the continuance and remembrance of happiness, relationship, soulfulness, passion, and connection.

Even if the crisis of the 21st century turns out not to be a material, physical crisis of human destruction, the crisis precipitated by the final annihilation of the authentic means to spiritual liberation will be every bit as disastrous. For if we lose the means to awakening to freedom, emotional and spiritual liberation, and self-realization—and especially if the loss is through our ignorance and abandonment—we forfeit the way to our essence, to our truth. If we sacrifice love, wisdom, peace, bliss, and compassion, we will have betrayed our deepest, most essential self.

The principles and the content contained here are endangered species. They may not live much longer unless we cultivate, learn, and remind ourselves of our inner vision, our intuition, and how we embody truth as essence in our souls. The fabric of the future may be rent in a way that can never be mended, unless we practice learning the wisdom that rekindles the fire of authentic spiritual insight. The way to the ground of being, to the field of consciousness, and the illimitable freedom that is our birthright and the only savior for humanity may be lost forever, unless we revive, connect, and expand our knowledge and ourselves all the way and beyond to a robust and real spiritual vision.

In the 21st century, it is crucial that we maintain a spiritual view that is: authentic, deep, and doesn't bow to populism or over-concern to make spirituality palatable, that retains its integrity, genuineness, and mystery, that can genuinely lead us to personal freedom and spiritual liberation. Reading this book, you too become a custodian of the future… and of the sacred, someone on whom sanity, love, and wisdom rely for their sustenance, for their practice, and for their survival. And this survival is also the survival of humanity.

Surviving is not merely physical, financial, commercial, or even global. It is spiritual and arguably if the spiritual is effectively annihilated within us then we will be wise to ask whether we want to survive physically, tribally, energetically, and desperately in a world that has lost meaning, real experience, authenticity, depth, and caring. Would we want to live in a world no longer sacred or divine? As the poets and troubadours have eulogized for hundreds of years, I won't live in a world without love or wisdom or sacredness or the Divine… not because we choose not to (as some modern day songs express it in this age of materialism and individualism), but because we *cannot*. A world without love is a world without life. Love and life go together. Love and life are indistinguishable.

What This Book Does

In the pages ahead you will discover how to go about saving and preserving the sacred principles for leading a truly spiritual life, the way to emotional and spiritual freedom, and guard, protect, and treasure the sacred-spiritual truths in order to live from your heart.

This book does many things. First, it dismisses, refutes, and argues against popularly conceived ideas about spirituality. Arguing that the contemporary boom in "spiritual" interest among people today has led to a burgeoning outpouring of diluted, superficial, often sentimental ideas and understanding aimed at people who trust the authors, self-styled gurus, and "spiritual" spokespeople and know no better (sometimes both the authors and the readers!). Sincere people are therefore kept in the dark about real spirituality and what it means and religious and spiritual "secrets" are on the brink of being entirely buried in the avalanche of "thin" spiritual ideas with mass appeal.

Second, ideas like "the special time," the coming of the savior, and a new spiritual era, the acceptance and induction into spiritual practice, the relationship with the spiritual teacher, the awakening "experience," time and eternity, "the Shift" in consciousness, allegedly occurring worldwide, the latest enthusiasm for Advaita Vedanta teachings, and the ready availability of too much wisdom are all criticized intelligently and in an informed way here.

Third, you will find here innovative ideas—philosophy and practices—that are offered in heartfelt response to the critical challenge that I believe we face today: the three stages of awakening, the need to work psychologically in preparation for spiritual discipline, grounded spirituality, the middle stage of authenticity, the Three Worlds, heart-centeredness, the *Philozovo* (the call of the Divine), the relationship of eternity to time, the Free

Individual, as well as others, either innovative, new, or restated, in a relevant way for the modern era.

Finally, this book encourages and empowers you to create and refine your own sacred calling. Don't accept what I say. Don't accept what anyone says. If you find some of the ideas here please you, while others grate, use it to find your own way, your own awareness, and your own vision of the sacred. One thing you can be sure about: your own vision is the only one for you. Because the distinguishing mark of contemporary spirituality in the present era is the way of the individual, not the rejection of the individual. The human individual is intrinsically free!

At the end of each chapter is a short summary that reviews the contents of the chapter, followed by questions and exercises to help you assimilate the written content into a personal experience of insight and understanding. My intention is that, rather than merely read this book, you will relate to it interactively, that it will elicit real emotions, insights, and understanding in you, and provoke your creative response.

Encouragement and Guidelines for Spiritual Practice

In my previous book, *Your Essential Self*,[1] I included a comprehensive and I am told very helpful section on Inner Work Practice. I won't repeat that here but refer you to it for a host of useful pointers. Now, I will give some gentle reminders and a broad sweep of how to set up an effective spiritual practice.

You need to establish a habitual practice (because habits are hard to break and you need to be consistent). A regular time—not too short, but neither too long—is preferable and I would advise scheduling a daily time if you can. Giving to yourself when there are so many other demands on your time in the contemporary world is often difficult, so I encourage you to consider a three-way split of time in your life. It is: a third of your time for yourself, a third for others and in service, and a third in work, duties, responsibilities, and providing for yourself and your dependents.

Creating a space for yourself and your personal inner work, which is aesthetic and comfortable, gives an appropriate sense of honor and respect to your endeavor. This space should be big enough and adaptable enough to allow scope for personal expression—painting, drawing, reading, lying or standing, writing, meditating, breath work, dancing, and movement. Take the time to assemble materials like paper, pens, meditation aids, inspiring pictures, icons, music, and objects, perhaps a special coat, shirt, or jacket you like to wear, which gives you a special feeling, a sacred feeling.

True spiritual practice is happy. You should enjoy it. Your spiritual practice is something you long to return to

---

[1] Richard Harvey, *Your Essential Self: The Inner Journey to Authenticity and Spiritual Enlightenment*, Llewellyn Publications, 2013.

and potentially it is the—or one of the—happiest and most joyful times in your schedule. Spirituality is a celebration of life. Do not forget this celebratory aspect of spirituality which has been spoilt for many of us by organized religion or institutionalized spirituality. Lose this association now, because it has nothing to do with deep spiritual feeling and sacredness. Enjoy your life, enjoy your friends, enjoy your world, enjoy your family, and in the time you take to renew, to refresh, to deeply relax and commune with your inner self, your deepest core, and align yourself with Being itself. Allow joy to fill you... and spill over. Be Happy.

The central question is generally, "Do I deserve it?" And the right answer is "Absolutely! Yes!" If you find yourself wrestling with selfishness and self-centeredness, just remember the work you put into your personal and spiritual journey really does benefit all humanity, all beings, *all* of life. So *please*—no guilt, no shame, and no reluctance to tend your own garden, this garden of your soul. Absolutely no one else can do this; you do have to do it for yourself.

Where We Are Going

Before we embark on this journey it is helpful to have some idea about where we are going. This is how *Your Sacred Calling* is laid out—following the introduction, the book consists of five parts:

- *Part 1: The Modern Context* presents a statement of the contemporary human predicament from a psycho-spiritual perspective and diagnoses the present sacred-spiritual emergency.

- *Part 2: Some Gentle Compassionate Demolition* provides a schedule detailing what needs to be removed to maintain healthy growth or performing surgery with compassion.

- *Part 3: Putting it Back Together in a New Form* provides a healing program for full recovery.

- *Part 4. Revolution: That Glimmer Could be the Dawn Light!* details a spiritual revolution, which is much-needed to establish a new sacred-spiritual vision.

- *Part 5: A Critical New Innovative Paradigm* offers an original model of human awakening, heart-opening, and enlightenment for the modern era leading to a sacred-spiritual life existence.

Inherent in this book then is a problem-solving strategy consisting of observation and assessment, intervention and action, stabilizing in the changes, extending into collective transformation, and envisioning a new future.

This is the process we will be undertaking together; this is the terrain we will be crossing together.

Introduction

The endangered, disappearing secrets of sacred life, spirituality, divinity and reality[2] are essential for the future of humanity and the world. Saving and preserving the sacred truths and authentic spirituality for future generations is now an urgent priority.

---

[2]To distinguish between the relative and the absolute sense of words like, for example, Divine, Reality, and Truth, I use the uppercase to indicate the absolute. Unlike these words when rendered in the lowercase, and therefore indicating the relative, these terms have no opposites. However, a profusion of uppercase words tends to make for awkward reading, so I have reduced the uppercase as much as possible, so when divine, real, or true are used adjectivally they are *always* rendered in the lower case or when a phrase expressing some aspect of the absolute is qualified, for example, "the immortal truth," I have also retained the lower case.

A Glass of Water

As all good books should, let us begin with a story. God and a disciple called Aatish were walking one day along a beautiful promontory regarding the richness of Nature, the expansive vistas, and the wonderful sky. As evening drew closer and the daylight began to fade, God looked at Aatish and said, "Would you please go and fetch me a glass of water?" Aatish scrambled down the side of a steep valley perceiving the lights of a nearby village where there might be a well or a welcoming house. As he got closer, he found a little house with lights burning in the windows and he knocked on the door. A young woman answered. She had a beautiful face and the warmth and light from inside the house felt welcoming and inviting. She invited him in and the family was insistent that he come and warm himself by the fire and have some supper with them. Charmed and captivated by the ambience and the warm welcome, Aatish passed a pleasurable evening, hardly able to take his eyes off the beautiful young woman who had answered the door,

It was only right that he should stay the night, so a bed was made up for him in the spare room and he went to sleep with a wonderful deep contentment filling his very being. In the morning he was woken by the cock crowing and came downstairs to share a delicious breakfast with the family. He offered to help with the household chores and one thing led to another, so as the days passed, he found himself feeling happier and happier and falling deeper and deeper in love with the young daughter of the house.

In time he married the young woman, and they had children. He enjoyed his life as a husband and a father. He was happy and life was good. One day a great storm came to the village. Everything fell into chaos. The storm grew stronger and the deluge caused a mighty flood. The man and his wife tried desperately to save their house and their belongings but the flood overwhelmed them. He watched as his wife was borne away by the waters in spite of all his efforts to save her. He was unable to save his children from drowning and the village was completely destroyed.

As the waters abated he was washed up on the side of the valley. When he regained consciousness, he found himself lying on the wet mud, barely alive. Aatish staggered to his feet and slowly, slowly realized what had happened and all that he had lost. He began to wander aimlessly, his body wracked with sobbing, and his freezing muscles hardly able to keep him from falling over. He cried until he had no more tears inside. Then with his fists clenched and his face turned toward the sky, he screamed out to God to save him from his misery and despair.

A voice replied to him out of the early evening darkness, "Do you have my glass of water?" The man suddenly remembered... and he rose and joined God again.[3]

෴

This beautiful story comes from an ancient Hindu scripture. I have told it in my own way and I use it to make the point that we have forgotten the Divine. We have forgotten the Divine to the extent that the Divine and us may soon be lost to each other. Not truly lost because you cannot ultimately, entirely rid yourself of the immortal truth of life, but lost in the sense that the means and ability to live a sacred-spiritual life in the modern era may soon

---

[3] This story is based on the dream of Narada in Heinrich Zimmer's *Myths and Symbols in Indian Art and Civilization*, Princeton University Press 1972.

be as farfetched as, to use the Hebrew expression, *hair growing on the palm of your hand.*

We have become seduced by the young daughter's innocence and beauty, the welcome of the loving family, the warmth and comfort of the home, our desire for pleasure, for propagation of the species, for human love and relative happiness. Death has become unacceptable—how can death be acceptable when you love life? When you have children and when you love someone? When you love, you don't want the beloved to die. How could you even imagine or accept such a thing?

And yet death is part of life—an inevitable part, perhaps the only certainty. Family life, friendships, lovers, even children, home, and happiness will all die... and end, as everything in this relative world arises and abates like the waters in the flood in the story. Everything arises, swells up, and subsides. In this sense everything is merely temporary, however real and permanent and resilient your life and its contents appear to you now.

For centuries humankind has sought the answer to the question, "What, if anything, is deathless, immortal, more lasting than this life?" It is the intention of the sacred life to not only find the answer to that question, but to live into it... to not only find the answer in life, but to live so that life becomes the answer.

Humanity at a Crossroads

At the beginning of the 21st century, humanity faces a strange paradox. While information technology floods our homes and minds with more knowledge and ancient wisdom than we ever had access to before, we have become increasingly ignorant.

Nowhere is this truer than in the sphere of spirituality, arguably the enduring concern of human beings since time immemorial. The trouble with spiritual matters is that they are not, and never have been, directly translatable. This is why traditionally they are transmitted from teacher to pupil, from master to aspiring adept, directly through practice, ordeal, and inner transformation to attitude, orientation, and relationship. There is also the matter of timing. When the master sees that the disciple is ready, he transmits the teaching through esoteric ritual, clandestine means, in appropriate and effective ways.

Today we live in materialistic times. This is also an individualistic era. The god of substance, cause and effect, and concrete facts rules, as does the doctrine of the small self, egocentricity, self-service, and self-fulfillment. Subtlety defers to efficiency, profundity to superficiality, the mysterious to the apparent, the sacred to the secular… and cooperation to conflict.

Your Sacred Calling is a book that presents the spiritual truths in authentic form. Some of these truths may be new to you and ground-breaking. Others you may have heard before, but they will be presented in a context and with connections that almost certainly bring them to you with fresh clarity and meaning. Throughout, the spirit behind the words, the unspoken wisdom ritual of teaching, inculcating and drawing out in you the truth is intended to realign you to your own inner reality.

In the age of extreme individualism, the powerful ego-processes emanate from a mask of strong egoity. Our inner conviction is that we are ourselves separate and separative, identified as self and differentiated from others. You don't have to be a genius to see the difficulties that arise from these assumptions—prejudice, competitiveness, self-centeredness, bigotry, blindness, ignorance of the plight of others, selfishness, detachment from nature and from the world, delusions, greed, lack of real boundaries and therefore the inability to relate to ourselves and to one another.

The ecology of the human being produces an individual and collective impact. In particular, today the de-humanizing of humanity alongside the de-sacredizing of humanity serves to disconnect human beings from each other, from other life forms and nature, and from our interconnectedness with all life. How an individual manages, organizes, and responds to their emotions and thoughts connects them to the manifest world. Our relation to our inner world is reflected in the outer world. Our awareness of energy in our own bodies anatomically, energetically, psychologically, and spiritually is transferred onto nature as affect and consequence. Our ecological concern for our planet and our environment has been approached scientifically as if we were neutral scientists observing in white coats. But we ourselves are part of the planet, neither distinct from it, nor separate. Psycho-physically we are participatory, included and intimately involved. Thus today the ecological concern for the planet omits the prior conditions of *inner* ecology that ultimately define it.

With projection as rife as it is today, many of us have turned to therapy or counseling as a way to develop personal clarity and cultivate awareness. Disappointingly, the early promise of the personal growth movement or Human Potential Movement failed to deliver. Today the world of therapy and counseling is woefully backward. It is surely a long discussion and one that would depress us immensely: how the excitement in the latter part of the 20th century gave way to fear and a backsliding of ideals and uncompromising risk-taking, pioneering trail-blazing, elevated visions, and expanded aspirations. It was all largely justified, real, and authentic. But what is it about human beings that, starting with an uncompromising promise, we atrophy into a remedial state of reserve and caution? For there are no real obstacles to being authentic, only the anachronistic fear of personal survival. This becomes apparent when we follow an ancient thread.

The Ancient Thread of Authenticity

Over the past 38 years I have been developing and refining my therapeutic approach. I have called it Sacred Attention Therapy. The insights, breakthroughs, and understanding I have experienced through my work with thousands of people in my therapy practice and training workshops informs this book throughout. My work represents the development of an ancient thread.

Sacred attention points toward the need for a spiritual and sacred approach to healing in the present era. It incorporates the central feature of healing therapy which is giving attention, and attention is a function of love. It is concerned with soul or the essential inner person.

Sacred attention references the etymological meaning of therapy: "attending to soul." It refers us back thousands of years to when a shaman, a priest, a holy man, a *sadhu*, or an eastern spiritual adept sat down with a pupil for Upanishads (literally "sitting at the knee") and practiced listening with the whole self to the soul of the other. This is what therapy should always be, or at least always aim at, because this is the profound depth of reverence and healing which "two gathered together in My name" can bring about.

Authentic Spirituality Disappearing
So much therapy is concerned merely with getting better as soon as possible. But today we have a much more complex and profound challenge. It is the disappearance of sacredness, spiritual values and practices. Authentic spirituality is disappearing so rapidly that we can hardly keep track of it. I would liken it to our disappearing rain forests, animal species, and other eco-disasters. Except this inner ecology is something everyone can and should attend to. As human beings, we have the potential to self-reflect. Not all inner disturbances are negative in origin.

Sometimes it may be a sane response to an insane world! Self-reflection enables and empowers us to discern what is right and what is wrong, not in an outward moral sense, but what resonates with our soul.

We have entered the age of the individual. There is no escaping this. Yet it is our very egocentric individualism that we should understand and embrace to liberate ourselves. This constitutes an entirely new paradigm of life, human spirituality, and global community. In the past we have sought organizations, religion, and institutions to mediate our relationship with our soul and spirit and provide meaningful guidance. In the modern era a new paradigm of direct relationship with divinity involves the individual in a great act of self-responsibility. This self-responsibility begins with clearing out the past. It is what has been called therapy, counseling, or personal growth over the last four or five decades. We will need a new label soon to denote inner work performed not from a pathological basis, a sense of weakness, or an inability to cope, but rather a paradigm of wise counsel and spiritual, soulful mentoring.

Effective therapy and inner work depends on the sincere motivation and openness of the client-seeker, the skillfulness and empathy of the therapist-guide, the quality of the healing relationship, and the ability to focus keenly on the most crucial issues of the process which is a constantly changing perspective. The most important of these is the healing relationship.

Healing Relationship
The healing relationship is the vehicle for the journey of personal growth and inner development. Without the deep robust vehicle which the healing relationship provides, the healing, insights, understanding, and changes which take place in therapy, between sessions, in the client-seeker's unconscious world, and in the healing energetic

realms have no containment or safe space for integration and stabilization. Without the vehicle, we don't really get anywhere.

The healing relationship should be healing in itself, ideally. Acceptance, attending, empathy, presence, and authenticity are just some of the characteristics that make the relationship special and unique. And the question arises can these wonderful qualities of acceptance, presence, and authenticity be taught in therapy training?

There are two kinds of therapists: the trained ones and the born ones. Get a born one if you can; someone who has always had a deep sense of resonance with the healing world through intrinsic truth and innate ability, a natural healer. A trained therapist acquires skills and learns strategies. It's OK for short-term counseling and relatively superficial problems. But in what is known as depth psychotherapy, at least some sense of deep life calling in the therapist is required. It is perhaps the best of both worlds to be both a born *and* a trained therapist.

The Romantic Myth in the Kali Yuga

Couples who come to therapy are crucially important in the modern era because we are struggling to transcend a romantic myth that is about two thousand years old and anachronistic. We must either transcend this myth or transform it to create an entirely new mythology to guide humanity in the times ahead. These times will either be extraordinarily dark or they will be the sign that we are emerging at last from the end of the Kali Yuga.[4] These end times are crucial because depending on which way humanity goes, what decisions are made collectively, and what values are followed, almost anything can happen.

---

[4] The Sanskrit term for this present age of darkness, ignorance, and conflict.

David Mitchell's book, *Cloud Atlas,* gives a terrifying account of a future in which the moral degradation of a McDonald's-style religion takes over, where base instincts toward survival, purpose, and higher spiritual intuition congeal around an animalistic center and debase humanity through uniformity and conformity. This is truly terrifying. Worse, it is entirely possible. This would be one of the darkest scenarios imaginable.

Let us hope that the alternative is tenable. The spiritual revolution, the inner revolution in world consciousness must precede breaking through into the light. Couples work is crucial because it is intensified projection. Whoever and whatever you are projecting your inner material onto, no one and nothing is usually as intense and concentrated as the person who is your loved object. The bitterness, the resentment, and murderous rage that accompany the end of relationships with its drama and betrayal are only equaled in intensity by the possessive love, loyalty, and attraction to the beloved at the beginning. The whole thing is a charade, of course! Take away the disowning of our positive and negative traits, and you see before you another human being, someone who you may or may not be able to love.

The New Mythology
The first stage of awakening in Sacred Attention Therapy offers a way through to personal transformation and takes you past this deluded state. The other is not yourself! He or she is the other! Regardless of the baggage you heap onto the beloved, the beloved is free. He or she is a person in their own right. Now how do you love them? This is a different question to the sticky, murky business of transferring mother or father and childhood images of attraction and aversion onto other people and—here's the tragedy—often basing your entire life on this relationship

and generating children who grow up to do the same thing: darkness begets darkness begets darkness.

The first stage of relationship is working with the central truth that *relationships show you yourself*; they act as a mirror. The second stage of relationships is learning to separate and be an individual attending to your own destiny, capacity, and potential with the beloved at your side as a loving companion. The third stage of relationship is the spiritual stage of oneness with all things and the role of relationship in this third stage has yet to be envisioned. In a sense it's not really time yet, because we are such a long way off. The new myth will have to address this and point the way to a sane and compassionate way of creating relationships between human beings. Whether the model is monogamous, exclusive, possessive and based on dependence and insecurity remains to be seen. No one can invent the new mythology. It must emerge from the level of collective consciousness humanity reaches. Then the old mythology fades and a new one emerges and this new mythology reflects the conditions of truth that contemporary human beings have attained.

Restoring the Balance
What can therapy do for us in the modern world? Among other things, psychoanalysis and psychotherapy have been criticized for encouraging conformism, and promoting a hidden consensus underlying the apparent liberation of the individual. What can talking about our feelings and exploring the inner realms do for the individual and the world today?

Inner work and therapy are crucial to the survival of the world—not only the physical, material survival but to the quality and culture of the world. This is because we are in a period of evolution where the world has expanded and developed outwardly and left the inner world behind. Our inner selves must catch up and restore the balance.

Humanity today is underestimated, marginalized, disempowered, disabled, and confused. Over and above this we are witnessing the atrophying of the sacred. The ancient thread of authenticity, sacredness, and spirituality is being eroded by a process that began hundreds and hundreds of years ago. Organized religion, organized society, organized morality, and an almost complete ignoring of the inner world have brought us to a critical juncture in humanity's evolution.

Manifesting the Divine
Today we are living from the mind and the mind is falsehood—we *think* our lives. Its extrapolations are false and its effect is neurosis, worry, anxiety, fear, guilt, and hate. In our hearts, we know this to be true. We need to live naturally from our wisdom and our hearts, with openness and vulnerable strength, sacred awareness and spiritual devotion. If these qualities are practiced, life will shine and reflect truth, life will be authentic and loving, and human beings will become natural.

This cannot be done while we carry the crippling baggage of conditioning and corrupt culture and a life dominated by mind. This can only be done through the heart manifesting the divine soul—the Buddha-mind, Christ-consciousness, and beyond.

This is the heritage of humanity, the promise that destiny holds us to. This is the response of gratitude and devotion that the gift of life naturally provokes in us. To become and feel natural is where the transcendent process starts. The response to this impulse is to clear the inner realms and to purify inner processes of guilt, hate, fear, lack, and desire. The way is through forgiveness. The processes inherent in sacred attention bring about healing and liberation from the personality in a deep relationship of trust, openness, and reverence for life.

A Tornado of Change: One Divine Body

We have reached saturation point, a time in human history where we have arrived at a crossroads and choosing the way now is imperative. Our choosing needs to be guided by deep inner wisdom, the innate certainty in our own self-regulating and collective self-balancing, but not self-serving, state of interconnectedness and love and in the way of compassion toward our fellow men and women to serve and to further the course of human evolution from a solid enlightening basis of real spiritual understanding.

The half-truths, the flaky methods, and quasi-healing practitioners, and the random way of wisdom-searching of the New Age, mind-body-spirit, psycho-spiritual populist arena must be challenged. It is my hope that the world of incompetence and good intentions, but little deep true effect, will be dissolved in a respectful ceremony of gratitude and honor, rather than ignominy and derision. We have all learnt a lot, surely though now we can see that the signposts were simply signposts, the images merely the play of light, the dictums and encouragement fuel for the journey. We have been led and we have led others. We have given and received help. There is no balance book, no calculations to make, no debt to pay. Each of us has or will soon cross the great water and everything we did to reach the other side served us—good and bad examples, pleasure and pain, wounding and nourishing. Of the many stones and stone-throwers in the world who will cast the first one?

This book does not provide all the answers by any means. It does not present a fully fleshed-out philosophy. But it does deconstruct the totems of superstition, expose the fallacies, and challenge the taboos, which have adorned (and some would say concealed) the modern upsurge of interest in psychology and spirituality. We will also not only deconstruct in this book, but also begin to plant the seeds of new thought, expansive philosophy, and fresh psychology; to muster the impulse toward insight and understanding, stimulate the real development of the inner world, and encourage and inspire others to go beyond. Nothing is free of evaluative criticism, nothing is so revered or holy that it cannot be questioned and potentially discarded. For all that is real will remain when the tornado of change uproots all that we hold dear and devastates the illusion of our world of attachments.

We are, have been, and will always be utterly free. We are not, never have been, or ever will be who we think we are. We will not be assuaged or content with a world dominated by thought, or even feeling, or mere separation and self-interest. We are human beings and human beings are spiritual beings. As incarnate spirit we are divine, not merely god-like, divine, and transcendent and not otherworldly and detached, not even separate. We are here, magnificent, pure, and free. May this book move us one step closer to our wholeness not individually, nor collectively, not interpersonally, but spiritually, transcendentally, and at last truly blissfully, peacefully into and as the One Divine Body, the abode of the Divine Realm.

In Summary

In this introduction we have stated the case for the present sacred-spiritual crisis in our world, for humanity standing at a crossroads in this age of individualism and ignoring inner ecology at its peril. We have also traced an ancient line of inner work and spiritual teaching to what has become known as psychotherapy and we criticized the modern day approaches to the sacred inner journey. Take some time now to let this information sink in and to consider it for yourself with the help of these questions.

1. What is the difference between knowledge and wisdom? Write your thoughts in your inner work notebook.[5]

2. If you were talking to a being from another planet who asked you to explain the reason for the human tendency to create the fake, the counterfeit alongside the authentic and the real, for example in spirituality and spiritual teaching, how would you reply?

3. On the matter of spiritual practice and inner work, many of us feel that we shouldn't spend time on ourselves, that we don't deserve it, because it is self-indulgent and we could be doing something more worthwhile. This stultifying idea has a deep root in self-abnegation, religious indoctrination, and educative moralizing. How did you learn to negate yourself? How did you learn that are not worthy? (Beware if your reaction to this question is to skip it. Your unworthiness may be admitted or

---

[5]Your inner work notebook is a sacred object. Select it well and treat it with respect. Record your psycho-spiritual journey within its covers. In times of despair and feelings of futility (which inevitably come), you will be able to refer to it and see just how far you have come.

rejected, lived in self-deprecating behavior or feelings of lacking in love and self-esteem or in a reactive compensation of rejection through a display of self-indulgence. Bear in mind that his theme of self-abnegation is cultural, which means it in unlikely you can escape it by simply ignoring it.)

4. How do identity and separation and the creation of the ego-self relate to prejudice and bigotry?

5. How do you think inner work relates to the outer world?

6. In this introduction I wrote, "… nothing is so revered or holy that it cannot be questioned and potentially discarded." Recall and record in your inner work notebook those occasions in your life when you questioned and perhaps discarded beliefs, teachings, and points of view.

PART 1:
THE MODERN CONTEXT

Let us discover a context together, a set of background assumptions and agreements on which to ground our journey of discovery, our exploration of modern day spirituality. Let us create here a base-camp prior to the ascent, as we assess, evaluate, and explore.

1. A Little Background

Whether we date it from Blavatsky, Vivekananda, or Gurdjieff, the New Age has been trundling along for at least 120 years. It has led us into a sad place devoid of its former promise, misplaced faith, and tired defeated glories. It has created in us a maudlin, worshipful, backward-looking attitude, confusing, inhibiting, and finally preventing personal growth coming to any real fruitful outcome or conclusion. Likewise, the psychological schools, all well-meant and pioneering, trail-blazing with burgeoning insights, concepts, and approaches, are somehow lacking, with their fascinating pieces, but not complete understanding of the human condition, not transcendent, not ultimately freeing. Is there no end to the human experiment? Spirituality, in the form of original heartfelt experience and transformative actions by unique and gifted individuals with extraordinary destinies has been led into the museum's warehouse, lashed down, dismembered, maimed, and neutered—mortally sacrificed, nailed into a coffin, and placed on a dusty shelf.

We sing, pray, marry, love, and give birth under the consensual, conformist banner of good behavior, common sense, and cooperation with our fellow man (unless we live in a war-torn country). So what? Christianity, Buddhism, and the rest have not resulted in a world of peace—cruelty and ignominy and atrocities still take place between human and human. Ultimately the institutionalizing of religion, whereby a great spiritual master and their teachings are organized, adapted, and compromised, lack the heart, the truth, the flavor of the original. The flavoring was chemical paraldehyde—the preservation of the pharaohs, the kings of old.

The sage, mythologist, and scholar Joseph Campbell commented on religious intolerance, "Each [religion] needs its own myth, all the way."[6] And that is an answer, but Campbell also said we are in desperate need of a new mythology for the modern era, because the one we've got is at least two, and in some cases several, thousand years old. Do we not need a house-cleaning of old religious hardware, worn-out beliefs and assumptions, the mother of prejudice and the enemy of awareness? Do we not need to radically question dearly-held, hoary, old chestnuts about kindness, health, and love which deaden important crucial concepts and render the key principles for the fulfillment of a human life useless? What better way to sabotage the great effort of humanity's efforts toward self-realization than to take the raw material and the building blocks of personal growth and use them as an obstacle to block the spiritual, emotional flow of teeming, wise, compassionate life within?

---

[6]Joseph Campbell with Bill Moyers, *Transcript: Joseph Campbell and the Power of Myth—'The Message of the Myth'* was originally aired on public television on May 30, 1988, A Production of Public Affairs Television and Alvin H. Permutter, Inc. © 1988.

Saviors and Charlatans

The situation today, as anyone knows who has even a glancing acquaintance with the MBS[7] arena, is that we are inundated with approaches and swamped with practitioners and teachers in the complementary-alternative, psychological, and spiritual fields.

It would be helpful if we distinguish the charlatans (and there are always some of those) from the healers, therapists, and spiritual teachers who are worthy. I propose we start by arranging them into three groups. The first group consists of the ones with little effectiveness who are not overly-gifted, who do very little good or bad, because people do not seek them out or, if they do, they see through them relatively quickly. Probably people in this group will stop practicing, becoming either resigned or embittered about their failure to do good in the world, blaming it on outer circumstances, finances, or geography.

The second group consists of the grey area. They are people of some knowledge, even wisdom and insight, who either use their understanding to bring people further on in their healing and personal spiritual understanding, or are simply cashing in, perhaps not intentionally. The New Age/MBS commercial constraints have pressured them to relinquish their vision from furthering in an organic way, so they keep content back and make inner material more palatable.

Disparaged and criticized as they are by the establishment and conventional thinking types, complementary-alternative medicine practitioners offer

---

[7]No, not Millions of Bytes per Second, but Mind-Body-Spirit. Loosely synonymous with the New Age, MBS is both a booming industry and the banner for neo-psycho-spiritual and philosophical, and particularly holistic, points of view.

some powerful healing for humanity. The weakness, like the strength, as ever is in the practitioner. Complementary-alternative trainings routinely neglect the central fact that at the heart of the effectiveness of their healing modalities is the inner development of the practitioner. This is really the key difference between so-called establishment medicine and non-establishment medicine. We could state the principle as: it is not something done *to* you, not some third element, but more a synergistic dynamic of complements and healing.

Specifically, in the psychotherapy and counseling field, we don't need just another psychotherapy or healing method. We need a deep philosophy and psychology of being and authenticity, aimed at the creation of a divine metapsychology. Opening to our emotional life, energy, mental and physical being, is no longer optional, but crucial—inner work is a matter of urgency and individual self-responsibility.

Self-Help Gurus and Do-it-Yourself Spiritual Teaching

In the West we have had an uncomfortable time with the guru-disciple relationship. We have been attracted to it, but somehow largely unable to embrace it, predictably perhaps, because of our cultural milieu. In the East, gurus are on every street corner; your uncle or your dad may be one. Just like here in the West a priest, a vicar, or a spiritual counselor may be in your extended family. But a spiritual guru is arguably more heavyweight in the spiritual sphere, and the relationship is much more demanding. Are we impoverished by not really having an accepted equivalent of the guru-disciple relationship in the West or is it simply just unnecessary in the modern era? Can't we just do it ourselves? Is a guru, a teacher, or a guide absolutely necessary?

The modern era is a rather do-it-yourself time. I live in rural Andalucía in southern Spain. It's a place that resembles England fifty to a hundred years ago. Everybody knows their place here. For example, when I was converting an agricultural building on our land into what was to become our *cortijo*, our home, I hired a *peón*, a builder's laborer, called Plácido. He was a very noble man, exceptionally strong and extremely efficient. His job was *peón* and he charged the same rate as all the other *peóns*. When a building team was working on a construction project there were *peóns*, builders, and master builders. Each one had their own specific status, daily rate, and job description. They knew exactly what they were doing and they would never think of intruding into each other's domains.

One day I tried to fit French windows into a wall with Plácido, but I was a hopeless builder. I was winging it. We didn't have much money. I was just making it up as I went along while thinking how hard can this be? Every now and again, I would meet a dead-end, and this was one of those times. How exactly do you fit a set of French windows into a solid wall? So we smashed the wall down and made a big hole, slipped in supportive timbers to act as a temporary lintel, stood the French windows in, and supported the frame as best we could. Then we had to fill in the gaps all around the window. I started but I couldn't see how to do it, so I feigned the need for a cup of tea and asked Plácido to carry on using bricks and mortar to fill in the gaps. But he looked at me like it was rocket science and said he didn't know how! I believe he had never laid a brick on mortar. His job was to carry the bricks, make the mortar, and sweep up. He never overstepped his work; he was a *peón*.

In my early life being brought up as a boy in 1950s England, there were tradesmen, delivery boys, office workers, salesmen, steam-roller drivers, and bus conductors. If you had a plumbing problem, you called a plumber. If a window frame needed painting, you called a painter, and if your roof fell in, you called a roofer and a plasterer. No one did it themselves. Everyone had a role, a profession, a trade. You were a something-or-other. It is still like this in Andalucía now. Rogelio, our neighbor, is a goat farmer just like his father Rogelio. Plácido's father was a *peón*, so Plácido is a *peón*. The line of heredity passes through the generations and brings name and occupation, and governs ambition and choice. It is medieval, a time before you had the ability to climb up out of your class level, improve your prospects, and better yourself.

In England all this changed in the early sixties when a man called Barry Bucknell appeared on British TV and popularized do-it-yourself (DIY). Within a few years every man worthy of the name had his own drill and toolbox and was making a big mess!

It seems to me that this usurping the place of the *especialistas*, as they're known in Andalucía, connects strongly with the present era of individualism. We seem to think that we should be able to do everything and that we are somehow lacking if we can't. Yet the truth is that people are all different with diverse talents and tendencies and capable of different activities. We exhibit a range of abilities, some of which are hard to detect when we standardize our idea of how people *should* be. So, for example, in reality not all women are great or even good mothers, and not all men are capable bread winners. We need a depth of tolerance and acceptance in society that embraces this and finds a place for differing temperaments, rather than creating a standard and expecting people to conform to it and damning them when they don't.

Among the impossible demands we make on others and ourselves has come the phenomenon of self-help, or do-it-yourself psycho-spirituality. And it's a mess! Of course, for some it works, as I am sure that some followers of Barry Bucknell found they were talented at home improvements. But for most, it simply doesn't work and they enter a la-la land of self-delusion, which is the very antithesis of self-discovery, because mostly it goes nowhere near deep enough. After all, in the modern era it has become a commercial enterprise. To authentically transform yourself and discover and live from your true nature, two essential elements are mandatory and inescapable… and these two things you *cannot* get from a book: the spiritual guide and your sincerity in the spiritual endeavor. The rest is suffering.

In Summary

1. How do you understand the arising of modern day New Age, MBS philosophies? How did you first become aware of them?

2. What New Age, MBS ideas are you attached to? What is your reaction to my comments and criticisms?

3. What is the meaning and the role of traditional religion today?

4. What experiences of inept or ineffective therapies, healings, and cures have you or your friends had? Alternatively, what successes? What conclusions have you drawn and what is your view of the field of complementary-alternative medicine (CAM)?

5. Write your own account of confusing personality with truth or of being taken in by the ego on your spiritual journey. If neither of these have happened to you yet, perhaps you have heard about it from someone else, in which case write their story. When you have completed the writing, *reflect*.

6. In your opinion does everyone really need a spiritual teacher?

2. Suffering in a Dark Time: The Age of Individualism

The ego-forces in this present age of individualism have never before been paralleled in human history. They have infiltrated all areas of human concern and obscured the real spiritual truths, path, and ways that represent salvation and the evolving teaching of liberation.

A Priceless Fresco

I am reminded of a rather odd story. The church authorities in a small Spanish village commissioned an elderly lady to restore a priceless fresco of Jesus. Her work on the fresco of the savior transformed a subtle, though timeworn and damaged, portrait, full of pathos, depth, and subtlety into a cartoon likeness of a monkey. Amid the predictable outrage and plans to amend the "restoration," an entirely unforeseen series of events occurred. The 80-something year-old pensioner achieved celebrity status as tens of thousands of people flocked to the tiny church to view the restored fresco, which was now roped off and protected by security guards. An online petition praising the woman's restoration efforts was signed by tens of thousands of "fans," as the tiny village church, housing a previously unknown fresco, became the vibrant center of a tourist boom unequalled in the village's history.

The granddaughter of the artist who painted the fresco pointed out that the elderly lady restorer originally merely painted Jesus' tunic, but that it was when she painted over the head and face that she destroyed the fresco painting. They hadn't seen it coming until it was too late and the damage was done.

We haven't seen it coming either. The efforts to make religious and spiritual truth and practice accessible have all seemed quite innocent, well-meaning, and reasonable. It is only now, as we find the head and the face are becoming obscured, that we see the whole picture is almost destroyed.

The eyes in the painting were the last to go. In the head there is a universe of difference between the subtle, otherworldly inflections in the facial expression and posture of Jesus' head in the original fresco and the two-dimensional soulless density of the cartoonish restoration.

The original suggests the condition of *ataraxia*, of spiritual, ecstatic transport, and the transcendence of the physical, while the restored version depicts starkly and tragically the lifelessness, unawareness, unreceptive, unseeing condition of modern-day humanity. It is a universe of difference.

We live in a time of overwhelming individualism. Egoic forces have become ubiquitous. We can hardly see ourselves through the haze of egoistic restlessness, vacuous accomplishment, pointless activity, fear, desire, competition and multitude forms of gross and subtle anger, violence and hate.

In ancient times the ego was overcome by necessity. When you have to work to survive and there are no state services or a social order that steps in to bail you out of the crucial business of living—eating, shelter, difficulties from injury, illness and disease—ego is caught up in simply staying alive. The plight of the Third World today, like the plight of primitive people long ago, receives much publicity and appeals to the heart and mind of kindness and compassion. But here in the increasingly Westernized modern world our difficulties have become internalized as anxiety, depression, emotional pain, confusion, and discontent. To judge these internal malaises as of any less consequence than the obvious outer ones is plain ignorance. Modern man and woman have succumbed to the barrage of toxicity in the modern world in the only way possible—by internalizing unnatural, negative forces.

Today we are suffering in a dark time. It is a time of individualism, self-doubt, and an almost total lack of enlightenment. In spite of what the world of natural healers and holistic psychologists may have you believe, much of what masquerades as spirituality is merely delusion.

The Shadow and the Eclipse

The difficulty for us today is that the ego has become powerful by default. Without our realizing it, ego forces have grown so strong in the world that we are content with diluted versions of freedom, spiritual revolution, enlightenment, wisdom, and happiness. Reaching this nadir appears to have taken a short time, but in reality, it has been a long time coming. It has occurred through a gradual accumulation of ennui, lack of attention, and inertia—reminiscent of the saying, "All that is necessary for the triumph of evil is that good men do nothing." This is rather like scaling a mountain when you never seem to be getting closer to the peak and suddenly you're there. In this case, what is there is the almost total occlusion of light by darkness, the eclipse of the sunshine of enlightenment by the shadow of ignorance.

To lift this veil, we are in need of a divine psychology, a philosophy of spiritual experience and values, and an inspired means to truth. It must begin with self-enquiry as a way of taking back from the arbitrary doctrine of individualism the power and the strength to change and transform individually and collectively. This means awareness of self in regard to ego-forces and their result, the psychological, emotional, behavioral, and repetitive way of acting that passes for a lifetime. This is what the ego finds acceptable because a superficial life, like the ego itself, is merely false, an illusion. Today people are apparently content to live within a systematically inauthentic milieu of falseness and unquestioningly adhere to dictums that merely glorify the ego and its accompanying shallowness in all its salient forms and disguises. This includes sentiment, personal opinion, reaction, dilution, cheapening, manipulation, control, and trickery.

The worst of these magical illusions must surely be the substitution of ego-driven forms to create spiritual deception. As if it was not enough to descend into ignorance the ego has now driven us into a complex lie. This is complex, but as well-hidden as Edgar Allan Poe's purloined letter and I quote, "The best place to hide anything is in plain view." This present era of individualism has produced a puzzling, downward spiral of selfishness, self-absorption, and self-indulgence.

The result is a lack of real pride, self-worth, internal reality, and authentic selfhood. Our deteriorating self-image, even meaning and experience, and our shallowness meets our indecent haste to have our desires met in the hollowest of ways. Isn't it curious how genuine self-respect, self-confidence, and self-reliance can be usurped by self-aggrandizement, self-loathing, and self-punishment?

What do we make of this? The age of the individual and the climax of intensity and the ubiquitous ego-processes have surely brought us to a point where only two possibilities exist. Either, the futile, foolhardy way of the individual self, the ego, will be falsely and misguidedly perpetuated toward material or spiritual oblivion (or both?), or the momentum of ego-forces will naturally subside and relinquish power in an authentic and much-needed spiritual revolution.

The signs are already here, as we might expect. But even they are ambivalent. On the one hand, the global financial recession seems to be inspiring interest in the quality of life rather than the accelerating scramble for material success, status, and money. On the other hand, humanity seems hell-bent on denying itself an awakened destiny, an enlightened and enlightening perspective, a spiritual and sacred life. It is a delicate balancing act: to the one side, darkness—selfishness, ignorance, and unconsciousness—to the other side, light—compassion, wisdom, and awareness—the fruits of illumination. We have a decision to make, for we are at the point of choice: on the one hand, magnificence, devotion, and reverence, on the other, superficiality, profanity, and irreverence.

The Magnificent Human

This is the time of the individual. It brings with it an ambiguous state. Now at last the individual is recognized, the wonder and magnificence of each note in the human symphony is available to be heard and seen for what it is… potentially divine, a shard of the numinous.

Much has been made—written, analyzed, sung and turned into art—about the foibles of humans. Their eccentricities, neuroses, psychoses, habits and strange appetites, perversity and perversions, flaws and imperfections have been cause for variously great art, shame and guilt, praise and fascination, eulogy and celebration.

To take only one of these, mental illness, *The Diagnostic and Statistical Manual of Mental Disorders* (DSM) published by the American Psychiatric Association has been developed into a compendium of terrifying descriptions used to diagnose what is wrong with individuals showing signs of mental disorder. Where is the equivalent, if we were capable of writing such a book, of conditions of positivity, wellness, happiness, centeredness, mental stability, loving kindness, forgiveness, skill in relationship, and acceptance?

Now, couldn't it be time to write the book of positivity? The book of well-being, health and potential, capacity and ritual and true methods for growing into love and compassion. We could describe the symptoms and behavior of human grace, the signs of wisdom and divinity and innocence, how we speak from the heart, the demonstrations of genuine tenderness, how love may sometimes be expressed in forthrightness and challenge, how we demonstrate courage and overcome our fears. This may sound silly or even superfluous. But unless we have words, concepts for the ideal forms, we cannot perceive their image in the world of appearances. This is the meaning of the Christian edict, "In the beginning was the word..." Without the word, there is no beginning or at least not a beginning we could know about, because it is inconceivable.

Now in this age of the individual we need to break through into new paradigms, new models of understanding and expansive behavior. The liberation of our internal patterning relies on these innovations, as well as the ageless paradigm.

The Ageless Paradigm

In inner work and the journey of self-discovery, personal transformation is surprisingly unspectacular, although the process of arriving may be endlessly dramatic, intense, and extreme. Everything changes and yet nothing has changed. It is analogous to dramatic "special effects" in Hollywood movies. The first special effect in life is early conditioning—the experience of real life is rubbed away by the hypnotic trance of conditioned thought and behavior. The hope for a human being is to realize his or her true nature by allowing the wise soul to guide the compulsive instinctual nature, not the other way round. Fear and desire must be tempered with a higher wisdom within the human psyche, or it will be consumed and overwhelmed by its baser nature. Let's explore this further through the Hollywood metaphor.

Harry Redmond was a special effects artist in Hollywood before cut and paste was a keyboard click. He was famous for his work on the film *King Kong*. Audiences in the 1930s were thrilled and moved to the edge of their seats by the effects of stop-motion photography and live action projected on to the cinema screen, as Harry and his team convinced them that a 25-foot tall gorilla could climb the Empire State Building—the world's tallest building—single-handedly while holding a wailing actress in the other hand.

Everything Changes and Yet Nothing has Changed
A little lower down on the totem pole, Redmond created the famous transition scene in the film *The Woman in the Window*. A film noir and famously the film that originated the genre, *The Woman in the Window* is a Faustian drama of an aging man's obsession with a femme fatale who effectively materializes out of a picture and seemingly lures the protagonist into the deepest debasement of

human tendencies—murder, crime, deception, treachery, and animal passion.

Hollywood at this time was infatuated with psychoanalysis and flaunted psychological conditions like paranoia and repression with risqué abandon. This fixated audiences who alternated contempt and fascination towards its own transferred desires. An audience could live out its deepest-held unconscious obsessions via identification with actors and celebrities who acted as scapegoats—as they arguably still do—for their shameful sins.

The prescribed conclusion was the suicide of the hero (or anti-hero depending on how we feel about our shadow side), but to avoid offending sexual mores, the church, and the Hays Code, it was commuted to a classic dream ending. Edward G. Robinson falls asleep and wakes up in his club - only to discover that it was all a dream.

The transition scene that depicts the transformation between dreaming and waking life demanded that Redmond and his team shift the background scenery of a New York apartment and exchange it for a gentleman's club. They did it in real time and the finished scene in the film has no cuts, splices, or doctoring of any kind: everything changes and yet nothing has changed.

The First "Special Effect": Early Conditioning
In inner work something similar takes place. The first special effect in life is early conditioning. From it we are condemned to wander in a wilderness of limitation and contraction. Everything is more or less as we expect it to be. The addendum to this is that we are unaware of it: it is as if the experience of real life were rubbed away by the hypnotic trance of conditioned thought and behavior.

Anaesthetized to life, we tend to act as if we are numb to experience, to others, to intimacy and touch, to beauty, and aesthetics. We may only respond to life's forceful blows or shocks, for example, bereavement, a serious accident, an illness, bankruptcy, a romantic obsession, or some other intimation of mortality. Then we may awaken momentarily and smell the fresh air of real life and enter authentic existence.

The Second "Special Effect": Human Transformation
The second "special effect" in life is the transformation of a human being. After a long period of application to integrity, honesty, and cultivating transparency a person seeking truth may, through awareness and non-clinging arrive at that point of freedom when they experience a rebirth. The precursor for this is the death of the conditioned self, the hypnotized, apparent being, the one invested in self-aggrandizement, self-inflation, and fear and desire.

Dramatic, spectacular, ecstatic, and despondent as the journey is, the transition and the transformation are comparably mundane and profoundly natural: a homecoming, a return to sincerity and spontaneity, somehow where you have always been. Just like when Harry Redmond and his team shifted the stage, the theater, and the background... and we have returned home at last.

In the movie Edward G. Robinson's character lurches from one realization to another, puzzling over his reorientation. His relief escalates into innocent joy as he realizes that all he dreamt is not really true. Everything has changed, as he appreciates the ordinariness of his life, a life that, apparently taken away, is now miraculously restored.

Behind Your Heart's Curtain
The transition scene and subsequent events recall the poet Rilke's words: "Who has not sat before his own heart's

curtain? It lifts: and the scenery is falling apart."[8] And this is the point: it was and has been all scenery and when it falls apart you realize what is true. The world lacks scenery and is devoid of backdrop, as well as assurance and certainty. When the scenery shifts and falls apart all that remains is dangerous uncertainty. Sureness is a chimera as we wander in life's adventure to awakening, afraid of death, and desiring what we do not have.

But when we have stopped doing all that we are doing to prevent reality, the truth from setting in, from informing us in everything we do; when we start to see what the heart sees, as opposed to what the eye sees, we prepare the way for wisdom to arise and present itself to us. This is the ageless paradigm. The muddy puddle clears from being left alone, undisturbed, and in the same way our inner restlessness, when it finally ceases from our disinclination to fuel it, allows the reflection of truth to become central and stable; it enables and empowers us to finally *see*. And we see with our heart, not the visible world of appearances, but behind, further in, and deeper, into the invisible nature of Reality, of Truth itself.

What is unconscious or invisible to the eye is the fact that most of us are spending all of our time holding up and supporting the structure of the ego, without realizing that the heart can see exactly what is happening.

In yet another accomplished piece of special effects work Harry Redmond has shown us this. The Marx Brothers' film, *A Night in Casablanca,* begins with Harpo leaning against a wall. An officious policeman making his rounds takes offence at his casual stance and asks, "What do you think you're doing, holding up the building?" Harpo nods vigorously and contentedly and then, as the exasperated policeman pulls him away, the entire building collapses.

---

[8]Rainer Maria Rilke, *Duino Elegies* 1922.

The ego collapses through the consistent, sustained attention of inner work. Occasionally, however, we get a preview, a preliminary peek through the veils when we experience the spiritual and the sacred—unbidden, suddenly, and unexpectedly.

Experiences of the Sacred

I have had many experiences of sacredness in my life. Perhaps I have been more fortunate than most. I don't know. I know that sacredness knows no distinctions of class, wealth, education, or status. I have been fortunate in meeting and knowing some exceptionally aware beings who have manifested sacredness, love, and compassion in breath-taking ways. Some were healers or teachers, waitresses or truck-drivers, mothers and fathers, close friends and strangers, people compelled to perform acts of consideration, awareness, and kindness.

One was a novice in the Zen temple where I trained. He was the chief junior monk. One day at a closing ceremony in the *zendo*, he padded on his stockinged feet to the altar with such presence and compassion. Writing this now I hardly know how to convey this to you. How do your footsteps express awareness and love? And yet his did to me. The ritual, the symbolism, the theme of closing, and the footsteps combined to swell my heart with longing, to fill my heart with love. It was a powerful, sacred occasion in my life.

My first therapist and teacher had great presence. He was a lovely man who could alternate great tenderness with bluffness. His compassion was balanced by his directness; his courage by his intense vulnerability. When he chose to, he could take your breath away with very simple gestures. He was full of grace and disarming innocence, alongside great wisdom. Once when he had returned to England from the US, he brought presents for a group of us who considered him our spiritual teacher and guide. Instead of giving the presents to us, he asked each of us to choose individually from a bag containing several gifts. He unwrapped each package carefully and mindfully until we mutually felt the rightness of a certain present and accepted it from him as our gift. Again it is almost impossible for me to express the patience, presence, and tenderness with which each gift was handled, unwrapped, and returned to its wrapping. But the experience remains with me to this day and informs me in everything I do.

I was one of those young people who, in the 1970s, felt compelled to journey around the world to find the sacred. Rather predictably perhaps, I found it in an ashram. The ritual of filing into the meditation hall and sitting in patient silence waiting for the guru to appear was filled with symbolism and drenched in significance and grace for me. The power of so many of us waiting with a single intent yields a wonderful insight into the collective power of humanity joined together in a collective focus of sacred devotion and spiritual intention.

I have to admit to not being able to hold and retain these depths of experience in my life at all times. I have taken the route of the householder, and the tests and challenges of family life are as intensely challenging and defeating, as they are precious and compassionately instructive in the ways of the heart. In my personality, I know that some part of me never left the monastery, and another part of me never left India. But I also know now that the sacred is everywhere; that there is no need to travel to other countries, to other groupings of individuals, or to change your life in any way. The sacred-spiritual truths and ceremonies, awareness, symbols, and intimations are present always, constantly beckoning, perpetually reminding you and so exquisitely, gently, and forgivingly waiting for you to participate through your presence. In family, relational, and everyday life I slipped as we all do many times... but Reality, the numinous, the Divine that works like a fragrance through sacred means never wavered.

My experiences, either individually or collectively, do not seem to be powerful or strong enough to express the feeling of sacredness inside me. Rather than dismissing this however I think it gives us a clue. The sacred is beyond description. It connects us to such a deep, profound, and core place inside that we may only fail in our attempts to express it, to communicate it to others. It is, after all, *sacred* (from the Latin *sacrare*, to consecrate, immortalize, or set apart). Remember that the teaching of profound spiritual illumination is not spoken or systematized, though it may be communicated through gesture, indirect means, and ultimately, transmission.

Transmission is a mysterious, intimate, wonderful conveying of spiritual truth, of divine wisdom, of enlightenment. Whatever else we might say about transmission, it is beyond words. So it is that the sacred, the spiritual, the Divine ultimately is beyond temporal expression.

One final experience of sacredness I would like to share. As a boy, I used to love to dive into the sea. So mundane, just ordinary, but I remember the profound feelings of the experience so vividly and brightly because it radiated with meaning and truth for me.

I am older now. No one ever tells you these things, but as you age, your relationship to your body changes. My body feels cooler sometimes now. I can't always walk comfortably on cold tiles. I have become acutely aware of drafts and sudden loud noises. Directionality in my hearing is sometimes inaccurate and background noise tends to make conversation in a crowded meeting-place impossible. I certainly cannot eat the sweet deserts I used to enjoy without paying the price of acidity. I cannot run and jump like I used to, and standing before the crashing waves on the beach, I no longer have that extraordinary experience of being at one with the elements as I inhabit my body. The body is more frail now, more vulnerable. I have to be more careful with it; it does not heal as quickly as it used to. The skin on my hands and arms does not snap back as quickly when I pinch it, and I am developing those age spots I remember Ram Dass talking about in a lecture when he said, "When I look at my hand, I see my father's old hand." When I heard his humorous consideration of aging, I laughed and I remember it seemed a thousand years away. I could not imagine getting old. Through the intellectual meanderings and irrational wisdom of youth I felt I would live forever.

The feelings of standing before the crashing tides waiting to be moved to throw myself headfirst into a wave were euphoric, transient, like growing wings, like merging into the vastness, like dying, like living, like Nirvana to me. When I dived, the tumult, the din, the serpentine movement, the tremendous power of nature—all gave way to the complete silence of the underwater experience: muffled cries like slowed-down music, distant tumult, and for the seconds or minutes, which seemed like hours sometimes, I was down there under the water, and I was entirely free of cares, worries, and my individual existence. I felt entirely liberated for this was a sacred experience... and so is aging to me now.

Aging too is like throwing yourself into the waves. It is liberating. No longer are you burdened with hubris. You have left behind youthful challenges. You no longer have the pressing need to prove yourself, to preen yourself, to further, develop, and embellish yourself with attractiveness, appendages, or restless striving.

ଓ

Aging, the grace of the guru, the ritual of gift-giving, the stockinged feet of the chief junior in the Zen monastery—all point toward the sacred as mundane, quite ordinary unremarkable extraordinariness, prosaic, and familiar blessing. Join me now as we throw ourselves into the water, with waves crashing around our heads, to embark, in Part 2, on some glorious perdition.

In Summary

In this chapter we have looked at the modern human being, considered the ageless paradigm—the way of the heart and arising of wisdom that leads to Truth, and the experience of the sacred. Before we move on to demolishing delusion in some rigorous questioning and ritualistic slaughtering of erroneous beliefs, please take a look at the questions below and spend a little time in inner work practice exploring the themes of the chapter before you leave it.

1. How do you think this is the time of the individual? Has our relationship to our individuality really changed? And if it has, how and why has it changed?

2. In your experience and appreciation, what writing, art, and songs express the wonders of being human? Having considered and chosen, ask yourself what your choice reveals about you. Now choose a complementary list of writing, art, and songs that express the darkness of humanity. What do your choices reveal about you?

3. In the discussion of the DSM-5 I imagined a book of well-being, positivity, happiness, and stability to balance our fascination with descriptions of what can go wrong with human beings with descriptions of what can go right. The DSM-5 is a thousand pages long and authored by thousands of professionals, so we need help to create the counter book. What would you like to see in the book of well-being?

4. How have you ever been anaesthetized to life and numb to experience, perhaps in reaction to a shock or trauma? How have you compensated for vulnerability or

weakness in your life with self-aggrandizement or self-inflation?

5. How do you prop up the structure of your ego?

6. What are your experiences of the sacred? Write these experiences (with drawings perhaps?) in your inner work notebook... and reflect on your accounts.

PART 2: SOME GENTLE, COMPASSIONATE DEMOLITION

Before we begin exploring how we could create a new structure of psycho-spiritual endeavor, thought, and methodology for the modern era, let's topple a few edifices. Some are new, but others are ancient, old as the hills in contemporary clothing, stale news masquerading as latest findings. It is ludicrous, in some cases, how these ideas have survived. We can only marvel at our and humanity's lack of discrimination and critical thinking in allowing these fallacies of spiritual reality to live on in us, in our culture, and in our hearts and minds.

For some readers this gentle, compassionate demolition will be hard, painful, hurtful, and relentless as it strips down attachments to thought-forms and shallow "spiritual" teachings or destroys holy idols and beliefs. Others will silently smile, as I try to express what they have felt and never quite taken the time to give words to. I am sure of this because it is true for me too. The psychotherapist Irvin Yalom said that he doesn't like to be "love's executioner," and neither do I. But I prefer to deny you this spiritual security blanket, rather than watch you suffer all the more as disillusionment gives way to a deeper despair that could have been avoided through the authentic initiation into the mystery of Reality.

3. Slaughtering Sacred Cows, Smashing False Idols

But just what is the role and value of destruction in our mission to re-establish the sacred in the modern world? First, let's try to understand the forces which give rise to creation itself, not to absolute Reality but to the world of appearances and arising and subsiding forms, the ones that comprise our universe in material and substance.

The Dynamic Interplay of Creation

Through a dynamic interaction of primal forces conflicting, harmonizing, smashing and reforming, merging and dividing, this whole creation comes into being. In Chinese cosmology, these forces are known as yin and yang while in Hindu philosophy they are rajas and tamas, and in Buddhism they are simply the arising of the opposites. The most basic way to understand this is in the experience of our personal genesis: getting out of bed in the morning. The dynamic interplay of inertia versus our impulse to action results usually in our rising from the bed. We get up and, responding to the call to action, we go about our daily tasks. If we turn over and go back to sleep, drink a cup of tea while staring into space, or phone in to work sick, we have allowed the death forces of lethargy and weakness to overcome us. But if we leap into action we allow the life forces, action and purpose, strength and assertiveness, to motivate and enliven us.

Through the dynamic relationship of death-forces and life-forces, action and inertia, a world comes into being. Although if we want to resist a world coming into being, inertia is not enough. We simply create a lazy world, a world of imbalance, and too much sleep. Nisargadatta advised the spiritual teacher Ramesh Balsekar, when he asked for permission to have his first book (on Nisargadatta) published, "Don't persist, don't resist." In these four words is the original meaning of *ahimsa*, non-violence, expressed and well-known in the world in the Ghandi-esque sense of passive resistance. But *ahimsa* cuts much deeper into the inner reality of the soul. It means "not to act according to habit." In other words, do not be reactive; do not be merely an automaton. An automaton gets out of bed in the morning according to habit and, thoughtless and unaware, goes about the day of tasks and duty. The automaton also lies in bed through ennui and an overriding desire for comfort and no demands.

Action is clearly desirable for getting a task done. But what is harder to appreciate is that inertia is also desirable for getting a task done. In the overcoming of inertia is our victory of will and motivation. It fuels our purposefulness, our energetic engagement with the task. We love the resistance, and we love overcoming our resistance even more. Passing the exam, adhering to the diet, clearing the chaotic garden of weeds and dense foliage, studying the subject to receive an accolade, completing the pilgrimage—all are examples of this triumph through overcoming *tamas*, inertia, surviving the ordeal, the homecoming of the hero after his journey. We need the *tamas*, the desiccation, the destruction, the forces of decomposition, disappointment, decay, and destruction. They are the resistance we overcome in the ordeal, the test, the challenge through which we prove ourselves.

The continuum of inertia or *tamas* or yin forces is strung between a mild, faint negativity at one extreme and a fully-fledged razing of the world at the other end. Destruction is that kind of generic. It speaks to us of a microscopic insect inhaled and annihilated in our nostrils as much as the post-apocalyptic world scenario.

Destruction *is*. It's a fact. It is neither good nor bad. It simply *is*. This insight was clear to our hunter-gatherer forebears who looked into the earth and the decomposing flesh and bones of relatives and quarry and pets amid decaying vegetation to strive to reach a primitive understanding of life. It pivoted on the dilemma of birth and death, rising or laying down, action or inaction. And this dilemma belongs as much to the contemporary human being as it did to Neanderthal man.

Death and Resurrection

In my days of attending spiritual therapy workshops in a wonderful experience with the therapist Paul Rebillot, we were invited to write a letter of inner guidance to ourselves from our wiser self. I was 28 years old. This is what I wrote:

'Beloved Richard

Hide your heart while you have to, but know that you will not have to always. The child teaches the parents, and there will soon come a time when you must be brave. At that time, you will need all your courage, but know that courage is not all yours. When that time comes your true mother will be beneath you—your support and your ground; and your true father will be above you—your nourishment and your sky. With their arms enfolding you, know that only you can limit your courage, your strength, and your love.

All your life is a learning—accept each task as a splendid gift because, when revealed, each yields a jewel. Accept experience graciously—receive it as it is given to you.

Your task, you know, is to see. So shall all be given to your eyes, so shall all be given to your ears, so shall all be given to your body. It is all.

Take care not to dig your heels into certainty. It is a mud that may trap you. Your worth is certain—do not mistake certainty for worth. You are precious.

Throughout all your loneliness, remember these things.'

This workshop was entitled *Death and Resurrection*. Over many days we evoked the forces of Thanatos, and we ended the course with a celebration. This is the cycle of life, the endless reciprocal sequencing of stages of birth and destruction, death, and creation. This is the mystery of life.

We crave and try to hasten the arising new life, like a pregnant woman who cannot wait any longer for her baby to be born. We want to speed it up. It always takes longer than we want it to. But the baby, the rewards, or the world, take as long as they take in the process of becoming. Only after the cycle has fulfilled itself does the next stage appear. Usually we are asleep, unselfconscious, unable to remark on its actual genesis, but as the sun rises we are able to say, "Hey, it's light," as the shadows appear to lighten and the forms of life appear.

Power and Fame

The spiritual master Sri Nisargadatta Maharaj talked of ages succumbing to their own perfection and new ones arising. Perfection of course is less of the human, more of the Spiritual-Divine. Yet through the trials and ordeals of human conscience, we are tested in our wandering and our life path to purify and clear our souls for the life of the spirit. One such archetypal test is in the Gospels when Jesus of Nazareth is faced with the temptation to forfeit his destiny for one of three worldly delights: riches, fame, and power. Each one is a fall from grace.

My dad fell for power and fame. He did less well on wealth, and settled for the appearance of wealth rather than the possession of it. However, he rigorously pursued local celebrity and succeeded. He was a hotelier at a time when large hotels carried some personal status and individual identity. Unlike today, a hotelier was personable and the success of the business depended on his character and personality. With my mother as an attractive appendage, he posed for photographs with national celebrities, singers, comedians, actors and actresses who used the hotel as a stopover during their national theater tours. His picture was regularly in the local newspapers and a local cartoonist exaggerated my parents' features increasing their Walt Disney character effect.

Predictably, my father paid the price of fame, merely local though it was. He was isolated, increasingly so, as he got older, friendless and alone. He spent long hours in front of the television with his feet up and a glass in his hand. On the occasions when I returned home, he would disavow any interest in the TV, while being glued to it like an addict. Occasionally he would read a forgettable, trashy novel. His life was all about his work, impressing people, and being 'a somebody' in the eyes of others—

fame and celebrity. The destruction to his inner life and the price he paid with his soul was immense. He was a man of his generation. His was a generation that didn't talk about horrendous experiences in the war and the hardships and tragedies suffered…but that suffering and destruction reflected onto my father's life.

Bringing It All Back Home

From the flimsiest, superficial teaching of spirituality in contemporary times to the deepest spiritual teaching of any time, all can be repackaged and regurgitated in a commercial bundle, an integrated product suite of quasi-spiritual initiation that appeases humanity's needs and desires. But understanding spiritual initiation, authentic spiritual practice, and preparatory disciplines, garnering the soul and pruning the self for the ritual of insight and enlightenment may not be considered, either deeply or superficially.

Both the shallow and the deep teachings are presented now in summary form. Advaita Vedanta grows out of a rich and varied source with a thick root extending back thousands of years. The lineage of many of the shallow teachings presented and summarized here may be lesser, but the extent of gobbledy-gook is seemingly endless. Over the years I have amassed and collected a number of populist texts which are instructive in their own right. They sit on my shelves alongside the most profound spiritual teachings of this or any other time—a testament to the variety of humankind in its apparently endless search for the answer to the perennial questions of human existence.

The extent of the confusion is so big we can only really examine the major themes here, but hopefully this will provide springboards to clarity for the beehive of details. Over this and the next three chapters therefore we will dispel the fascination with the "special time" and other ephemera of desire (in this chapter), present the Ten Tenets or a heretical creed for clarity and navigation through the mirage (in chapter 4). We will delve into the darkness of the spiritual celebrity and entertainment (in chapter 5), and examine the spiritual phenomenon of Advaita and its complex difficulties (in chapter 6).

Spurious Themes of Contemporary "Spirituality" (and Psychology)

The Special Time
We are *not* entering a time when there will be a planetary shift, when the earth speaks, and a biblical tide of destruction ends the lower phase of consciousness for humankind forever, and we enter into a new heavenly phase of compassion and empathy and a divine existence. This kind of idea is prevalent today, but it has been prevalent for thousands of years also. It is—like all evocative, meaningful ideas about life—*symbolic*, which means it points to something *beyond* itself. The key word here is "beyond." In other words, we need not expect natural disasters, world political events, reports of leaps in collective evolutionary consciousness, or any other worldly event to be anything other than what they are—events in time and space.

The important thing to keep constantly in mind if you are a spiritual seeker or aspirant is that events in time and space are never spiritual events. They are instead worldly events, events in the spatio-temporal realms. They can be understood and appreciated as such only so long as no special significance is attached to them. They are what they are, and that's it!

Now obviously the notion of a special time (the one we just happen to be living in now), a special place, special events, a special person, or special teaching all have a strong allure to the heart touched and motivated by longing. But the heart untouched by longing, the open free heart, will see that this is a self-aggrandizing idea, an elaboration of self-indulgence and of the primal need to be loved and respected, as substitutes for acceptance and inclusion. "Special" has no basis in a real spiritual teaching and is even less a valid interpretation and understanding of the outer world.

Things happen, phenomena arise, randomly and spontaneously, without any specific meaning or connotation, *other than that which we ascribe to them.* We will not find real meaning where we seek it; we will find it where it truly exists.

The need for a paradigm shift, one away from the egocentric, subjective, personal point of view is never more relevant than here. Consider: sentiment may substitute for love, nostalgia for present-day emotion, and melancholy for profundity. Experiential surrogacy has become so prevalent today that the core, instinctive, energetic, human-defining qualities of our lives are becoming obscured in the thought-pictures and fantasies of pretence and consensus. We need to belong. We are reluctant to question and disagree. We deeply desire to be accepted and acceptable.

And yet the random events of the relative world are of no fixed spiritual significance whatsoever. Spiritual events are those which have significance in the spiritual realms. This is obvious and clear when we stop to think about it. For those people who don't wish to face the challenges of the spiritual realms, the notion of concretizing the ephemeral, the etheric, the magical, and the spiritual into something they can understand, touch, feel, conceptualize, and experience is overwhelmingly attractive. When enough people come together to reinforce the enthusiasm and the delusion it becomes even more compulsive and exciting. But it is clear to anyone with real awareness of what is going on that this crowd mentality and collective hypnosis reflects a deep inner longing to have the inward spiritual rewards, which can only be attained through hard and dedicated spiritual work *in the inner world of a human being.*

The symbol of the special time, the special place, or the special event is real. But it must be understood and it can only be understood when we see what it stands for.

This special time awaits everyone on the spiritual path. It is the time of their liberation, of the fulfillment of their spiritual work in transcendence and awakening. This experience is entirely real and it will not be simulated, acted as if real, faked or replicated in any way. It is the experience of otherness, the event of spiritual illumination in the human heart-mind. The sublime, ecstatic meaning of this divine event is the realization of human existence.

The sounds, the lights, the revelation, the atmosphere and the sense of belonging are all aspects of the inner state of enlightenment. It takes place in a very special environment: the human heart. And the event is singular, more than special; it is unique. It can happen once for every person, and life is never the same again. It is the relinquishing of all and everything. It is the utter surrender of the personality and merging into the truth in the form of the Divine Person who is at the same time both everyone and no one.

One of the obvious difficulties in talking about this spiritual event is the fact that we are not present. No one is there! That is the condition for the condition-less state to occur. An individual life finds its meaning in the transcendence of identification with itself. The illumination of truth in the individual entails not merely a knowing, although that must be present too, but the acceptance and active receiving of the invitation to live in and as truth. This means being absolutely present, involved in the present condition as the only condition, with total attention.

To summarize, the shift or revolution in consciousness that is so often depicted as an objective, outward phenomenon is actually a symbol for the inner transformation of the individual who is on the spiritual path. It is therefore subjective. The associated themes of destruction, natural disasters, and prescient occurrences are likewise symbolic of the inner process. While obviously signifying catastrophic events outwardly, in the inner world they represent the breaking down of the old order of thinking, feeling, and organizing experience in the individual inner world. Finally, events in the relative world of time and space are never fundamentally spiritual in nature.

So, no special time… and yet, no time that is not special.

Outer "Reality"

Does this mean that we should ignore outward reality? Outer reality is exactly that—outward. Our responsibility is to see ourselves and the world clearly and not through the filter of our past experiences, fears, traumas, prejudices, and judgments. When we do that, and this is what most of us are doing all of the time, all we see is ourselves reflected back to us in changing forms of fear and desire. To see the world as it is we must see ourselves as we are. Only then, when we are clear, can we engage in a genuine and real relationship with the world.

We relate to the outside world with the very best of intentions, as a pale copy of our more profound tendencies and our innate capacity to engage with selfless love and true compassion. But inevitably, in spite of these well-meant intentions, we fall short of the ideal. We need not feel guilty about this, but rather strive towards the higher energy centers, the spiritual reservoirs of human capacity that will enable and empower us to be true to our deepest self.

So how do we do that? Please read on.

Awakening "Experiences"

Awakening experience is itself a contradiction in terms. We are already awake, but we do not necessarily realize it. The view from the egocentric perspective is that there are experiences that comprise a journey to start and complete, but from the transcendental point of view, it looks very different. With no process, no ordeal, no pain or joy, and particularly no experience as such, there is only the Absolute—God, Love, Truth.

My awakenings have been many. Coupled with that, I have had the privilege of accompanying many people on their spiritual journeys and intimately and vividly sharing in their awakenings. Is there any doubt now that the awakening of individuals in our society is the only route to radical change, to a natural loving world of sacredness and spiritual intelligence, compassion, and real divine-human living?

The divine moment of awakening is never an experience per se: it is an eternal occurrence, an action of Love outside of time.

Someone once asked me a question about the Buddha's successor Mahakashyo and the moment in which Mahakashyo was the only one of the Buddha's disciples to "get it" and become awakened when the Buddha delivered his famous flower sermon.

"Have we not missed our opportunity?" he said to me.

"No," I replied, "the Buddha is forever delivering the flower sermon, and we are Mahakashyo, and we are Buddha who is forever offering the flower of spiritual enlightenment to the world. We are also the flower and, in just the same way, we are the Buddha offering ourselves back to ourselves for acknowledgement and recognition, for love and compassion toward ourselves, toward the world, and toward each other. For we are the same."

The world religions have told us this repeatedly. Perhaps we weren't listening? When St John of the Cross laid his head on the Divine, he forgot himself and the world. In the *Bhagavad Gita,* in recollection or remembering, you withdraw from the world of the senses, and you cannot speak of the eternal Tao. In the *Mandukya*

Upanishad, the Self is realized in the unthinkable and indescribable essence of Consciousness.

The moment of awakening is purely unselfconscious, and this is how it must be when you are transcending the self—the petty self. You are not present, you have never been truly present, and that is one of the meanings of spiritual awakening.

The term attracts comparison with waking up from sleep and it is apt. Because what concerns the "dream body" and even the identity you experience in your dreams is not the one you become conscious of in your waking life. There is a rupture in the flow of experience as you are set into the circumstances and requirements of the "real" world which is how people tend to refer to waking life.

Awakening is confused, or at least merged together, with insight, understanding, breakthrough, and smaller scale realizations. As such it is rather like a plethora of terms in the New Age, MBS, personal growth pantheon. Although we do not need to resort to the removed superiority of the rational mind, we can use our words precisely, clearly and accurately with apposite meaning, giving words the power to transport us, to ensnare us, to drop us into an experiential, feeling, emotional, and energetic receptivity to Truth.

Awakening then is a generic term. We should speak of levels, stages, and depths of awakening. The complexities of the human experience deserve that. We will return to a further discussion of awakening in chapter 9.

Discovering the True You

The often referred to true you, real self, or authentic self is not someone to discover, manipulate, or create. It emerges as a natural consequence of applied inner work. Likewise, your innate abilities, talents, challenges, purpose, and potential arise spontaneously and effortlessly as a result of the deep inner processes of clearing and releasing deeply suppressed emotional experiences. Seeking quick results by removing negative behaviors and patterns carry the risk that you throw out valuable, irreplaceable raw material for growth and compromise your chances of achieving wholeness. You may be doing more damage than good to yourself in your so-called healing through this kind of method.

Again, we cannot help wondering who, if anyone, is really listening? This insight, ignored by so many popular healing practitioners today, was expressed by Jung almost a hundred years ago in a dream interpretation in which a patient, slithering around on mucky treacherous rocks by the sea, scratches one to find that beneath the muckiness the rocks are made of pure gold. *Don't be too ready to get rid of your shit; it may be gold*—the dictum from the 1970s growth movement was quite likely built on this anecdote.

It is a crucially important principle. Perfectionism, the repression of the saboteur, idealization, addiction to faultlessness defeat your efforts at self-development, as much as in any other field. The true you is discovered through awareness, acceptance, and compassion toward yourself.

A Second Coming

We should smell a rat immediately when we see that all the world religions, as well as lesser religions, contain a doctrine of the second coming. If they all contain it, what truth could there be in it? They can hardly all be true, there would be far too many second comings! The concern about the future is not a spiritual concern; it is a human one. So once again, we have a clue. Jesus, Buddha, Da Kalki, King Arthur, Hiawatha, and all the great heroes will return... of course they will, and the truth of this is that they will return *in our hearts*. In their first coming they are an impersonal message of divinity in the form of a courageous life. They tell us that we ourselves are divine and that we as human beings are destined to realize our Self, our divine nature, here in this world—not in another world, at another time, or in another body. You are already divine. Your divinity is the only Reality... Come again? What for? You *are* divine.

End Times

End times fits in well here because along with the second coming you find end times abound. The Day of Judgment, the Apocalypse, and eschatological themes proliferate throughout history, in religion and mythology, and trickle down into popular thought. Let us restate, the Spiritual-Divine is not of this time-space continuum. The legends and myths and religious stories are maps, road signs, encoded instructions for our reaching spiritual enlightenment in the only place and time where that can ever occur—in this eternal moment. To "experience" this eternal moment (and experience must be in quotes to make the point that eternity cannot be experienced) we must become aligned to our eternal spirit beyond fear in the realm of Truth and radiance and the light body of Consciousness which is our human destiny.

Many atrocities have been carried out in the name of the end times. Predictions of the Apocalypse include the Essenes and the Mayans, two Millennium Apocalypses, Christopher Columbus, Jehovah's Witnesses (many times!), Charles Manson, and, of course predictably, Nostradamus, among many others. Perhaps we might be forgiven, in light of the extraordinary list of predicted end times, for thinking that humankind wants the end, but I suppose the choice between salvation and damnation is not much of a choice.

My wife, Nicky, once had a curious conversation with the leader of a small group in Totnes, England. He subscribed to Lee Jang Rim's prediction that the end of the world would be at midnight on October 28, 1992. He urged her to join him at an undisclosed location outside of town and ascend as a member of his small group of believers to avoid the coming devastation of the end times.

Lee Jang Rim was the head of a Christian religious movement called Dami Mission which had 20,000 followers in South Korea and the United States. Lee declared that the "believers" would ascend on the fatal date while those left would face seven years of intense suffering culminating in Jesus' second coming. His prophecies were communicated in his book *Getting Close to the End* and advertisements in the *Los Angeles Times* and *The New York Times*.

As the date approached, the predictions caused a social crisis among Lee's 20,000 followers in Korea. There were suicides, abortions, military desertions, and mass fasts, amid calls for the Dami Mission church to be closed down. In September 1992, Lee Jang Rim was arrested for fraud, about 30 members of his church were also charged, and Dami Mission churches were placed under constant surveillance.

On 28 October, fifty-four followers dressed in white burned furniture outside the Dami Mission headquarters, while one thousand pilgrims attended the Dami Mission church in Seoul where police sealed off stairs to the roof and barricaded the windows to prevent mass suicides. At ten minutes past midnight, a boy shouted through a window "Nothing's happening!" to the assembled crowd which included 1500 riot police, 200 detectives, 100 journalists, emergency vehicle crews, and dozens of plainclothes detectives who had infiltrated the organization—and it was all over.

A day or two after "the end of the world," Nicky passed by a wine bar in Totnes and happened to notice the leader of the group sitting with his followers looking rather sheepish.

Spirit Guides and Channels

Spirit guides and channels are projected images offering psycho-spiritual support and as such they are reminiscent of the idea of a universal deity or personally supporting entity, communicating, advising, and helping. All these images and ideas merely represent symbols pointing you toward absolute Reality. These personalities, even as supra-personalities, are nonetheless identifiable as individual identities, so they are not the Real, impersonal Truth. Mere disembodiment does not make you a wise teaching conduit of the Divine. Whereas the symbols themselves are transitional, the reality they point toward may be authentically and utterly real. Therefore, release yourself from attachment to these kinds of symbols as soon as possible so you don't fall into the trap that befell religious institutions through the ages, as well as misled cults and regressive fundamentalist religions in the present time, which is to elevate the symbolic means of spiritual transformation to the level of truth which it is not.

Create the Life You Want

The popular hope that you can create the life you want is based on the idea that freedom is license and fulfillment of desire. In whatever form it is presented, this is flagrantly untrue. Speculating on alternative paths for a human life is absurd. They are of no consequence to the serious student of spirituality. There is only the true path, which is the path of surrender and devotion, and the false paths.

However, distinguishing what you want in an inner world of multiple conflicts, the relationship of subpersonalities, and pulls from your many needs may not make this so easy. Most of us cannot distinguish between need, desire, and love. We are extremely resistant to having what we want, because desire generates its own dissatisfaction, which makes it an endless, rather than a fulfilling, pursuit. So starting to create images, lists, and visions of a wished for outcome, a desirable lifestyle, a sought after destiny… these attractive phrases are fraught with inaccuracies and unreality and as such they are only for those of us with un-enquiring minds who want to sop up this kind of zealousness for falsely appeasing the desire body, which is always a futile task. (I have a little more to say about this later in this chapter in *Matching the Frequency of Reality*.)

Acquiring Knowledge Furthers Your Enlightenment
Knowledge is of no use on the way to spiritual fulfillment. Knowledge gives you collections of data that you actually need to shed in the spiritual endeavor. I have a personal take on this, which may be helpful. In question and answer sessions sometimes the question has arisen that the questioner-seeker feels they do not know as much as I do. They perceive me as having a wealth of knowledge, and that without that depth and breadth of knowledge they would not be equipped to progress in the spiritual realms. In answer, I point out that my own therapist-teacher knew far less than I do now and that he wrote a page or two maximum on only one or two occasions because he had a lesser tendency to express himself through writing, and I am presently much better read than I believe he was. I do, however, consider myself a would-be scholar, because in the end I fall short of the tendency to study and accrue knowledge.

Do you remember the old Zen story of the professor who comes to the master for teaching? The master has the professor's teacup filled to overflowing, and when the professor complains, the master says that the cup, like his mind, is overfull and he should go and empty it before asking for spiritual teaching. The old Zen story, perhaps one of the most frequently told, should not blind us to its almost universal pertinence simply because it has been told so often. Instead perhaps we should consider that it has been told so often purely for the reason that it is so universally pertinent.

For some reason or other, spiritual seekers still persist in the erroneous idea that the more knowledge they pour into themselves and store up, the more enlightened they will become. Perhaps I have made my point now. Here it is anyway: knowledge is not wisdom and your wealth of knowledge will have to be forfeited in your bid for spiritual attainment—no exceptions.

Dissolve Your Problems
It's much more complex than this. Saying, "Dissolve your problems; make them go away, or rise above them," is like saying, "Relax!" You instantly acquire the additional problem of having to dissolve your problems, as you immediately feel extra tension in having to relax. To really make sense of and benefit from the past (which is where your problems come from), you must work with the subtle and gross inner dynamics that hamper your freedom by allowing yourself to re-experience, release, integrate, and stabilize in a complete healing process. This is not taking the long way round simply for the sake of it. The long way round is not only the more thorough and lasting route, it is also the way that brings the most long-lasting benefit.

Find a guide who knows what he or she is doing, focus your intention clearly, and set out for a longer journey than you imagine. Along the way, simply enjoy the process. You will make it, you will get there, and it is most likely to take longer than you had hoped

Find the Perfect Relationship
Good idea perhaps? But a perfect (in the sense of idealized and problem-free) relationship will never yield the fruits you need to process your inner world through seeing yourself in the other, which is, for a very long time the real purpose and function of a primary relationship. So aspiring to a "perfect" relationship too soon could be uninspiring, unhelpful, and extremely unwise, since all that can possibly do is generate complacency and a false sense of ease. Heal the relationships you have? Well yes, but depending on what you mean by heal. If heal means that perfect idea again, then no. How about accept it—warts and all—and be willing to compromise and allow all you can in the name of love to sweep you up and give you the key to successful relationships between two people, which is to value above all the opportunity to love.

Three Temptations: Pleasure, Wealth, and Power
Let's look at three proponents of the pursuit of worldly joy as a be-all and end-all, three Don Quixotes jousting at windmills, living in their imaginations, chasing the chimeras of youth, wealth, and power respectively. They are: the publisher Hugh Hefner, the entrepreneur Jack Ma, and the TV personality Martha Stewart.

Hugh Hefner, the Peter Pan of Porn: The Chimera of Sex and Youth
Hugh Hefner is the creator of Playboy Enterprises. He is 89, a multi-millionaire and lifelong playboy/womanizer. His sexual conquests are legendary. In the Sixties he boasted that he had been involved with "eleven out of twelve months' worth of Playmates" who appeared in his pinup magazine's centerfold. Forced to tone down his wild lifestyle following a stroke at 59, he married Playmate of the Year, Kimberley Conrad, who was nearly

40 years his junior. After he and Conrad separated in 1998, she moved into a house next door to his mansion.

Hefner developed a domestic arrangement with between seven and fifteen girls who lived in his mansion simultaneously in rather degrading conditions. They received a thousand dollars a week and had a seemingly unlimited allowance for breast and cosmetic surgery in exchange for attending a bi-weekly orgy, having sex with him, and appearing by his side in public on club visits to reinforce his playboy image. Alongside this arrangement, Hefner would favor a "Number One" girlfriend who shared his bedroom. He married his third wife, Crystal Harris, who was 60 years his junior, after ending his relationship with two "Number Ones" who were 20-year-old identical twin models.

Allegedly, sex for Hefner, now Viagra-fuelled, may be less frequent. Notwithstanding, the twice-weekly orgies persist with porn showing on two TV screens and all the girls dressed in pink pajamas with identical essentials—long blonde hair, doe eyes, and large breasts. The girls also have to observe a nine o'clock curfew and there is a total ban on recreational drugs, excluding Quaaludes, which are meant to put the girls in the mood for sex.

Do you think Hefner is truly happy?

He hasn't ever admitted to unhappiness. However, commentators note that he may have become obsessed with his legacy in his senior years. It seems he hopes to cultivate an image of himself as a cultural revolutionary, political spokesperson, and philanthropist, rather than a pornographer. Meanwhile he clings desperately to his youth through his exploitation of the female body and macho sexual image.

Jack Ma, the Reluctant Multi-Billionaire: The Chimera of Wealth and Value

Jack Ma is one of the richest people in the world. At 50-years-old, he is the Founder/Chairman of the Alibaba Group, a family of highly successful internet-based businesses. His estimated worth is over 20 billion US dollars. In 2014, *Forbes* ranked him the 30th most powerful person in the world.

Ma had failed university exams twice before being successful in getting a place in one of the worst universities in China. When he graduated, he taught English for $15 a month. In time he applied for many jobs getting turned down for a secretary's job at Kentucky Fried Chicken.

He saw the internet for the first time on a trip to Seattle as an interpreter. In spite of knowing nothing about computers or e-mails, he borrowed $2,000 to set up a company; he had never touched a keyboard. Speaking later of setting up the business, he said, "I was like a blind man riding on the back of a blind tiger."

Eventually he gathered eighteen people together in his apartment and explained his vision to them. Everyone put their money into the venture. His bywords for inspiration became value, innovation, and vision. The reason the company survived, according to Ma, was because they had no money, no technology, and no plan.

But Ma had a global vision and he called it Alibaba after the Thousand and One Nights. His motto was "Don't give up." When Alibaba went public, the company was valued at $26 billion.

But Ma seems to blame his business success for his personal unhappiness, which he has declared "my great pain." He complains that people have too high expectations of him, and he says he worries and thinks too much about the future. He hopes to alleviate his unhappiness through philanthropy. He has said that he wants to be himself, and that as one of the richest men in the world, people look at him in ways that inhibit that, but he just wants to be authentic, relaxed, and happy.

Martha Stewart, the "Brander" of Womanhood: The Chimera of Power and Influence

In the 1990s, Stewart was the definitive American woman. Her definition of womanhood was displayed in her lifestyle TV show, her *Martha Stewart Living* magazine, and her holiday specials. The former model also restored old properties, decorated homes, and produced books on: gourmet cooking, entertaining, wedding planning, and Christmas. She also wrote a mass of newspaper articles on homemaking.

The variety of her business ventures proliferated to include publishing, broadcasting, merchandising, and E-commerce. As a guest on many prestigious TV shows including Oprah Winfrey, her influence and popularity grew exponentially.

In 1999 Martha Stewart Living Omnimedia brought her TV, print, and merchandising ventures all together along with a new online catalogue business and a floral delivery business. When MSO went public, Stewart became the first female, self-made billionaire in the US.

In 2001, she sold shares on insider information to avoid financial losses and faced public and media scrutiny. The magazine Newsweek called it 'Martha's Mess' on its cover headline. In 2004, Stewart was convicted of charges related to insider trading. Indicted on nine counts, including securities fraud and obstruction of justice, she stood trial in 2004.After a highly publicized six-week jury trial, Stewart was sentenced to five months of incarceration, two years of supervised release, and five months of electronic monitoring.

But her comeback was spectacular. Within a short time, she had launched a new ready-made home furnishings business, produced several more TV specials, and published several books. By 2006 her power was more than recouped as she earned Emmy Awards for Best Host and Best Show for her daily talk show, and started selling homes based on her own. A year later, *Forbes* declared her the third richest woman in entertainment.

This embodiment of the American dream was the second of a family of six children. Her father was apparently strict, demanding, and disappointed with his life. Her mother was cold, unhappy, and resentful. Martha grew up under the constant threat of poverty. Her humble beginnings are thought to be linked to her need for power, control, devotion to perfectionism and material success. Her presentation of childhood seems to have been as much of a fantasy as her marriage and family in adult life. Her husband left Martha for one of her former assistants. The smart business woman image is balanced by accounts of her disorganization, short temper, and tyrannical behavior.

In 2015, her only child, a daughter Alexis, published a book revealing a strange childhood and revealing her mother's eccentric, antisocial, and often unmotherly behavior.

CB

We have considered the major chimeras of popular "spirituality" and considered three outstanding examples of success or failure, the three temptations. In conclusion, the Special Time, Awakening "Experiences," the True You, Spirit Guides and Channels, Abundance, and so on betray our inner collective paucity, and it's all show, all front, and all compulsive and seductive consensus making. Why should we be living at any better time than anyone else at any other time? What gives us the right to assume that human history and humanity's evolution may have converged here at your birth to make such a huge difference? This theme of time and spirituality is so important let us consider it in depth now.

Transformation, Time, and Modern Nonsense

Spiritual transformation does not occur in time. We transform in eternity out of our eternal nature. No explanation for this exists, because the time-bound mind is created from our thinking mind and the mind of thought is enslaved to the past, memory of past hurts, experiences, fixedness, divisiveness, and separation. Our liberation is predicated on our transformation, which is never conscious, but always emerging from that borderline of conscious and unconscious, inner and outer, human and spiritual worlds.

We are living in a time of profound transformation, but transformation does not occur in time. We might well be living in such a time, but when was it not a profound time for transformation. Transformation does not occur in time or space or the relative world, because it is just that—transformation—which, in spiritual terms, means a raising of consciousness to a higher spiritual or transcendental level.

The Right Time and Real Spirituality
This week (at the time of writing) a popular western guru releases his latest book—a book on spiritual realization. He is reported to have several thousand followers, as have many other western and eastern gurus around the world. The boom of interest in spiritual enlightenment is said to be greater than ever, greater perhaps than the time of Buddha. A leading spiritual spokesman and prolific author has praised this new spiritual work and adds that he is sad he isn't living in the era of the great masters, Buddha, Krishna, Jesus, but that maybe this is the right time to be enlightened.

What is this nonsense? The rallying cry of an earth-based spirituality is enticing and seductive. We—or perhaps I should really say "they" because it is not for me—are enthused, filled with camaraderie and mutual embracing, arm-linking and marching on to a brilliant enlightened, irresistible future. Commercially this is a good marketing ploy. How to get people together in spite of their differences in culture, dress, religious convictions, lifestyles, thoughts, habits—how to transcend all that and feel instant unity in a kind of idealistic, John Lennonesque way. We don't need to knock it any more than we need to knock the available personal growth holidays in the company of celebrity spiritual teachers, but I will simply say what must be obvious to anyone who takes a step back to look at it clearly: this has nothing whatsoever to do with real spirituality.

And how do I or we know? What do I base this on?

Hardly Anyone is Enlightened...
Well, for one thing there's 5000 years of ancient teachings. The word spiritual, if it has any meaning at all, is distinguishable from human and this doesn't mean that a relationship between the two does not exist, it means that we have to objectively and authentically discover, understand, and live the relationship between the two that exists in reality, not some mumbo-jumbo, feel-good, pie-in-the-sky, warm and fuzzy feeling that we wish spirituality was all about.

After the 5000 years of teaching there is the surely incontestable fact that, following fifty to a hundred years (depending if you date it from the New Age or the Sixties) of contemporary interest in spiritual matters in the West (the East had a good head start after all!) hardly anyone is enlightened. That's why we can have a spiritual teacher basing his teaching on this mix of terrible rubbish with some good stuff thrown in, so that we are confused or unquestioning, because we are rather like the audience at a tennis match looking this way and that, while we are being hypnotized by the charisma and bonhomie, plus a dash of genuine ego-challenge, always an added attraction that sells spirituality to the masses.

And masses it is too. Recently a famous author opened a telecast, cost-free, with the news that 15,000 people had signed up for his new course. The whole flavor of the presentation is unchallenging, feel-good self-improvement, while having all that can be desired in the material world as one's right. But can any of this truly be achieved without challenge, without the reality of surrendering ego-identity with its concomitant pain and loss?

Losing the Life Divine
If you fall for this stuff, and judging by the figures you probably have, the horse has already bolted, so who am I talking to here? We have truly lost ourselves and our spiritual way. If we lose our spiritual way we lose the means to transcendence, the location of the Divine. We forfeit what Sri Aurobindo (one of the spiritual masters who has provided much of the source material for the modern day teachings) called "the life divine." As our appetite and tendency toward the diluted version of spirituality persist, so we move further into the shadows.

Perhaps these are the truly dark times, the Kali Yuga, the days of ignorance and the eclipsing of enlightenment. What better way than to rig up a false and compulsively attractive system of quasi-spirituality with the truth ripped out of it, parade it on national TV, develop best-selling books about it, paint it in lurid colors, package it up with free gifts (I am not making any of this up, but you know that, I am sure), and sell it to the kowtowing, bowing masses. Wracked with guilt, carrying a burden of shame they are not even conscious of, filled with self-doubt, self-criticism, and negative judgments, they rush forward to claim a stake in the spiritual teaching that will absolve them from blame and vengeance and offer them contrition and redemption for their deep remorse.

The Secret to the Sacred Life
The victory in life which I and others have discovered is to be proud and alive, to celebrate and relish the moment, to greet life with passion and meaning, to live experience and be in all the multi-dimensional, present content, and challenging, mindful, joyful intensity of precious existence in this lifetime. The secret to making life sacred is to accept profoundly that life is a gift. It is a gift of learning and playing, and feeling and creating, movement and stillness, wisdom and bliss, ecstasy and fulfillment, mundaneness and extraordinariness, freedom and laughter. The motivation today is strong—most everyone involved would agree with these last sentiments—but the false guidance, the seduction, the manipulation, the ignorance, disguised as transcendence, is baffling.

When ego-forces are as strong as they are in the present era, the integrity of human beings is compromised almost beyond retrieval. These are dangerous times. It sounds so absurd that it is hard to take it seriously. Like waking from one of those super vivid dreams in which we are convinced of a death, or our culpability in an atrocious act, or our re-meeting and coupling with an old flame, or the loss of our home, our livelihood, or our partner, and the" reality" we find ourselves occupying is not authentically real. Like breathing polluted air, swimming in waste-infected water, exchanging all our other senses for the predominant visual sense, a deep love for superficial attraction, subordinating our rich, varied, and complex taste buds to merely sugar, sweets, synthetic food tastes, and abrasive deep fried foods, pop spirituality has sentimentalized, saccharined, and hideously processed the life force and the essence out of true spirituality.

People have become sophisticated in a predominantly urban modern culture. They read a little and think they can learn a lot from a little. They regurgitate truths as if they have experienced them for themselves when they haven't. They fall prey to the modern preeminent myth of facthood: I think therefore I am (when the reverse is more clearly the case). Any amount of Buddhist sayings, Advaita dictums, and other quotable spiritual sources will not make up for the lack of real wisdom gleaned from substantial spiritual practice and irrepressible consistency in dedicating ourselves to what is sacred.

Matching the Frequency of Reality
Most unfortunately of all, many fail to distinguish between their lower chakra concerns,[9] which are known to them, and their higher chakra concerns, which are not. The reflective nature of energy centers becomes a further source of confusion. For example, people band together to enjoy gathering and group interaction. Primarily this relates to the second chakra concerns to do with the security of the tribe, family, or gathering together to ensure safety and survival. By reflection the sixth chakra concerns are of a higher nature, a higher calling, yet they relate to the tribal chakra.

The spiritual process is long and hard—usually longer and harder than we think. Our desires, preferences, and requirements for how it should be must all be discarded over time. There is no other way. Any approach to authentic spirituality must reflect the same principle or it is counterfeit. The true world of consciousness and light is not subject to or influenced by our ego-identification in

---

[9]Chakras are the seven energy centers ascending through the human body from the base of the spine to the crown of the head. They represent survival, relationships, self-worth, love, self-expression, intuition, and pure consciousness.

any form whatsoever, for the simple reason that spirituality is about reality, and ego-processes are about illusion. They can no more coincide than we can spend in our waking life tomorrow the million dollars we possessed in our dream life last night.

A popular recent quote states: "Everything is energy… Match the frequency of the reality you want, and you cannot help but get that reality. It can be no other way. This is not philosophy. This is physics." (This is usually credited to Einstein, but it is actually Darryl Anka channeling Bashar, a "multi-dimensional extra-terrestrial being," in 2001). The level on which this statement is possibly true presupposes such a high psychological and spiritual attainment it would entail that you know exactly what you are doing, not only in your actions, but also in your conscious mind, your subconscious, and your unconscious; that you are fully aware of your emotional life and able to track it; that there is an advanced sense of harmony between your body and mind; that you have deepened in awareness practices to become consistently and fully aware of the totality of your organism, and ideally that you have transcended the ego-tendencies toward identification, separation, and division. So it's absurd from the point of view of the average person who is unlikely to ever put the time and effort in to achieve these advanced psycho-physical states.

Collecting Rubbish in the Wake of the Guru
The truth contained in these kinds of feel-good maxims, which are so popular among the spiritual fraternity, is often so unqualified as to be useless or even untrue to anyone other than those who want to live in a world of delusion. While delusion may manifestly be what spirituality is not about, it has in its history attracted a fair amount of it.

This is because the interpretation into words and expression of spiritual truths is inevitably filtered through a personality, albeit a spiritual personality, and a particular culture at a specific time. For example, it would be hard to pull off the mustard seed analogy today, but Jesus used it most effectively in Galilee 2000 years ago. The cinema screen projector simile used by Ramana Maharshi was of its time and not available to previous Indian saints for reflections on time and eternity. Finally, the carriage, horse and the coachman analogy used by Gurdjieff (but probably derived from either the Katha Upanishad or Plato's *Phaedra*) is certainly archaic today as modern and relevant as it must have sounded when he used it.

In a sense, this could mean that anyone can say anything (cynical view), or any genuine spiritual teacher exhibits enlightenment through all that they say, think, feel, and do (positive view). The latter is like the female spiritual teacher in Mumbai who, according to Mariana Caplan in her book, *Do You Need a Guru?*, walks the seashore collecting rubbish. As her disciples join her, they too take up the practice and silently begin collecting rubbish in her wake.

Spiritual Enlightenment is Located in the Eternal Moment
A mysterious event takes place in the contact between the spiritual teacher and the genuine disciple. It is called variously transmission, opening, grace, revelation, initiation, awakening, illumination, purification, or enlightenment. More accurately it is less mysterious than it is genuinely spiritual, so to express it in words is almost impossible. Instead it must be expressed poetically or metaphorically. This is the point at which the literacy, poetic sensibility, or disinclination to speak of spiritual matters kicks in according to the temperament of the spiritual teacher. For a spiritual teacher is not necessarily

literate. Neither is an enlightened being necessarily a spiritual teacher. When enlightenment meets the teaching ability or gift (or function, as it is sometimes unattractively called), you have a spiritual master, one who imparts understanding and illumination to others.

To return then to where we began—*we are living in a time of profound transformation, but transformation does not occur in time*—this mysterious or spiritual and consequently inexpressible phenomenon or event happened outside of time in the eternal moment where all spiritual enlightenment is located.

In Summary

In this chapter we have begun the process of taking away the false so that what will remain is the real. We have considered how our world comes into being in a discussion of action and inertia. We contrasted the cushioned death of habit with the vitality and spontaneity of real spirituality, discussed the temptations of power, wealth, and fame, and the price of delusion. We deconstructed some of the staple beliefs of popular spirituality and superficial teachings, and I hope, once and for all, established some clarity in the relationships of time and eternity, stagnation and transformation, the human and the Divine. It has been a tough ride, this insurgence of light into the murky underbelly of New Age assumptions. Integrate and stabilize in the personal insights you have gleaned from this exploration using the following exercises and questions.

1. In what ways, if at all, was this gentle compassionate demolition difficult or painful for you? Do you still hold on to any of these ideas I have attempted to discredit or deconstruct? Do you disagree? If so, state your case (in writing using your inner work notebook) and "flesh out" your point of view.

2. Meditation on the three *gunas*: In my book *The Flight of Consciousness*,[10] I wrote of an ancient Vedic teaching:

> In the ancient *Vedas*—literally "sacred teaching" and the oldest texts of Indian literature—the world of

---

[10] Richard Harvey, *The Flight of Consciousness: A Contemporary Map for the Spiritual Journey*, Ashgrove Publishing 2002, 123.

appearances is made up of three *gunas*, or qualities—goodness, passion, and ignorance. These three qualities both conceal and are born of Brahman—Absolute non-duality. Goodness represents the inner purity that we need to realise the Self; passion stimulates activity and is regarded as the obstacle to goodness and ignorance produces immobility, which is needed to overcome passion. According to the *Vedas*, we need to balance these three qualities so that nothing appears in the realm of *maya*, then all is in perfect poise and the Higher Self can be fully realised.

Sit in a comfortable meditation position and allow yourself to feel relaxed and alert. Now take a deep breath and begin to follow your breath in and out. Spend some time meditating on the arising of the three *gunas*: the qualities of goodness, passion, and ignorance—purity, action, and resistance. Everything that arises, arises from the interaction of these three qualities. Deepen into your awareness of this interaction and see what insights it yields.

3. Experiential exercise and question (*koan*): walking in nature, contemplate the endless differentiation of natural forms—no two leaves, no two rocks, no two clouds are alike... no repetition exists in nature. Now your *koan*: what is the relation between this relative world and the eternal moment?

4. Have you ever had the experience of being taken in by a chimera or succumbing to a false temptation? What was it like for you and what did you learn?

5. Desire feeds off the frustration of ever possessing its object... no? If that is the case, then what about the

desire for spiritual understanding or enlightenment? Could this desire be somehow different?

6. "Imagine all the people/Living life in peace"[11]: How could this ever happen? Is it possible?

---

[11] John Lennon, *Imagine*, © Sony/ATV Music Publishing LLC.

4. The Ten Tenets (or the Heretical Creed)

Decimation and Tithing

Now let's be a little quasi-religious, irreligious, sacrilegious and bring a tablet down the mountain... momentarily! To finish our gentle demolition and raze the building to the ground, I propose a heretical pagan creed of ten main points to hang the wrecking ball off. They will serve as links in the steel chain to swing the ball... and decimate delusion.

The original meaning of the word "decimation," which now means destruction or loss, was "the removal or destruction of one-tenth" (from the Latin word *decimare*). Decimation is related to tithing—the giving of a tenth. The first recorded instance of tithing is in Genesis in a transaction between Abraham and the priest Melchizedek following Abraham's defeat of the Elamite army. In the following ten tenets, I trust you will find some decimating truths.

The First Tenet: The State of Ignorance
The world today is unsacred, Divine-less, a-spiritual, and love-poor. Only a spiritual revolution can change this state of ignorance into one of understanding, compassion, co-operation, and spiritual enlightenment.

The Second Tenet: The Child-like Condition
People today are prevented from rising into the heart chakra because they are centered in the child heart, which

is not unlike the *puer eternus* in Jungian thought. Trapped in a child-like condition whereby the needs and desires of their early life development are unfulfilled, they are doomed to a life of repetition, frustration, and unfulfillment.

The Third Tenet: The Image of the Spiritual Teacher
Spiritual teachers in the modern world are considered in the same way as a beneficent father God or Santa Claus. The image of the spiritual teacher is less one of discipline, challenge, and rigorous truth-seeking, and more one of kindly parent who comforts, protects, saves, and delivers.

The Fourth Tenet: The Cult of Personality
This is the age of the individual who expresses him- or herself through personality based on character. The cult of personality that surrounds popular spiritual teachers today is identical and equal in importance to the fans' relationship to pop idols, celebrities, and actors (who are sometimes considered spiritual spokespeople). This is the projection of the self-serving ego-state.

The Fifth Tenet: Spirituality is Not Neurosis
People must learn to mature and closely examine their relationship to "spirituality." Nearly everyone I see who professes to be "spiritual" reflects an anxious, angry, unconscious need in the psyche, which is not spiritual at all, but merely neurotic.

The Sixth Tenet: Deepening into Presence
If you are following a spiritual path (see the Eighth Tenet) you are almost certainly misdirected, caught almost exclusively in childhood and early life patterns, and not thinking for yourself. Release from your conditioned path

begins with your active deepening into presence and innate intelligence.

The Seventh Tenet: The Preparation for Spiritual Practices

Who cares how *you* see it? Who cares about your opinions, your personality, your habits, your conflicts, or your arguments? Mainly—if not exclusively—*you*. So long as you have still a fundamental, ego-based attachment to yourself, you are not yet prepared, ready, open, and willing to enter the spiritual-transcendent journey. So you must work hard to release your attachments to your ego-self. This work is not spiritual, but merely psychological. It is, however, preparation for spiritual practices.

The Eighth Tenet: No Path to the True Self

You should know and be aware that, ultimately, there is no spirituality, no path, and no method. The divine transcendence you seek is here already, manifestly present. It requires no seeking to discover; seeking only takes you further away. So the only spiritual practices that are worth anything at all are the ones that assist you in that endeavor.

The Ninth Tenet: No Spiritual Attainment

The true spiritual state is the one of being purely as you are, without adapting or interfering. There is no spiritual attainment, only ceasing to do what you do out of entrenched habit to inhibit the natural state of enlightenment. Effort is mostly unconscious; hence, most people will not begin to authentically understand this tenet.

The Tenth and Final Tenet: Reducing the Spiritual

Spirituality may not be witnessed through the individual focus, anymore than you can fit a quart into a pint glass. All aspects of the spiritual are misunderstood in this ego-activity and reduced to material worldly quasi-spiritual events in what I would call the "sacred" Walt Disney effect. In the commercialized modern world, a human being is reduced to a representation, a quality turned into a cartoon appearance. Actors play two-dimensional parts, and love is reduced to sentiment, a travesty of the sacred.

In Summary

An old teacher of mine used to say that the inner journey is so serious and dark sometimes that you have got to be able to laugh to save yourself from going under. In the Ten Tenets, I have brought you some serious matters in a perhaps humorous form. Each one is important, if not crucial. Spend a little time contemplating each one and recognizing its significance in your life. The following exercises are given to aid you in this endeavor.

1. Is a spiritual revolution the only way to radical change in the modern world?

2. Why and how do human beings cling to their childhood state?

3. Why shouldn't the spiritual teacher be a kindly Santa Claus or beneficent God-like figure?

4. What, if anything, is wrong with cults?

5. How do psychology and spirituality relate within you? We release our attachment to the personality—identity and separation—in preparation for spiritual practice per se. This preparation brings up the question: Who am I without my personality, my opinions, my preferences, my story, and my argument?

6. *Contemplate* these three statements: There is no path to where you already are. Seeking only takes you further away. Stop what you are doing to avoid your present state.

5. Spiritual Celebrity or Spiritual Teacher, and the Cult of the Individual

Specialness and the Spiritual Celebrity

The spiritual celebrity cults today, far more than any genuine spiritual longing or transcendental motivation, demonstrate a childish need to assimilate oneself into a family grouping, to be seen, to be given attention, and to be loved. Spiritual celebrities proliferate because individual egos are caught in an endless dance of reinvention and rejuvenation. Thus, the cults of spiritual celebrities paradoxically ensure the survival of the ego.

Seriously reflect and ask yourself: do I really long for the Divine more than I long for money, pleasure, status, power, fulfillment, or for human love in my life? If the answer is no, you are not yet engaged spiritually. You may be engaged psychologically in inner work and development, but unless you are seeking the spiritual, the transcendent, and the Divine above all things—simply because that is what is Real—you are not sincerely, wholly, and practically ready for the spiritual fire. If you were to enter it, you would incinerate instantly.

Spiritual celebrity is a contradiction in terms. Somewhat like personal enlightenment, spiritual experience, or real illusion. The Truth has been assimilated into the human, commercial, entertainment culture for public consumption, ground in the pestle and mortar of ignorance, watered down into palatable food for weak stomachs, and distorted to fit. A number of methods prevail to bring this about—mock inclusion, embracing and accepting blindly, adulation, the need for a good daddy, mommy, and savior, or impossible idealization. In spite of a little knowledge, we are not always wise... at least in matters of reality, projection, and delusion.

Yet authentic spirituality is in need of our serious engagement for the sake of the world, for the sake of ourselves, and for the sake of Reality or enlightenment itself. In these dark times when the light of enlightened souls and the great wisdom of the perennial philosophy are all but entirely eclipsed, we may substitute wisdom with knowledge, seek *upanishads*[12] as self-help, mistake ego-aggrandizement for ego-transcendence, and chase experience at the expense of realization, immersed unconsciously, as we are, in a psychological straitjacket of self-obsession.

The cult of spiritual celebrity that prevails today may be due to the powerful filters of mind-body-spirit packaging, as well as the transference of ourselves onto closely admired and identified-with glossy or intentionally un-glossy figures, celebrities or anti-celebrities, who spout a body of knowledge that is now freely available on the internet to anyone who can read and which according to people's proclivities appeals in grandiose or paltry ways depending on our psychological makeup.

Perhaps it is my prejudice, but I cannot help reflecting on the paleness of the contemporary spiritual teachers when compared to, say, Vivekananda, Yogananda, Gurdjieff, Krishnamurti, or Steiner. Not only are the contemporary teachers far less deep and charismatic, they are merely derived and superficial. The century of the self that began with teachers of obvious spiritual character and

---

[12]The Sanskrit meaning of *upanishad* is "sitting at the feet of the teacher to receive esoteric knowledge."

uniqueness has ended with teachers of pale imitation and second-hand vision.

The fawning cults that have formed around these straw dog teachers, that are themselves an interesting image-personification of our perceived flaws and weaknesses, are based on the insecurities and unfulfilled desires of early life: the need to belong, to fit in, to be welcomed. The passive, listening, upturned faces of disciples of these cut-out spiritual teachers are usually an unconscious response to the unmet needs of childhood to be loved and given to, sitting mesmerized, fascinated, less listening, more longing, and unable truly to receive. It seems that the need to be, or at least to feel, special, reflected in the mirror of the spiritual celebrity, bathing in their aura and brightness of their "light" while imbibing the "teaching" has become irresistible to many in the 21st century.

An Individual Path to Spiritual Enlightenment?

Like so many half-thought out and partially understood principles, the common belief in spiritual circles that each human being has or possesses an individual path to self-realization points to a more complex truth than is at first apparent.

The ways to spiritual attainment are as many as there are human beings. But this doesn't preclude the usefulness of following a valid spiritual path, as part of or as our entire individual journey. Certain prerequisites are mandatory in spiritual practice. Particular thresholds must be crossed, sometimes timing is essential, and sometimes psychological or spiritual work left undone holds us back. It is a far cry from the teachings of instantaneous enlightenment or the liberal contemporary school of do-what-feels-right spirituality. This is because discipline has a fundamental place in spiritual life and practice. When I am asked about spiritual practice without a guide, I have to answer, "Yes, we may all want to do it ourselves, but—and it's a big but—*we can't.*" Why not? Ego forces are far too strong to handle on our own.

Self-help spirituality is like living on your own. When you live alone every moment is an opportunity for self-delusion. You have no idea if you're in a good mood or a bad mood, angry or afraid, resentful or contented. But if somebody is sharing your life, your space, your meals, your living room, they become a mirror—and often an unforgiving, uncompromising one. When you are in a bad mood, you may take it out on them. Even when you don't, they will feel it anyway because it's hard to hide in relationship.

The spiritual teacher is like that domestic mirror, but far more intense. He or she may feel you, be clairvoyant of your inner states, and know you better than you know yourself. The challenge to your integrity is enormous, because there is literally nowhere you can hide. Curiously as your deep inner desire to be known truly is manifested, you experience the farther side of desire—how you resist being known at all. Caught between desire and fear—your desire to be known and your fear of being known—your ego processes are driven into the shadows... or into the light if you are ready to change.

The teaching of your chosen teacher may be verbal or silent. There is a mélange of methodologies including verbal teachings, *satsang* (the company of truth), experiential energetic wisdom, ecstatic infection, hands-on spiritual healing, transmission, and *mouna* (teaching in silence). In spite of all these ways, the assertion is often made that there is no best way, and no required or mandatory practice.

Well, we may all walk and walking may be a common experience. But have you noticed how everyone, without exception, walks in their own unique way? Think about this for a moment: how do you recognize someone across the street from behind, as they walk away from you into the distance? Do you see? Their walk is uniquely expressive of their character. There has never been anyone like me before, and there never will be again. There has never been anyone like you, and there never will be again; we are all utterly unique.

This rather obvious yet crucial insight brings us to the questions. Is there a personal path to spiritual enlightenment? How can we drop the personality if our very path to realization is personal? Shouldn't we have a depersonalized, impersonal path to what is after all impersonal Self-realization? Please allow me a brief detour.

As I loathe generalizations, I have often had an aversion to writers, sages, and gurus telling me what's happening to me, as if I were a broad mass. I have been known to throw books across the floor and leave them to gather dust! I have justified this stance, as you might also have done, by reasoning that if I was offended then I obviously belonged in the group the teacher was referring to. It is perhaps easy and clearer to point out how this works. There are three general types of human beings—the simple innocents, the complex ones, and the authentic ones. Most people are in the middle group, the complex ones, which is why the generalizing on the whole works, because generally speaking that is where you and I are likely to be. More specifically, most people by far are in the lower bands of the middle group, which is to say they have lost their innocence to the complexity and conflict, the sacrifice and the general neurotic state of modern humankind. When I speak of spiritual challenges and tasks, I am addressing those who are interested enough to read, study, or enquire for themselves and/or for others into spiritual teachings, practices, and methodologies. They, or perhaps we, since you picked up this book, belong in the third group, the authentic ones.

Now to the role of personality: the first group—the innocents—are oblivious to personality as to most else; they simply do not question or enquire. The second group—the complex ones—wrestles at best with personality, with the desire and the fear of it, the clinging and the cost of holding onto it, and finally the third group—the authentic ones—clearly sees the role of personality and the need to shed attachment to it, while recognizing that as a human being your personality provides a vehicle through life.

The individual today as personality and character is not only unavoidable, he or she is one of our greatest assets in self-exploration, insight into truth, and ultimately in providing fuel for the spiritual fire. (We will discuss this further in The Free Individual, chapter 14.)

Therefore, it is I who chart my own awakening. But is it and could it be desirable that each person is creating their own individual path to awakening? The answer is no. For the simple reason that ego cannot work against itself, and desire cannot work against itself. We can no more do it on our own than we can look around and see ourselves.

Spirituality is Not Entertainment

Spirituality is not synonymous with entertainment. The search for truth, the desire to know the Divine, and the opening of the heart to compassion are not matters to be taken lightly. They are easily distinguishable from entertainment.

We can leave it to scholars and sociologists to trace the history; the downgrading of the spiritual into the purely secular, the descent of the transcendent, particularly over the last few decades. No doubt the New Age will feature in the examination, the rise of the flimsier mind-body-spirit publishing too, the manipulation of the public mind and heart by half-baked spiritual teachers, bathing in adulation, turning a quick buck, and resorting to easy sentiment and playing with suppressed emotions. Our thirst for self-knowledge, our need for self-improvement, and our attraction toward the appearance of depth has been enormous. It has revealed a great gaping hole, as the open mouth of oral endlessness—need, desire, and love plaited together beyond distinction—opened and closed over the objects—books, magazines, poetry, films, workshops, courses, ashrams, trainings, ancient and modern masters, spiritual practices, psychological exercises—of our manic devouring. And somewhere among this conflagration… authentic spirituality sidled into the realms of entertainment.

Spirituality is not entertainment and since so much is these days, we really need to distinguish between the two. So let us look at three main points of departure—preference, happiness, and choice.

Not Conforming to Preferences
First, the question of preference. You do not have to prefer or necessarily even *like* the spiritual path that you are

drawn, often inexplicably, toward. The character of the teacher, components of the methodology, appearance of the organization or movement has absolutely nothing to do with your attraction—from the spiritual perspective.

This is because authentic spirituality is not a reinforcement of your ego-self. Neither is it a support or a challenge, nor any kind of invitation to your ego-self. The spiritual in whatever way it appears in your life poses a threat to your ego-self. It may ignore, conflict, oppose, or demolish the ego-self altogether—if not immediately, then over time. Therefore, if you find yourself, as your ego-self, attracted to spiritual discipline, be wary. The spiritual path you follow should at least be rigorous enough that you feel the very edges of your comfort, your defensiveness, and your identification with your ego.

In contrast, of course, with entertainment the very opposite is the case. We are drawn to personalities, celebrities, and characteristics presented in the media that draw (and manipulate) us toward certain personality images (not real people you notice) and, by association, their products: movies, music, T-shirts, websites, and so on. The association through desire is enough and it's simple to understand: we say we like someone or other and we are now sided with this package or image-streaming product, aligned with it or on its team, so to speak. If you like the same as me then we are brothers and sisters together. If you like another opposing celebrity or celebrity field or group then we are opposed to each other, exhorting the virtues of our preferred entertainment over yours. All good fun perhaps, but a million miles away from spirituality. This competition incited by entertainment (sports, pop culture, movies, dining-out, classical concert-going, opera …) is centered in the lower energy system of a human being. It is the base chakras that emanate and exploit this "need" to be associated with the strong or weak of the tribe for survival and for status. Thus in the eat-or-be-eaten world of animalistic concerns, we become one of the elite (or at least favored by the elite) few who are assured of their physical survival due to their elite status.

Even if the spiritual path we are deeply drawn toward is initiated by attractive appearances, characters, and so on, we will arrive at a point fairly soon where we wish we had been drawn in some other direction. The spiritual path, the path of loss, yielding and surrender concerns ordeal, challenge, unrest, embracing suffering, heartbreak and the radical, gritty journey to our core, and then further sacrifice. This is not entertainment; it does not conform to our expectations or preferences.

Not Pursuing Relative Happiness
Second, the question of happiness. Entertainment does provide a rush of excitement, short-lived euphoria even, and a certain human passion and pleasurable, tortuous longing (toward the desired object, unattainable and therefore more desirable). This kind of happiness and satisfaction is unstable and usually short-lived, because it is attached to an object through desire. When the object is present, fleetingly and tantalizingly, suggestively and teasingly and the object of desire appears to be in our grasp or *almost* available, we feel happy. When the object of desire is denied to us, withheld, ignoring us, or abandoning, we are not. This kind of relative happiness is obviously based on desire. Spirituality does offer happiness. The joy of self-realization is unequalled. But it is vastly different to a joy based on desire, happiness founded on "I want" with the corollary of unhappiness founded on "I don't want."

Very closely associated with the demise of the ego is the eroding of desire—desire which thinly masks frustration and chronic dissatisfaction. Desire is like the reins that you pull the donkey of the ego-self along with.

The happiness you reach through spiritual ways and mean by contrast is not dependent on any object. Neither is it a see-saw between desire and frustration.

Not Having Choice
Third, the question of choice. We love to think we have choice; don't we? We become outraged at any suggestion of the opposite. But what if we really do not have choice... at all? Time to wake up now! Your conditioning through your early childhood years has prevented choice on the authentic level. You have learned to settle for third—no wait, twenty-fourth, may be thirty-fifth best! I am joking a little here because this point is so truly serious. You do not choose. Inside you is a pantheon of splintered personalities. You are as used to them and as accustomed to their rivalry and conflict as you are to the microorganisms raining micro-blows all over your face. In other words, you are oblivious to it.

A little humility can go a long way here. Consider any moment or any field in which your eyes were opened and you realized that something wasn't what you thought it was. A lot of this kind of thing is happening today. Politicians, royalty, celebrities, public figures who embody some quality, some values, some aspirations for us are falling off their pedestals in disgrace. We realize then that they are not who we thought they were... and choice is not what we think it is. Neither is love or freedom or anything else, until we have surrendered to the sacred-spiritual life fully.

You notice perhaps that something all three of these—preference, happiness, and choice—have in common, in the context of my criticism here, is that they are individual and personal. Thus they are participating factors in the ego-processes. As such they give support to separation, division, and identification.

Today we are subject to the pressures and demands, insidious, ubiquitous, and seductive as they are, of a youth culture. This youth culture has insinuated itself deeply into the collective psyche and gorges itself on fear and, unsurprisingly, on desire. From its vacuous celebration of the persona or mask to its superficial parodying of real energies, like sexuality, worship, ecstasy, and spiritual attraction, through glamour and manufactured charisma, the point is lost, the reality is trundled, raked, ploughed over, disintegrated, and interred in the burial—the personality cannot deliver the rewards we long for.

Personality is Merely an Impression

You do not grow authenticity or spiritual enlightenment out of the personality level of your humanness. You cannot develop reality from the imaginary. This appears obvious but human beings are subject to egoic forces and the ego's principle justification and point of view is that the egoic perspective is all there is.

The claim is absurd, but the argument is compulsive. We sometimes deny the simplest of truths. For example, we are created out of fear and desire. Consider the life of someone you know; isn't their life dominated by fear and desire? You don't need to look too deeply to see this and yet people are inclined to deny it, as if you are catching them *in flagrante*, with their trousers down or on the toilet. Fear and desire are nothing to be ashamed of because they are the necessary beginning for embarking on your spiritual path. They establish your human status and assert that you possess the potential for Self-awakening.

The absurd claim that spiritual enlightenment grows from your individual personality is the misguidance of your ego's resistance to its own demise. What better way to preserve itself and you in your suffering than to pitch the argument that ego is all, as rational fact? Now, if you are inclined to better yourself, improve your life, or change your character, inevitably you must begin at the ego level. For some time then you suffer the futile defeat of failure, over and over, until you understand that some attitude, some fundamental stance, poise, or alignment in you is simply off beam. You are not going to succeed because you are approaching this all wrong.

It is a steep learning curve and one that we have to endure and overcome more than once to emerge each time renewed and more insightful. The ego is so extraordinarily resourceful; it deceives us time and time again. And each time we discover a little more about ourselves.

Now when you have brought attention to your personality or journeyed around the self so that most of what you were previously unaware of in yourself is now perfectly visible, you are ready to move on in your personal process. This preliminary work calls for great self-regard and belief, a fundamental sense of worth, tremendous honesty, and openness.

Despite how it looks and feels, personality is merely an impression. In a way we already know and are aware of this. Even a vivid and genuine feel or experience of life *as it is* can be enough to usurp our habitual ego-based viewpoint. In those times when we penetrate into a fresh vivid realness and sincerity or experience truth or a transpersonal, ecstatic vision or event, we discover a deeper experience of truth behind the veils.

In Summary

In this chapter we have considered the cult of spiritual celebrity as projections of individual ego-states, the personal, unique nature of the spiritual path alongside, versus or complementing general mandatory requirements common in spiritual practice. We talked of the dangers and necessity of generalizations, preference, happiness, and choice as anathema to the true spiritual pursuit, the impossibility of growing enlightenment out of the seed of egoity, and individual personality as illusion in contrast to the transpersonal realms of reality. Deepen into these themes now with these exercises.

1. Pick a "spiritual" celebrity and look closely into his or her work. Examine their character, personality, and the prevalent themes of their teaching. What aspects of egoity do you find are reflected in their persona? How deep do you find their teaching?

2. Identify and explore, first, the uniqueness of your own spiritual path and, second, aspects of spiritual discipline you may find challenging or hard to accept.

3. Give yourself some time in an expansive place—on a hill, near a river, at the ocean—now let the sense impressions of the place you are in fill you—sound, sight, taste, smell, and touch—allow yourself to merge with the experiences of the senses and, in time, settle into *union*.

4. Intentionally refuse to follow your preferences at home, in a restaurant, in a bookstore, in your leisure time—in different milieus, experiment with making choices that bypass or even oppose your preferences and watch... notice the effects.

5. Draw a picture—using expressive crayons or paints—of your persona.

6. Write a short autobiography centered and focused on the twin themes of fear and desire.

6. The Form of Nothingness

One spiritual teaching that has become rapidly popular, surprisingly so, is the profound teaching of non-duality or Advaita. Perhaps it is the epitome of our over-eagerness and our emotional precociousness that we should embrace such a teaching and inevitably reduce it to a parody of itself. Perhaps it was predictable that our enthusiasm to transcend repressed emotions should have resulted in the need for a premature "payback" in the form of a spiritual teaching that negates the separate self. For Advaita offers us the ideal of healing in the form of nothingness. "Never born and never died" makes emotional healing either worth it or worthless, depending on how you look at it.

Advaita is the teaching of Vedantic non-dualism. It denies the separateness of any aspect of reality from the impersonal oneness of Brahma—everything is God. From the point of view of personality, it provides absolutely no comfort or compromise. It eradicates ego from the very beginning.

Is Advaita the great liberator or a greater torment? While answering some people's questions about life, it has got just as many into very deep waters of despair and confusion. Both magnificent deliverer and fiendish bewilderer, it manifests paradoxically both clarity and confusion, spiritual profundity and human distress.

The Advaita Answer—the Distress of Non-Duality

Many people today have stumbled upon the new and ancient writings and transcripts of the wisdom of non-duality, derived from the teachers of Advaita Vedanta. Pre-eminent among them are Ramana Maharshi, Nisargadatta Maharaj, and Ramesh Balsekar. Modern western teachers, like Eckhart Tolle and Andrew Cohen, have been considered proponents of Advaita, too. These teachings have seized the spiritual world, and there are currently far too many less well-known teachers to even begin to name them all. They are arrayed all around the world coming from different walks of life, may be literate or not, sophisticated or not, but the basic principles they share are that the world you see does not exist (or may not matter at all), you do not exist (ditto), and that each of us is the totality, as summarized in the classic phrase of Advaita, "You are That."

These teachings are among the very highest spiritual teachings in the world today, and possibly the highest. Yet they cause a great deal of pain and distress to ordinary people on a spiritual search. I have counseled some who felt unemotional and indifferent about life, dejected, futile, or suicidal. Because of their attachment to their personalities and characters, they were most definitely not ready for these teachings.

The essential Advaita principles are that absolute reality is formless, non-dual awareness, and the goal of life is self-realization which is not separate from the Absolute reality. These beliefs can lead to a solid, encased circle of philosophical thinking that acts as a tourniquet on the individual life-force standing in an egocentric vessel... a circle that can only be ruptured by the catharsis of inner distress at the assault on one's fundamental sense of self.

This tourniquet effect is surely ambiguous. It is both Advaita's great strength and also its "weakness." In what has become known as the "Ramana effect" (because he propagated it), Advaita today has been criticized for disregarding preparatory practices. Traditionally, a spiritual practice to bring the aspiring student to a level of maturity and one-pointed desire for enlightenment preceded the transmission of teachings of this magnitude. The lack of adequate preparation for the Advaita insight may, for example, account for this person's experience:

> This Advaita philosophy has really disturbed me. Reading Nisargadatta's books has damaged my emotional life. I think I should become solely analytical to save myself. Absolute truth, nothing exists, we are never born and never die—the language and ideas confuse me! Does anything truly matter? Or exist? If I think anything at all, apparently I am simply wrong! Everything is a lie or a dream or a fantasy or deceitful. And in reality I am God, or something, or not, or neither! And non-existent! Where does this end...?

This person, who had found their way to me for therapy, was not only intensely emotionally disturbed, they were also contemplating suicide.

Advaita Vedanta reflects truths that are extremely difficult to accept or even tolerate before you are ready for them. This doesn't mean that Advaita itself is flawed; neither does it make the human being who is unable to hear the teachings flawed. It is simply a mismatch, a relationship that cannot be, an arrangement of parts that don't gel yet, and may never form a creative whole.

Let me try to illustrate this. In a previous chapter of life, I was a guitarist. Playing my guitar, I would try to put phrases together that were meaningful, emotionally exciting, musically rhythmic, and melodically expressive. Around this time a young guitarist emerged who set a new benchmark for melodic, rhythmic, and expressive guitar playing and, in particular, improvisation—Mark Knopfler. As I puzzled on his phrasing, which I was unable to emulate, and the quality of his musicianship, what baffled me was that he was using the same basic eight notes of the scale as I was, yet the difference was as heaven and earth.

Here's another illustration. A TV documentary I watched about Picasso showed the master daubing paper using only a thick felt-tip pen (a modern invention at the time). Using only this mundane medium, he produced lines, form, texture, and composition that took your breath away. Working spontaneously, he seemed incapable of drawing a mediocre line.

In the hands of Knopfler or Picasso, wood, paint, strings, and paper produce worlds of transcendent art. They are prepared, practiced, and gifted, but also full of mature artistry; they are ready to express greatness. In Picasso's case, he assimilated the rule book before he discarded it. In Knopfler's case, some inner daemon fuelled him to bring the staple rock 'n' roll instrument into a postmodern era through his innovative interpretations.

Advaita, too, is greatness; it is a transcendent spirituality, but one you cannot possibly take in without meticulous, authentic preparation. I do not want to labor this point here, since we will look at this in more detail in Part 4, but the free availability of the secrets needs to be tempered and governed and taught by a genuine spiritual instructor or teacher. Such a one would be sure to gauge the readiness and openness of the pupil or student and guide them along gently and encouragingly.

The Advaita Question—the Peerlessness of Non-Duality

Advaita teachings have helped me to arrive at my three-stage model of human awakening as a radical response to the spiritual crisis of this new century. My model is designed to help people work through their personal psychology in preparation for deeper human and spiritual truths.

When you are stuck in personal psychology the deeper truths of spirituality may only be experienced through an ego filter. Not only are they veiled, liable to be misinterpreted, and beyond your comprehension, but they are also inappropriate—a practice you are not ready for and should not have posed to you as a challenge.

One of the most curious aspects of Advaita is that when you hear, or more likely read, the words of a genuine master they carry enormous weight. They penetrate to the core of your soul, and you are drenched in the truth of the utterance. I have experienced this first hand and must admit to reading *I Am That*, Nisargadatta's book, purposefully before workshops and training presentations because it incites my mind and heart with such incredible clarity. The effect of the utterances in this book remains profound and almost peerless in my estimation.

The problem is not with Advaita itself, it is with the readiness of humanity to hear Adavaita's message and that message should and must be heard at the right time. It is (and I say this with humility and compassion, but I must be direct) *way beyond* most people's understanding. We are simply not ready for it yet, collectively.

For some, this is patently obvious. They simply refuse Advaita on their first encounter. Others weigh in for a time and then reject the teaching. But the most dangerous and serious difficulty we have in the modern era is with those who "think" they have heard Advaita, believe they have understood, and proceed to preach it from a point of view—a point of view of limited understanding.

There is no precedent for the power of the words of the masters of Advaita, like Nisargadatta or Ramana Maharshi. We cannot utter the words of truth and give them any power at all. It can only be genuine. Neither can we pretend to hear.

In conclusion, Advaita is a spiritual way suited far more to the oriental mind and heart than to the West. The western mind and heart set has been largely adopted in the Orient. The contemporary sophistication and complexities of twenty-first century consciousness of the self, self-identity, separation, and division are supported by and symptomatic of the ego-processes. We can say with some certainty that Advaita—sublime spiritual teaching that it is—presents modern humans with a bridge too far in term of spiritual aspiration unless adequate preparation has been made. This preparation includes the gentle processing of attachments and confusion associated with the early stages of life through infancy, childhood, and adolescence. It also involves the thorough dismantling and healing of the refined and calcified ramifications of early life conditioning in the form of emotional-behavioral patterns, character defenses, and fixed assumptions and beliefs about life. And the way to do this is through personal, rather than spiritual, inner work.

Let us now end this gentle demolition and turn toward a reassembling of our parts that is entirely consonant and redolent of truth and realization, authenticity and reality.

In Summary

We have devoted this chapter to Advaita because it is the preeminent, arising, popular spiritual path. Without detracting from the teaching itself, it has become a torment or a false hope for many spiritual seekers around the world. Not yet prepared psychologically for the potent challenges of Advaita, would-be disciples have fallen through the cracks, the great divide between a partial psychological preparation for spiritual discipline and the powerful demand of a spiritual path as advanced as that of non-duality or Advaita. In this chapter we considered the popularization of Advaita, the dangers inherent in the teachings of nothingness, and the power of words spoken or written by a genuine spiritual master.

1. May I suggest that you make a study of Advaita Vedanta, regardless of what you know about it so far, and span the work from Ramana Maharshi and Nisargadatta to modern-day teachers like Gangaji and Mooji. Once you have some knowledge—and perhaps understanding—see what you make of this modern-day spiritual phenomenon.

2. What approach do you think we should take to the problem of people taking in the teaching of nothingness and reacting to it with despair and perhaps acting it out in mental illness?

3. What are the virtues and the drawbacks of interpreting "You are That" as "I am God"?

4. Other than through inner work to release attachments to the personality is there any other way to embrace and accept the teachings of Advaita?

5. What is your response to the passage in this chapter (in the section "The Advaita Answer") beginning "This Advaita philosophy has really disturbed me…" written by the emotionally distraught person who was contemplating suicide?

6. From time to time, through your day, simply pause and bring all your attention in to your awareness. Remain for a few seconds or minutes in a state of acceptance and integration, receiving the boundless welcoming embrace of existence.

PART 3: PUTTING IT BACK TOGETHER AGAIN IN A NEW FORM

Having pulled down some false idols and trampled on some tightly-held taboos; let us now offer some basic spiritual truths to support the vision.

We have said what spirituality is *not*. We have sacrificed some mainstays of the "pop" spirituality field on the altar of truth, annihilated some assumptions, and stuck a needle in the balloon of our complacency. Our need to build our practice, spiritual endeavor, and indeed our collective culture and world, on a firm and real foundation begins with this clearing, this raking out the debris of unthinking, cobwebby traditions, unexamined beliefs, and unawareness.

But the collapse of the old forms is a preparation for the arising of truer, better, more lasting ones. We have a responsibility, if we are to embark on a process of dissolution, to reassemble, to rebuild, and to avoid the mistakes of before, the superficial ideas and downright lies, to go beyond the limitations and resist the seductions of the past.

So let us put in some preparatory groundwork, lay some foundations, put in some basic planks, and propose the fundamental ideas that will hold and support the new vision. But planks are no good if they are infested or eaten from within. We must beware and make firm, intelligent, and heartfelt decisions and watch our backs... and the backs of our friends.

7. First, Fix the Car—Then, Start the Journey

When Should I Begin Inner Work?

When should you begin inner work? How long does it take? And particularly how long will it be before you become you—your authentic self? These are all questions that are frequently asked by newcomers to inner work. They are difficult to answer, because we human beings are so varied and diverse. It is as well to remember too that short cuts are not necessarily the best way even though our time-obsessed orientation tends toward *quickest is best*.

You must transcend your attachments to your personality before you can open to the truly spiritual life. Any serious commitment to spirituality *begins* with freeing yourself of the personality traits. Your entire life is on hold while you live within the limitations of personality. Unless you work at going past your personal limitations you can never really become yourself.

So when you ask when should I start inner work, how long does it take, how often should I do it, when will I experience a breakthrough, the answer is you're missing the point. If you are drowning in the sea and someone throws you a lifeline, do you test the quality of the rope or ask if it will support your weight and if there's a guarantee? No, you grab it hard, desperately and gratefully, and you hope someone is pulling you in.

The Zen command, "Train as if your hair is on fire," encapsulates the truth of the human predicament. But human beings can be incredibly complacent, self-sabotaging, ignorant, and self-destructive.

Begin your inner work as soon as you can. Do not delay. There is nothing for you in the past and even less in a fantasy of the future. Unless you free yourself now from the limitations of yourself you will die having missed your life.

Find someone who is able to counsel you, listen to you, empathize and resonate with you (They are not very far away I assure you!). See them regularly, as much as you can, and use the contact wisely. They are known variously as therapists, psychotherapists, counselors, teachers, guides and healers, but whatever they do and whoever they are be sure they know of a life beyond the personality and make sure they have made—or are making—the breakthrough themselves. If they haven't, they are using you, so don't bother. Spend some time everyday on your inner work to invite your discoveries, insights, and deepening understanding. Work hard, persist, bring great effort, inner strength and fuel to your endeavor. Don't give up and know that you will prevail.

However long it takes you, it is merely remedial preparation for the fullness of heart life, for the life of love and compassion, for your authenticity and the blooming of your true nature.

Look around at your friends and enemies, your relatives and lovers, your colleagues and acquaintances. They are adult-looking people with childish concerns. You actually know it's true because when their lives meet a chicane, or narrowing, they are afraid or angry or controlling. And the source of the problem is always the same: the basic childish concerns of ordinary life—fear and desire, dependence and independence, action and passivity, abandonment and control, rejection and betrayal.

You aspire in your deepest unknown heart to the impossible, to rise like the ugly duckling or the creature that tired of clinging in Richard Bach's book, *Illusions*.

Something in you knows there's nothing for you here. You must transform and, though it seems impossible and you know of no one who has ever done it, you are compelled by its irrefutable verityit's simply what you have to do. After all, if the one-eyed man is king in the kingdom of the blind, then isn't the mad man sane in the kingdom of delusion?

Blindness is a symbol of wisdom. It involves the idea of opening the inner eye and cultivating a deeper, wiser inner vision. Deeper because more original, more prior... wiser because only the person who can see within is able to truly see the outer world.

The Inner Eye

What do we see when we look inside and practice inner work?
The following passages are based on a spontaneous talk which gives a summary and a wide sweep of inner work as I saw it at the time. Over the years I have been involved in the psycho-spiritual journey, among the many things that have amazed me is how the work always appears different or at least I can always describe it differently. Rather like a garden or a landscape—something living, vibrant, and organic—it never looks the same; there's never a duplication or repetition.

The text includes a guided meditation, but all of this section can be considered a meditative-contemplative exercise. Try closing your eyes and either by listening to a recording of these passages or by having someone else read them gently and slowly allow yourself to respond, physically, energetically, and emotionally, and be open to images, inner experience, insights, and even breakthroughs to occur.

☙

When you look inside with the inner eye, the first things you discover within you are those emotions, relationships, and dynamic forces that have created, and continue to create, your personality. Fear, anger, sadness, grief, hurt, and pain produce an underlying inner restlessness. This inner restlessness may be the beginning of a deepening awareness of the inner world. For many the restless feeling precedes the experience of the emotional states that lie beneath.

These restless aspects of your inner world must take a form in the outer world. Although you may be familiar with them as you look inside and acknowledge that you feel angry, afraid, or hurt, they go much deeper. It is like looking on the surface of the ocean: underneath there are many fathoms of subterranean world, yet all you see is the surface.

In the same way when you look inside you see and become aware of inner experiences that feel deeper than your experiences in the outside world. Following the ocean metaphor, the creatures from the depths manifest in your relationship to the outer world through reactions and defensive behavior. But as you practice inner work, you start to know the inner terrain, rather than merely see its reflection in the outside world. Thus, you begin to see how the outside world as the world you are creating.

Inner and Outer Experience
Inner exploration helps you to stop externalizing your inner world. It also stops you from creating a world that merely reflects your restless nature back to you. Your restless nature is based on fear and desire. It is restless inside you. What you create outside you are myriad forms of desire and fear. Now instead of creating it outside, you confront it inside and only when everything in front of the eye truly disappoints you do you truly turn inside. Everything: sex, food, pleasure, drugs, or whatever you are addicted to, obsessions, dependency, fear (because fear is something you are attracted to), desires (before desires are repulsed by their opposites) are in you. And when you take full adult responsibility for them, you gradually cease to create the world in your own image. You must contemplate this deeply to become aware of how the inner and outer experiences relate to each other.

Now, looking further and penetrating in to the second, deeper realms of the inner subterrain, you begin to detect what lies beneath the emotions, relationships, and dynamics which sustain the conditioning as personality, character, and defense.

Adulthood, Happiness, and Authenticity
This second level is the location of authenticity and it is characterized by a lack of reaction, because it is not, like the first level, based in memory. Response, rather than reaction, is the defining characteristic of the second inner level, plus a certain amount of release and freedom. You are also able to experience the kind of joy here that is not dependent on outer, or even inner, events. This is the kind of happiness that has no reasonable basis and which may extend unexpectedly into intense, spontaneous joy.

Happiness is really a by-product of authenticity, a consequence of abiding in your true heart. You become intimately acquainted in this second level with your intrinsic nature as the specific and unique human being you are. In the outer world, you are able at last to practice compassion as a direct response to the world. This doesn't necessarily manifest in action. It may be a deep, consistent, and growing experience which develops over time into a state of open-heartedness and empathic resonance. Deepening into the second level of human experience may be accompanied by the attainment of genuine adulthood, the maturation of a human life from a psycho-biological perspective.

The Realization of Spirituality
The spiritual challenge usually associated with middle-age and more advanced stages of a human lifetime await the spiritually-inclined traveler through life. Of course people very often have spiritual enthusiasm and application before their senior years. But we have learnt to associate spirituality in its accomplished, realized aspect as being an older pursuit, which is often true, both metaphorically and literally.

The realization of spirituality is the final destruction or the death-in-life that becomes a reality for those who wish to fulfill the principle of loss, relinquishing all and surrendering all to what is sometimes referred to as the spiritual fire.

The spiritual path to attainment is no airy-fairy business, no pie-in-the-sky ideal, or unattainable fantasy. Entrenched as we are in the age of the individual, where ego-forces have run wild and unconsciously subverted too many subtle expressions of the human life form to count or process, the irony is that the human being is ultimately a spiritual being. Spirituality is the essence of humanity, so a human being is hardly human without being spiritual.

Now the word spiritual may be used in several senses, meaning essence, soul, depth, intellectual, visionary, sensitive, immaterial, and so on. Sometimes a spiritual person is entirely unselfconscious of their spirituality. They may be irreligious, agnostic, or atheistic. Yet something shines in them which is translucent, generous, giving, and merciful. They may embody spirituality while disavowing God as Divine or Absolutism in any form. They can be pragmatic types, salt-of-the-earth people who have "no time for nonsense." Yet their spirits shine.

Everything we speak about concerning spirituality is image and metaphor. Throughout human history we have been interested or even obsessed with the inner world in the form of death, God, the unchangeable, the immortal aspects of being, morality, ethics, and much more. And all of these themselves are images and metaphors. Primarily we speak about the spiritual realms in symbolic language, using words that express more than their literal meaning, like light, ocean, or sky. To pursue the realities behind their symbolic expressions is an act of faith.

The Beginning of Faith
The Divine is not only beyond seeking, but also beyond description, words, and images—even doctrines and

beliefs. All the authentic, transcendent, mystic, spiritual paths—from mystic Christianity to Gurdjieff, from Sufism to Zen, from Hasidim to modern day paths like *A Course in Miracles*—have one thing in common. And it is exactly what I chose as the starting-point for my book *The Flight of Consciousness*.[13] The beginning of all of the approaches over thousands of years and all over the world start with a single insight: *you do not see the world as it is, you see the world as you are*. This insight is the beginning of faith.

Only when everything you see with the outer eye disappoints and dissatisfies you and you feel hopeless and defeated, do you withdraw inside with all of your attention. It is necessary that that happens, because otherwise you're like someone with a telescope who is trying to look at the planets in space, who keeps seeing something up there and reports it in various different ways—it's down there, so many degrees left, that latitude and that longitude, it's over there and it's flying through space on its own, when you find out it's just a fly squashed on the lens of the telescope! There's nothing up there at all! You have superimposed your own way of seeing in many different forms, so the fly became a meteorite, a lump on Mars, a crater on the moon, many things, everything, a whole new planet, but there's nothing there, only your projections.

Clearing Assumption and Expectations
So, this is the beginning, the very first stage of the mystic path, the inner journey: *you do not see the world as it is*. This is your first struggle, your first endeavor to clear yourself of the history of your assumptions and expectations of how the world should be. Many of these

---

[13] Richard Harvey, *The Flight of Consciousness*, Ashgrove Publishing 2002.

assumptions and expectations are hidden from yourself and from others. The hidden ones are even more difficult. You can learn a great deal from other people's feedback about how they experience you, how fixed they find you, how critical you are, how judgmental, what incites you to intolerance and anger or to not accept them or aspects of the world. All of these comprise your confrontation with the world, your argument against the world and this shows you your assumptions and expectations. They lead you back to who you think you are, which leads you back to: *if you see the world as you are, then you don't see the world as it is.* The inner eye is not open when you can't see past yourself.

Is your self calling to you, insisting that you see it, see yourself and *know* yourself, as the ancients expressed it? Yes, it is like that. If you are an industrious person you see jobs that must be done, work to do, tasks that will take time to do, duties that you will struggle to do, endless activity that you will never stop doing, so much work, such a long way to go, exercises and methods to do, and how much you'll get from doing them. In short, how you will be a valid human being for being immensely active. It's a difficult quandary, because it would seem that the solution is not to do so much: if I don't do so much, I'll feel more, I can be more, and I will have more time for meditation, pleasure, and leisure. But you have to be aware and take care not to simply take the character and reverse it, because the reverse is exactly the same. You become very busy not-doing. Being busy doing or not-doing is still being busy.

The Middle Path of Acceptance
Before you know yourself, you have to accept yourself; don't you? It's a relationship with *you*. It's very much like being in a relationship with somebody who you really love and then one morning you wake up hating. You hate

that you love them. You hate that they are so beautiful. You hate that you want them so much. You hate that they are the recipient of your love, and you cannot be alright on your own without them. You hate them. If you take that far enough and if you love them enough, you may fantasize destroying the relationship completely. Then you're shocked at yourself and you wish you hadn't had that thought.

Hate can only be incited by love and violence by gentleness. These are the opposites; this is the world in which we live, and this is how we come to project a world of self. We don't project a world of self that says the other is just like me, he behaves like me, and he looks just like me. We project a world of people who *don't* appear to be ourselves, because even inside us we are not ourselves; we are pushing this feeling away, that experience away, this behavior away. When we feel like spontaneously jumping up and putting our arms round someone or saying you are so beautiful, we inhibit ourselves. We say to ourselves: I had better not do that because it would be rude, or I can't say that because I would be in their power, or they would take it the wrong way, or they would get the wrong message or something would be expected of me, or I would expect something from them. By the time we have finished inhibiting who we are in our natural expression and in our inner world, we create a million orphans. The orphans of our consciousness have no mother and father, no belonging and no place to be. Some of them are magnificent, wonderful, and they lead us to pleasure and joy. Others would get us in trouble by leading us into rejection, humiliation, and misery.

The orphans are the parts of us that we disown. We believe we haven't created them, because they shock us so much. We marginalize them, put them in a corner, and pretend they are not there. It is what we don't want to know about ourselves. Some of them are wonderful, some are disgusting, but they are really all us. In the outside world, we meet these orphans through projection. The beautiful person who attracts us and the ugly person who repels us are both parts of us that we are unwilling to include. We see the world as we are. We don't see the world as it is.

The Journey and the Guide
Personal exploration—the journey of self-discovery—is a courageous, sustained effort, an act of faith that shows you that you contain so many unconscious urges, desires, fears, violence, separating, dividing, dominating, repressing aspects of self, and a great mishmash of different personalities. In an accepting therapeutic relationship, you can bring those different parts forth, reveal them to yourself and your therapist, because another needs to see them. Otherwise it would be enough to have nightmares and bad thoughts where these hidden aspects of self appear. But it's not enough to merely see them yourself, because you are human and too tricky. For the healing ceremony to be effective, there must be a witness.

You need a guide who you can trust to take you through your journey. You need the support of a group who are honest enough to give you authentic feedback, appreciate, support, and challenge you when necessary. Sometimes you fight, and sometimes you are in harmony with them, but you see it through anyway. Then there is what in Buddhism is called the *dharma*—we can call it the teaching or life, as it manifests what you need to know in the moment. For that, only one thing is required and that is your attitude. You will need to be open to *dharma* in your attitude, not selective nor closed off. You need to consider yourself a pupil, a student of life, learning and allow life to teach you in every moment.

Digging the Tunnel from Both Ends
I teach my students to start digging from both ends of the tunnel. One end I have just explained in detail. It is the personality end where most people are submerged. They are down a hole, and they will never get out without a great effort. Whether they are eight, eight months or eighty years old, they are still submerged in the same pattern and not awake. For some there is no prospect of awakening; there is only ignorance. They will never meet anyone or move in the circles or be attracted to the kind of environment where anything could change.

When you find yourself attracted to change, transformation, and spirituality, your attitude is the only thing that you have any power over at all. The rest of it you must work on. From opening up to letting go, you open, experience, and learn. And you carry on emptying, all the time becoming less, until you realize that as you empty and become less, so experience can enter in. You begin to see things more clearly, more honestly, more true. You begin to find out who you are.

Then I add the spiritual dimension to it. I throw your will ahead. I say you are not a man, a hurt child, a violent psychopath, a 38-year old with a broken family who was badly treated by his mother and father. I look at you and I say, "You told me that you are devotion, love or consciousness, and now I say it back to you, and when it's true this devotion or whatever your spiritual nature is, your expression of *satchitananda*—which means truth, consciousness, bliss, which itself is the natural state of humankind—I say you are consciousness and in this life your manifestation of truth is…"

When that is spoken to someone with a spiritual tendency, the devotion itself will start to wind them in. It is the same with you. I cast your will forwards so that love, spontaneity, and surrender open. The heart in you is always winding you in. So you are doing the hard work of personality, of lessening, and the Divine already has a hook in you, is pulling you into that state of absolute love, which you've heard about, desired, and intuited somehow is the natural state—which is already who you are.

So you are being pulled toward your natural state even while you are working in the lower regions of personality and survival, fear, and desire, where all the comings and goings of coupling, eating, drinking, smoking, your normal feet-on-the-ground life seems to create its own intrigue, dramas, and disruption. In this way you are digging the tunnel from both ends: The Divine enters at one end and the personality, the character, the defenses are being released at the other end.

The Ground of Being
Now, you meet in the middle, in the true heart, what's known as the core or the essence or heart. It is a place of absolute peace, tranquility, being-ness. No tendencies are followed at all. In the ancient scriptures it was called the "ground of being" because nothing appears on it; it's just the ground, the flat place where nothing comes up, being before any doing, any tendency, before any thought even emerges. In India, it was called *Samadhi*. This blissful state which emerges in God, Buddhists would call *Samadhi*. Christian mystics would call unity in God, the Kingdom of Heaven. Jewish kabbalists would call it the stages of the *sefirot*, and Sufis would call it "seeing God's face."

My Day—My Ashram
People who engaged with inner work and spiritual discipline in days gone by entered the monastery, the convent, the yogi school, or the ashram. Whereas many people, who meditate and do inner work today, practice amid the vicissitudes of secular life. By embracing a spiritual path in the world, you are saying yes I have roles,

yes I have loyalties and allegiances, a mother, a need for sex, for food, recreation and I dedicate myself to a sacred life and a spiritual path with sincerity and application. Who can say that we are any less spiritual or serious about our *sadhana* today? Who would say that this secular world is a less worthy setting for sacred-spiritual life and attainment?

The monastery, the holy place, the blessed, cool cloister is my heart. The ashram is my room, my day from when I wake up to when I sleep.... and when I wake up the next day, I am in this world but not of this world, because I realize that as awareness, as being-ness, I reflect the Absolute. This is what Christians call God, and what Sufis call Allah, while Buddhists call it Buddha Nature. It is quite ordinary and appears in quite ordinary form in this world *now*, never at any other time. And where? In India, in China, and in ancient Japan? Yes and no, but *here*; it is all here.

So to recap, you do personality work just like you have breakfast, just like you telephone and talk to your children, just like you maintain your schedule. It's ordinary life. I am a father, a worker, a lover, a breakfast-eater. You don't have to worry about that. It all just goes on and you use it as grist for the mill, as raw material to burn your way through the personality, so that you come out on the other side no longer imprisoned by your biological family, your early conditioning, your childhood, no longer subject to the life statements of your early life, like "I must think and not feel," "feelings are chaotic," "the woman in me is childish," "I am worthless," and so on *ad infinitum*. All this—or at least your belief in this—merely creates the delusion of ego-self.

The Divine Reels You In
Now you can see how personality keeps you in a certain place and you begin to release yourself from its

limitations. That's one end of the tunnel then at the other end love, compassion, or God reels you in because you are *as you are* and the Divine insists that you *be* as you are—it's crucial that you become yourself. You are no longer ignorant, caught in the realm of the senses and the trappings of fear and desire, delusion and illusion. You have all of the attributes to awaken and the Divine reels you in. In the middle of that you look to one side at therapy and the personality and on the other side you look at the Divine reeling you in. In the middle of that you sit quietly, tranquilly in equanimity and bliss, because you don't have to do anything. You don't have to make anything happen to be as you are. The less you do and the more you get out of the way, the quicker you will be stabilized in who you really are.

The Essence of Meditation
Now how are you going to do that? I have known hundreds of people who have practiced all kinds of psychological and spiritual ways to realization and enlightenment. But how many enlightened people have you ever met? We may now have run into millions of people who have done meditation and spiritual practice. But how many spiritually-realized people have you met? Probably not many, if any, and could that be because they missed the essence of all meditation, of all yoga, of all internal spiritual practices, which is do nothing—*do absolutely nothing.*

Identify the engagement of the five senses and withdraw, withdraw within the skin and identify the processes that take place there—thinking, feeling and the functioning sensations of the internal organs: respiration, breathing, digestion, all those processes by which we assimilate vitamins, minerals, nutrients, food, and water. All of that is going on in your body constantly—withdraw also from that. You make it tiny and small because it isn't really of dimension, time, or space. Come away from the external senses and then away from the inner experience which is usually unconscious. What is there then but a sense of I AM, existence, being-ness, because without being whose heart is there to beat, whose mouth to receive the food, whose hands to work?[14]

Whose nose and mouth to take in the enlightened air, the *prana* of the universe? Whose mind to think, who to feel sad, scared, hurt, angry? Whose skin to touch, feel? Whose eyes to see, smell, taste, and whose ears to hear? Within just these few small words is the physical person, the intellectual, mental, rational, tactile, physical body person, and all the range of emotions and the soul manifesting through the senses. Withdraw even from all of that and the inner and outer functions of the inner life, particularly thinking.

For many people thinking is all there is. You ask some people "did you taste the food" and they say "no" because they have been thinking too much... and no one tastes the food. No one is being aware; they're thinking about what they are thinking about the food.

A Guided Meditation
Let go! Take in the I AM, the being-ness... very tiny inside, at first... with no physical place, no tactile, physical sensations... neither any other sense impression whatsoever, but merely empty, open, fullness... full of potential and capacity... and possibility. But none of this great, immense possibility is realized. You just hold it... the potential and capacity and experience... feel.... the humming, the vibrancy, the immense promise inside... within.

---

[14]This paragraph is a brief summary of the contents of the Consciousness Meditation, see the Appendices.

A sense of possibility, of initiation... but without any form... just initiatory feeling, initiatory energy. Now this energy gravitates toward the heart... experience it in its purity... without association or intuition... or physical or psychological narrative or consequence... In this point of absolute emptiness and potential there is nowhere to go... nothing to consider... no action is necessary... no associations made. There is nothing, merely pure being.

It encompasses and includes everything, everywhere... intuition, heart, consciousness but stabilize in pure consciousness. Sit now... take a deep breath... and immerse yourself in pure consciousness...*only*.

Three Practices
So these are the three practices: therapy on personality, casting yourself ahead and allowing the Divine to wind you in, and standing in the middle of both and accumulating openness and fuel for the journey.

From your meditation on being-ness you receive great strength and centeredness. Deepen in the intensity and significance of this practice and it will yield insights, breakthroughs, and ultimately understanding. Everything proceeds from this sense of I—the existence of self. When you have a pure sense of yourself in this awareness of I and completely distinct from personality, the fly on the lens has gone and you see the world as it is. Authenticity and the life of the heart are now possible, and you learn from everything and everyone.

In your awareness there is nothing between you and the other, no attraction or aversion. You center yourself regardless and increasingly you are less affected by the vagaries of the outside world. As the dramas and the intrigue lessen, so you feel the world fully in your awareness, not in a superficial way, but in deep profundity and resonance. When you feel you feel fiercely, emotionally, and uninhibitedly and the feelings refer you back to yourself as your interactions in the outer world now reflect your longing for the Divine.

Stages of Healing, Maturation, and *Sadhana* (with reference to Maslow and Jung)

What happens when you are healing and transcending your personality? What stages do you pass through to reach the next level of your psycho-spirituality?

Transcending the attachment to personality is the journey to wholeness. It was presaged in the work of Jung and Maslow as, respectively, individuation and self-actualization. You become yourself fully as a human being in the spatio-temporal realms. You realize your true nature by living from your essence. With light and dark aspects of your total personality, both inner and outer (emotional and behavioral) now fully accepted and incorporated, you contain no inner conflict and you blossom into personal authenticity.

For that to happen, you must pass through certain key stages of personal growth and self-discovery. In summary, these key stages begin with the healing process of awareness, re-experiencing, releasing, integrating, and stabilizing in the changes, taking back projections, discovering your defensive character and expression, through the stages of forgiveness, dissolving your primary attachments to the ego-structure, perceiving your Central Character Dynamic[15] or the axis around which the drama of your life revolves, healing your original wound and arriving at the bridge of authenticity.

In the work of Maslow, Jung and others there is much room for obfuscation and lack of clarity. In particular, is individuation or self-actualization the same as spiritual self-understanding? How high are the views of Jung and

---

[15] The Central Character Dynamic (CCD) is my original concept. It comprises the hub around which the structure of the false self or façade spins. The function of the CCD is to protect the essence or core self.

Maslow? Were they transcendent psychologists or transcendental spiritual visionaries and teachers?

Jung and Individuation
Is Jung's individuation merely the process of integrating the personality or the realization of the Self? Should Self be understood transcendentally as it was understood in the *Upanishads*, for instance, or is it an expansion of the individual psyche?

Jung stated that the Self includes consciousness, the unconscious, and the ego. In Jungian psychology, the Self equates with wholeness, an original, innate impulse or state that is aligned somehow to unity consciousness. Individuation is ego differentiation, which means a process of release from the small separate self which Jung felt took place over the first half of life. Psychological and physical health also relied on the Self and we could reach these healing forces by way of myth, initiation, and rites of passage.

In the second half of life, through a wounding of the personality, the Self is consciously rediscovered through integrating the shadow (or unconscious personality), the anima and animus (or soul or even Self or mediating force with the ego, depending), and finally the *Mana* (or wise man or woman, the collective unconscious or perhaps the wisdom of the Self).

This sequential archetypal revelation climaxes in the appearance of the Self, "the total, timeless man…who stands for the mutual integration of conscious and unconscious." But we are still perhaps not any clearer about whether this Self is transcendental or merely transcendent. Is it developing subjective personality or individuality, a process of inner maturation either abstract or concrete but in the final analysis psychological or spiritual in nature?

Maslow and Self-actualization
Maslow's self-actualization underpins humanistic psychology and in particular the notions of fulfilling your potential, abundance consciousness, and taking a positive view of human nature. Self-actualization is usually taken to mean realizing your potential or your true self. Self-actualizers are those who feel themselves, are secure rather than anxious, accepted and loving, alive and fulfilled.

Self-actualization is inherent in Maslow's hierarchy and, as such, you might expect it to have a clear definition with regard to human and spiritual. However, its meaning is often confused with self-discovery, self-reflection, self-realization, self-exploration, and even self-transcendence. Maslow felt that self-actualization was growth-motivated rather than deficiency-motivated and that it could not be reached until the lower order necessities of his hierarchy of needs (physiological, safety, belongingness, and esteem) were satisfied. He also held the view that self-actualization was rare, occurring in less than 1% of people.

The examples he gave included: Einstein, Thoreau, Albert Schweitzer, and Mother Teresa. Maslow believed that each of these people had discovered their unique core-nature.

Self-actualization was the summit of human fulfillment and involved becoming fully human. He defined fully human as living creatively to your full potential, seeing reality "as it is," accepting yourself and others, relying on your own experience, being natural and spontaneous, having a mission to fulfill in life beyond yourself, being resourceful, independent, innocent, and appreciative, creating deep loving bonds, feeling comfortable in solitude, and being able to laugh at yourself. In addition, the self-actualizer achieved *peak experiences* with feelings of ecstasy, harmony, deep meaning, and being at one with the universe. Finally, he or she was socially compassionate, having few friends but those few friendships were deeply close and intimate.[16]

Maslow talked about integrating painful parts of the psyche and this and other aspects of self-actualization resemble Jung's individuation. It has even been suggested that self-actualization may bear some relationship to *satchitananda* (being-consciousness-bliss). But can we seriously take this smorgasbord of references seriously in terms of spirituality? I don't think so. Respect, by all means, while being critical of, the father of humanistic psychology who was a pioneer in personal growth, and pioneers command our respect. However, it is hard to refine the path while you're cutting a way through the undergrowth.

A Developmental Summary
First, the personality must be explored, discovered and integrated in both its light and dark aspects. Second, in an act of sacrifice and loss we inhabit our hearts until we are capable of compassion and the mantle of authenticity, which comprises the first transformation of a human lifetime, which is the surrender to the heart of compassion, the middle stage of the journey to self-realization. The life of compassion gives way in time to subtler holdings of fear and desire, and adherence of the ego-self. Thus we enter the third phase of human awakening and development. Through spiritual, transcendent, and divine levels of spiritual attainment we finally emerge into the higher stages of divine reality, peace, wisdom, and bliss. This development of the human soul may be seen as participation in three sequential worlds.

---

[16] See Abraham H Maslow, *Motivation and Personality*, Longman 1987.

The Three Worlds: The Grey, Bright, and Brilliant Worlds

If you could peer into the light of unity you would see a prism dispersing light in three different directions. Three worlds appear out of the unity, joined and separate, appearing different yet emanating from a single source.

The three worlds manifest and echo through stories, fairy tales, myths, and dreams that you may have read or heard, and are most certainly influenced by. They are contained in the perennial philosophy of humanity and also in the great tradition of enlightenment seekers. These three worlds are echoed and reflected over and over through space and time and successions of evolving moments. Sometimes it seems like there is nothing else and in a way it is true that there is nothing else—only these three planes of existence, revealing, radiating, and blessing. These three planes are very different.

The First World: The Grey World of Three
The first is the world of three—I, you, and the action that takes place between us. Although everything exists in unity, this first world separates and splits all arising phenomena into three through mental, left-brained perception.

Essentially this separation is a survival strategy, and therefore it presupposes that it is itself the tacit cause of personality, defenses, and character. The world of three is based on the ego-assumption of causality or self-centeredness. "I am the center of my universe," says the ego-self. You are someone, they are others, and all arising phenomena arise around this central domain of I-ness, me-ness, and mine-ness. The illusion of subject, verb, and object arises unchecked and eventually becomes established as the overriding background assumption.

Our early education supports this. The first grammatical rules introduced to begin the young child on the road to a conditioned perception of the universe are subject-does-to-object. Here's an example: "The cat sat on the mat."Sometimes the subject is described by the object, "A heart is pretty and red." So the implicit and explicit rule of experience, doer and done-to (verb, subject, object) is that one object acts upon another.

The first world is grey because inherent in this grammatical construction are all complementary opposites; guilt and blame, victim-mentality and "power-over" dynamics, bullying and cowering, self-responsibility and vengeance, and finally individual forgiveness, which is one of the greatest delusions of humankind.[17] The world of the opposites, or the relative world, though bright with logic, mental objectivity, and divisiveness is opaque to spiritual revelation. So the spiritual journeyer must release herself from all attachments to it.

But the world of three is also revelatory. In the grey world, people do not really see, think, or feel fully. They don't truly care about themselves or each other. They cannot respond and love and feel rightly, because when they were born here as spirits in bodies they became scared and hurt. When that happened, they had to find a way to survive, to live and not get defeated. So they became desperate—desperate to live, survive, and preserve their lives at all costs. All forms of life are like this. They have an instinct, a compulsion inside to survive, to cling to life and exist. The difference is that humans are very complex. They are so complex, so that when they are involved in the struggle to survive, they invent extraordinaryly involved and intricate structures of

---

[17]See "The Seven Stages of Forgiveness" in my book *Your Essential Self*, 114-120.

defense and control. Once these strategies have worked, they find them extremely difficult to give up. They settle for a less than complete and fulfilling life because their defenses have worked so well. Because they have succeeded in surviving, they become attached to how they survived, and they will not let go.

To persuade a human to go further, to strive higher than mere survival is really hopeless; in fact, it is futile. Humans have to find this impulse for themselves. When they do, there is help, love, and wisdom, such that they could never have dreamed of. They have to take a period of adjustment to get used to the new conditions, to embrace the new freedom, to expand and fill the new space of relationship, spontaneity, and freedom.

The liberation of a human being from their personality is no small thing, as we have seen (in "The Inner Eye" above). The grey world is also the world of discovery, deep self-exploration, and transformation. This is the very pinnacle of the grey world, and for the beings who get that far, the significance of the grey world is completely re-visioned as the gateway to unity.

Within the world of three, we experience the unity of all things as three, because we are dominated by the I-thought. Everything is perceived through the lens of this I-thought. The principle spiritual practice, which represents the way out of the world of three has traditionally been the question "Who am I?" The sustained and applied practice of internalizing this question through a variety of methods leads through the veil of illusion. This practice may be started consciously or even unconsciously when we come to inner work to deeply explore ourselves.

In the world of three, love is always compromised because of the belief in a separate self. Even the person who is partially motivated occasionally questions altruism or selflessness in themselves. The first step then is to admit to yourself that outside the lower levels of role identification and engagement, you are devoid of real love. This is not intentional or even necessarily conscious. It is merely to say that when you are fighting for your life the subtle refinements of the feeling life are out of reach.

The Second World: The Bright World of Two
The world of two is the authentic self-experience when self and other are largely eroded, and we strive for a life of truth through compassion and interpersonal relationship grounded in the transpersonal insight that I and the other are one. The process of surrender into service is a reality in this stage. As we live, the insight that self is other and the other is ourself, we answer the traditional question in the world of two: Who is the Other? The other being myself as I help or feel towards, or resonate or empathize with the other, so I experience myself in multiple forms of differentiated being.

When liberated from the defenses of character and personality, we enter the great adventure of authenticity. The second world is the bright world. Its nature is to radiate selflessly in the heart and the light of compassion and truth, because here we really care, feel, and love. Compassion, the activity and natural inclination of the human heart, is ubiquitous here. The relationship of person to person without selfishness, with consideration and loving kindness, is everywhere. That's why it is the bright world. Not only is compassion ever-present, authenticity abounds here too, and real relationship flourishes in intimacy and receptivity. Communication between beings takes place in reciprocity, love, and forgiveness. And yet even this world has to be transcended, and there is great sadness for anyone who becomes ready, or who is called to leave. The call is the genuine spiritual call, the path to transcendence and liberation, the call of the Divine.

The Third World: The Brilliant World of One
The third world is the brilliant world. It is characterized by perpetual illumination and the use of wholly different reference points for interaction, centeredness and existence. Intuition and spiritual vision, radiating love, blessing ritual of everyday life, self-sourcing divine reality are all the unconditional conditions of the third world of brilliance. In fact, this third world is very difficult to talk about or express. The facts, the state and conditions of a being here, are otherworldly, numinous, and divine. This is where what we have for so long called God becomes finally a living reality. It is and always was real; it's just that you could not have talked about it really with any relevance or real meaning before. This is because it must be felt, not just seen, visited, or philosophized about. It must be touched and allowed to consume you. The power is so strong that it must be allowed to entirely annihilate your thought that you are someone, and that you are separate and self-interested... in any way... whatsoever.

When you arrive in the brilliant world, you begin to practice inner work seriously, very seriously indeed. You move through realms, levels, and stages, but it is not that which makes the difference; you are already awakened, and you are already enlightened, and everything that you considered natural in the first two worlds seems very distant, absurd, intangible, and even unreal now. Finally, you look out though and there it is again, like it never really went away—the old world, the grey world, the relative world, the world of day and night and good and evil. You see it, only now it is transformed, now it is transfigured into heaven, and you understand like you never did before that heaven is, was, and always will be on earth. Before you didn't see it, and for a while you thought you created it, but now you see, understand, and are compelled to be it. It is you, your relationship and communication with it that is absolute as is everything else. In fact, there really isn't anything at all to worry about or become attached to. You are entirely, absolutely, and timelessly free.

What, if Anything, is *Absolutely* Real?

Human beings stand between heaven and earth, our heads in the air and our feet on the ground. When we first embrace spirituality, we have a tendency to fly off into unreality because the mind is so extraordinarily creative. Through mere thoughts—flights of imagination, fantasy, self-aggrandizement, dreaming, egocentricity—we "create" an extraordinarily spectacular version of spirituality that is really based on ourselves, rather than on any objective truth or higher intuition. If we are not careful, we fly off into fantasy, become embedded in it, and never return.

When you enquire into a person's approach and view of spirituality, you notice that often they have never cleared out their old ideas before filling up with the new. So their inner world is polluted with emotional and mental debris and spiritual half-notions, and these are mixed up with past experiences, traumas, opinions, and prejudices. When you meet someone whose spiritual practice is flourishing, this is not the case. They have reached a point of surrender and emptiness. They are receptive and available. These are the circumstances under which spiritual practice is able to flourish meaningfully in a human being.

But a lot of confusion and conflict arises from a basic misunderstanding of spirituality, particularly of the process whereby human beings reach spiritual attainment. Why is this?

The ready availability of ancient scriptures, easy access to age-old methods, and a smorgasbord of spiritual practices now accessible to anyone who can read and surf the net hasn't helped. People get hold of a little knowledge and erect a philosophy. They think that a personal philosophy can help in the spiritual endeavor, and based on particular beliefs, they create healing and "transcendental" methodologies, schools, and even cults that have all the appearance of legitimacy.

Legitimacy implies authenticity, correctness, and some basis in fact. There are spiritual facts just as there are physical, chemical, or logical facts. And in just the same way, for example, as a psychological fact emerges and relates to a different context and set of criteria, so spiritual facts emerge from a spiritual background or milieu. If you don't know that spiritual background then the spiritual facts don't make sense, so if you only know and understand a physical milieu then you have no context in which to view and understand spirituality. All that is left for you is the dichotomy of belief or not belief, faith or atheism, religion, or physics. When there is so much more than either-or to choose from it is an absurd choice, isn't it? In any case, whatever happened to the truth, authentic sacredness, and real spirituality?

Spirituality is not a matter of belief; it never has been and it never will be. It is a matter of knowing, of experiencing, of dynamic process, of arriving, of truth, of *what is*. Belief is the concern of religion, as well as concepts like faith, redemption, sin, guilt, and otherworldliness. The basic stance of religion is the separation of heaven and earth; dealing with the problem of spirituality in a human body by separating the two into the religious and the secular when they are really the same, because both grow from the same single root.

Spirituality, in contrast, pertains to, points to, and stems from what is *absolutely* real. This is the basis and the totality of what spirituality is all about. It is not a matter of opinion; it is a matter of what *really is*. An individual point of view or a collective point of view of the spiritual will always result in conflict, fighting, and holy war, not because it has anything whatsoever to do with spirituality—it does not—but because it is the extension of egoic forces and the mind. The mind compares and separates, and so it is divisive and self-aggrandizing. The mind is competitive, possessive, jealous, and egocentric. Ultimately it serves unreality. A mind that is not firmly grounded in the truth will imagine and fantasize and create a world that is unreal. Anyone who has meditated or stayed in an ashram, a monastery, or adopted a serious yogic discipline will understand this. The predominant experience as you begin and persist in practicing a psycho-spiritual method is one of arriving in reality, of having an altered state experience, not unlike a drug-induced altered state, and along with it comes the conviction that you have been living in a fabricated world, a false reality that you have somehow adopted, created, endured, and sustained. So, your initial insight on taking up a spiritual discipline is the one that precedes all genuine spiritual practice and is the basic tenet of all valid mystical paths since time immemorial. It is that the world you see, experience, and know is not the real world.

The Three "Ds" —Dissatisfaction, Disillusionment, and Despair

This is a humbling insight and the ego—or more strictly speaking the ego-process, for ego is more rightly a verb than a noun—is resistant to that. Imagine now the plight of the middle-aged person who has worked all through their life only to have everything taken from them. This is a modern-day phenomenon. People work: to climb the tree of status and material gain, to get somewhere, and to be certain of having a desirable life-style in later life. Today in the worldwide economic crisis people are finding the pension they saved toward has disintegrated, or the age for eligibility has been moved on past a time of their life when they may still enjoy it. People have woken up to find their principle investment in property or their home has fallen into negative equity. Natural disasters, redundancy, crippling hospital bills over-extending people's financial reach, and children staying at home for longer than they used to due to lack of employment opportunity are among the many and varied ways that people fall into disillusionment and dejection with the world.

Or—and this is peculiarly Western and modern in its potency and effect—the inner world of a person rises up, enthused, motivated, and longing for truth, for something more in middle years when they realize that their career is futile, because it does not address the deeper needs of their soul. In a host of possible ways, an individual's life is proved pointless and meaningless and then that person feels their lack of value acutely.

The spiritual insight that the world you know is unreal carries the potency of this sort of invalidation a hundred-fold. The whole world view is unraveled, the fabric of the psyche disintegrates, everything is in question, and all you have really is the unknown, which you may in no way be prepared to handle.

From the point of view of the inner world, this is immensely positive. One obvious way to see *how* positive is when it makes sense of what I call the three "Ds"— dissatisfaction, disillusionment, and despair. These are common progressive human states. People tolerate them without ever really understanding that they are calls to the Divine. That's why they don't go away. Positive thinking, "cheering up," medication, sports, and self-esteem may work, but whatever you do, these three states remain, plaiting in and out of your life, calling out and beckoning you to cross the spiritual threshold. But it all depends where you place your loyalties and concern. If you are attached, enmeshed, and oriented to the outer world then, of course, it is immensely negative.

When it propels you into a mental and emotional condition that is interpreted as a pathological state, you may choose to take medication. Or, you look for a good therapist, which is the other alternative. Now whether you find one who doesn't operate under a pathological model of inner states and can really help you is the next crossroads or crucial point, because your fate depends on that basic orientation, unless you have learned to think for yourself. But most of us not only don't think for ourselves, we are not even aware that we are thinking or what we are thinking about orr feeling... It's more or less the same thing at this juncture, because both are subsumed beneath the shadow of unawareness.

Unawareness is being oblivious to experience, and it is the fundamental condition of modern humanity. With some exceptions as ever, but you know you'll get by better on unquestioning unawareness, disempowerment, and adaptation to the common collusion to fit in at all costs and suffer than you will get by on questioning and awareness, being present, empowered, and true to yourself. That will inevitably get you into a great deal of trouble in the modern world where the basic ethos is: fit in, get what you want, don't "weaken," manipulate others, work hard, and don't feel, experience, or align yourself with reality. In other words, *stay mad and stay grounded.*

Grounded Spirituality (and the Life of Compassion)

The process of spiritual attainment requires a sound foundation of psychological maturity. Prior to psychological maturity, all that takes place in a human life relates to and is bounded by the earlier stages of life.

Spirituality must be firmly grounded in the initial stages of psycho-spiritual work, which I have called the first stage of awakening or the process of self-discovery in my book *Your Essential Self*.[18] Unless you have resolved and discarded your personal character-creating conditioning and released your attachments to your emotional-behavioral patterns, your personal biography, and everything that supports the fiction of self, you will not survive one step in the spiritual realms. You can practice a meditation technique, breath work, self-help, emotional opening, mantra, *yantra*, yoga *et al*, but it will not be a genuine spiritual practice, rather a spiritual dalliance, dilettantism, or merely light involvement to adorn your outer life.

So are monks and yogis and *sadhus* beyond personality? Religious spiritual images, roles, or functions, like the monk image, may be idealized (they are, after all, archetypes), but they are also life choices and roles to aspire to. And in that case, yes, there is some truth that the true monk will be beyond personality. But the reality is that monks, yogis, and sadhus are people. They are human beings with flaws, attachments, and personal limitations. The important question is: what are they doing about these flaws and limitations? Are they healing them? And, if so, how? It has been well documented that you can reach high spiritual states and yet be truly neurotic or remain attached to anxiety, lust, anger, or selfishness in your personality. The vital question is: how

---

[18]See *Your Essential Self*, 17-137.

do we go about a practical realistic spirituality—a truly spiritual way in which the character and attachment to ego-processes, the continuity with the past, the emotional glue that attaches to past trauma and the formation of defensive character is annulled, so that the body-mind may be offered as a vehicle for divine realization?

This is the practice of "grounded spirituality." Practically speaking, it is what has come to be known as psycho-spiritual (previously transpersonal) inner work, which is a powerful resource of specialized approaches, wisdom, and practices for dealing with the inner work of character and defenses from a spiritual orientation, as opposed to a psychological one.

My own work—Sacred Attention Therapy—is a progression of psycho-spiritual psychotherapy in which the precise relationship between the small self, the heart, and the spiritual life can be followed clearly and understood in their relationship and relevance to each other. You simply cannot put the cart before the horse. The Three Stages of Awakening in the Sacred Attention Therapy model clearly describe the relationship between the horse, the cart and the harness: personal psychology, spirituality, and heart.

What is the difference in the psychological and spiritual approaches to the ego-self? From the psychological viewpoint the health and the building up of a healthy sense of self and ego-functioning is paramount. Whereas from the spiritual perspective even if the ego-processes need to be healed and made healthy for better functioning, it is merely a temporary state, a precondition for erasing ego in the spiritual fire.

They are not necessarily poles apart in intention, or diametrically opposite. You need a healthily functioning ego to enter the spiritual realms and engage in spiritual practice. If you don't, try as you might, your spiritual practice is really only a "neurosis fest!" All this should spoil your idealized image of the archetypal monk, meditating as a way of hiding his neuroses and his attachment to his mother!

As has been said before, everything before your eye must disappoint you if you are to discover Reality within, God within. So we are back with that initial insight of genuine spiritual practice we talked about earlier, we have come full circle, when you understand that the world you see is not real. The real world is the one that may only be lived when you have become all that you are.

The Fable of the Flower and the Sun

Look at it this way. If you were a flower, then for a while it's all darkness and growing underground and moisture and dampness and earthiness and so on. That's the whole thing! Then in a powerful breakthrough you shoot through the ground and you're blinded by light. You don't know where you are, but you're warm now and there is a balance between dark and light, dampness and dry. Then you reach or tend toward the bright globe in the deep blue that's always there. This nourishes you like a divine source, and you reach and bow toward it in an act of great worship, and all your impulses are dedicated to it. Then one day you break, and you transform. You don't know what you're doing, and you realize yourself as a wonderful flower.

Now you can commune with the sun and soak up the light, heat, and nourishment, because you are liberated! Later on, there is one more step. Either you return into the ground by dying only to be reborn as something else, some other tendency of form and intention, or you seek the way out and the way out that you seek is the way of dissolution. You don't die back into the earth; you die into the sun, and you and the god of light become the same thing.

From that exalted viewpoint, you find at last that you are the sun and everything which the sun shines upon, and that there is no difference between you and everything else. This is the great liberation, the perennial insight, and the end of attainment in the spiritual quest. It is the realization that you are consciousness, and that there is nothing apart from consciousness. You are perfectly free and beyond fear and desire, because there is nothing that is not you. Thus you release yourself from the round of birth and death and find the True Self.

At each stage of the way as a flower, you are convinced that this is *it*! But it's only once you have found the True Self that it's really *it*. Everything else, all other states, are only partial. And there will be restlessness in you to keep on going, to try to become all that you are. That's the point; you cannot short-circuit this or really pretend that you are anything other than all of it, because you will be uneasy in your heart and mind until that day when you fully merge with Truth—and *the flower dies into the sun*.

With your head in the clouds and your feet on the earth you stand connected to yourself, the authentic life, and the fulfillment of your human-divine destiny. The ground is the beginning, the foundation of Self. Stand firmly and you may reach higher and merge with the divine Spirit.

Grounded spirituality is a means, not an abiding philosophy. It means that when you feel like you are on shaky ground in your humanness, you don't fly off and lose touch with the reality of the relative, even non-spiritual, world. But I say not abiding, because at some point when you are ready and able—and with capable and compassionate guidance—you do. You experience your rapture, the spiritual swoon, your epiphany.

In Summary

In this chapter we have asked when we should start inner work. We have taken a peak at some of what we see with the inner eye and considered the relationship between the personal and the Divine in self-exploration. We touched briefly on two of the old masters—Maslow and Jung—in relationship to transcending personality and discussed the three worlds we pass through as we evolve. We asked what is real and discussed the three "Ds" before looking at how we establish a strong foundation of psychological life to support our spiritual attainment (in grounded spirituality). Lastly, we reflected on the cycle of birth, life, and death in the fable of the flower and the sun. Here are some suggestions for grounding further into the subject matter we covered here.

1. Attachments to personality are reflected in the unfinished business you have with your biological family. Take a few minutes to consider your early childhood. What events carry an emotional reaction with them, even now? Write these down in note form and don't be afraid to cover a few pages, if necessary. Later on you can go back and start to explore each one in detail.

2. In your inner work notebook write afraid, angry, sad, and hurt in the middle of four consecutive pages. You should write one emotion on each page. Over the next few weeks, make associations with each emotion by writing a word, a phrase, or a memory alongside the appropriate emotion until the pages are full. When you have sufficient time, contemplate each one and see what insights this exercise yields.

3. How do you project desire and fear into the outside world?

4. With reference to the passage entitled "The Beginning of Faith" complete a writing assignment about the experience of your own initial stirrings of faith.

5. Consciously practice living your life as if your day, the moment you presently occupy, and the circumstances you find yourself in, are the ashram—meaning the location of your sacred life. So long as you feel ready to accept the challenge, commit yourself to this *sadhana* or spiritual discipline, starting now!

6. Buy yourself some expressive crayons or paints and a large pad of drawing paper. Illustrate "The Fable of the Flower and the Sun" as beautifully and accurately as you can.

8. The Last Spot on the Sun: The Guide meets the Seeker

What role does the spiritual teacher, the guru, or spiritual mentor have in the sacred-spiritual process?

The Return of the Whole Enchilada

Two Essential Elements
There are two elements to personal growth and spiritual development that are essential for genuine awakening.

First, we make a deep commitment to ourselves through aligning ourselves to a method, a teaching, and a practice. We do this through meeting an extraordinary person who surprises, even shocks us out of our habitual complacency. The teacher-guide may appear to be an ordinary individual; he or she does not have to exhibit magical powers or appear exotic. Someone's guide may be another's mundane person! But this person provokes us to be *who we really are*. He or she is uncompromising, unpredictable, and natural, and inspires us to go beyond our ordinary limitations.

In practice, the teacher is likely to be a spiritual mentor, a psychotherapist, a healer, or similar. The roles and the relationship really set themselves. You cannot go in search of a spiritual teacher; all you can do is inwardly prepare yourself. Then, when the time is right, the teacher appears. It's mystical, magical, yet oddly scientific as well. If you look and watch carefully, the teacher really does appear when the pupil or the disciple is ready to receive them. Trying to make it happen doesn't work, wishing and hoping doesn't work, neither does thinking yourself into a place you are not. What works is surrender and cultivating your willingness and your openness to receive.

Second, we are prepared to do what we do not want to do to attain the goal of awakening. Doing what we do not want to do locates us in our real center by taking us outside our ego-self. Without meeting this challenge, we merely play at the edges of self-discovery and spiritual attainment, longing for happiness, hoping to improve ourselves, or being motivated toward acquisition and personal increase.

Doing what we do not want to do may mean going that extra mile in our inner work, staying in therapy past the point of comfort, persisting in meditation past the place where you feel how excruciating it is to remain there any longer, staying in a relationship when you know there's still something there for you, something that you cannot quite see yet. Sometimes it's listening to the teacher or to your own inner guidance (these two should coincide) or to insight or inspiration in your life.

Through these two essential elements, you reach deep acceptance of the present moment *just as it is*.

The Final Veil

The paradox is that when you finally see everything just as it is, through deep acceptance, everything changes, because change is a constant event and it's the life blood; it's the only certainty, really. The movement of the cosmos and the cycles in your body are so connected that in reality they are the same. It is within this incredible mystery and in quite extraordinary circumstances that the teacher and the disciple meet to penetrate the final veil.

The final veil is the last speck of separation or the final illusion. It is the only spot on the sun, the last belief that you want for anything, the final fear, belief, or opinion and at the same time everything, all the illusion, delusion, and unreality in your soul. The whole enchilada returns for your delectation! And just to reassure you that there truly is no progress! Not that it has all been futile, merely that there is no attainment in the place where attainment would be futile. This is how you are aligned and reoriented to Truth.

The Golden Halls of the Stars

Divine Truth is unchangeable. We are not referring here to the truth that is relative, changeable, pliable, and subject to matters of opinion, preference, and ego-tendencies. That kind of truth is another matter altogether and it is rather gross, rather like picking up a stone and hitting it on your head to prove that it's hard. That kind of truth is relative, scientific, fashionable (or not, depending), and fleeting—the truth of insecurity and certainty, of reliability and dependency.

Spiritual, divine Truth is of a different order. It is unchangeable, undying, and eternal. It is what we have tried to describe and understand as God... Brahman... Zen... Tao... *satchitananda*... and to understand futilely. Unlike objective and scientific truths which reveal facts along a continuum of fluctuating certainty and uncertainty, divine Truth may not be understood in the intellectual sense, at all. Neither may it be experienced in any accepted sense of the word, neither can it be thought about since it is beyond thought, nor opined since it is beyond opinion, or argued about since it is beyond differences or logic. The nature of Truth is unity and therefore it incorporates all differences. It is truly Unknown, Unknowing, awe-inspiring, and numinous... the golden halls of the stars.

Shams and Rumi
In an enigmatic story from the 13th century, the futility of understanding God or the Eternal is illustrated in the poet Rumi's meeting with his teacher. Not only is Rumi's lyrical poetry a precursor of modern day pop song lyrics, the entrance scene of his spiritual teacher is like a scene from a Hollywood movie. From early westerns like *Hop-along Cassidy* to Robert Rodriguez's *Desperado*, the man dressed all in black making his entrance into a saloon has

been a staple of the western genre. What has this to do with the mystic poet Rumi?

One November night a man dressed from head to toe in black entered a bar in Konya, Turkey. He claimed to be a traveling salesman looking for something... or someone. His name: Shams Tabrizi.

Eventually Shams (Arabic for *sun*) found what he was looking for: a master-student and his name was Rumi. Rumi was sitting next to a pile of books, reading. Shams passed by and asked Rumi what he was doing. It is important to bear in mind that Rumi was educated and of noble class, whereas Shams was a spiritual wanderer, to outward eyes merely a beggar. Rumi replied to Shams, "Something you cannot understand." At which Shams took the books and pitched the whole pile into a pool of water. Rumi scrambled to retrieve the books and found that they were all dry. Rumi asked Shams, "What do you think you're doing?" Shams replied, "Something *you* cannot understand."

In an alternative account of the story Rumi sees an uneducated stranger, who of course is Shams, passing by. He asks, "What are you doing?" Rumi replies, "Something you cannot understand." No sooner are the words out of his mouth than the books burst into flame and Rumi turns to Shams and demands an explanation. Shams replies, "Something *you* cannot understand."

Looking for Yourself

Shams became Rumi's life-changing teacher, and he poured out his devotion to Shams in heart-rending lyrical poetry. Later, when Shams disappeared in suspicious circumstances, Rumi searched for him in mounting grief and despair, until he had this realization, expressed in verse: "Why should I seek when I am the same as he? The essence of Shams speaks through me. I have been looking for myself!" Rumi attributed his poetry to Shams as a sign of love. For Rumi, the teacher channeled God's love for humankind, like a sun he shone the light and guided Rumi's heart, mind, and body to Truth.

You cannot *understand* God, the Unknown, the Divine—the Truth. You can only become One with it. When you do, you enter the brilliant world, what has become known as the world of Unity Consciousness.

Fear and Desire Create Illusion

Illusion is what is not ultimately real. Illusion is the condition of humankind. In spite of the encouragements of the sages and seers of modern and ancient times, who were the ones who saw through the illusion, humankind has not embraced the notion of what is unreal and therefore it has not become free of illusion. Confrontation, conflict, inhuman treatment of each other, in war, domestic violence, prejudice of all kinds, callousness, and irreverence are the habitual routine obsessions of human beings leading the un-sacred life. It manifests in jealousy, possessiveness, low self-esteem, anxiety, chronic depression, and a host of human ills. What all these conditions amount to is ego.

Ego is the process of identification, separation, and division which we go through to ensure our individual survival. Once we have survived childhood, this mode of living becomes stuck in us and all future life is led through the veil of our survival strategy. Ego revolves around the twin pillars of fear and desire. It relies on a competitive, selfish, confrontational relationship with the outside world.

The outside world in Hinduism is called *maya*—the temporary reflection of the Divine. Everything is divine, but *maya* is merely a modification, a reflection, illusory. To find the truly real at first, we have to look inside. This is why psycho-spiritual practices are called collectively inner work. Passing through stages of awakening, we turn the world upside down and inside out. We locate reality within ourselves, because that is the location of all that is real. We are consciousness, and consciousness manifests in the authentic state of awareness. All else is unreal, illusion. Inhabiting our natural condition, the world transforms before us into blessing, into reality, and love.

So this illusion is what we have to transcend and its source is our identification with an individual self, the small sense of self, the ego and the projection of a world of illusion, which is simply the creation of desire and fear. The illusion is the perception we are separate from the Divine. Our illusion ends, and so too does our desire and fear, when we realize we are one with the Divine.

Meditation: The Joy of Your Eternal State

We have looked at the essential role of the guru, teacher, or guide in inner processes. And we have discussed other crucial aspects of the inner journey. What about meditation practice? Is it essential to have and maintain one and, if so, what kind of meditation is best?

No one should be without the gift of meditation in their life. It is a wonderful treasure, freely offered and simply waiting to be chosen. And what an absurd joy in the modern world to experience how precious, irreplaceable, and profound such a simple occupation can be. But the ability to sit quietly with oneself, watching conditions coming and going, and to fall by chance into deep states of peace and ecstatic revelry is really quite wonderful.

Meditation is irreplaceable and also necessary. But we should understand what it really is. First, what it is *not*. It is *not* the performance of some method, or some technique in the hope that something will happen. It is *not* some form of relaxation or technique for improving your health or well-being. It is *not* a form of hidden attachment whereby you invent a new, albeit "spiritual," role for yourself.

Meditation is the intense and whole-bodily communion with the Divine. It is the demonstration of your eternal state; it is the expression of individual awareness in unity consciousness; it is the sublime expression of devotion, bliss, Samadhi, surrender, spontaneity, Reality—everything that comprises Truth! How absurd though to say to someone in this predominantly material world that when you close your eyes you are rich beyond your dreams, that you are connected to all things, to everything, to the All, intuiting all conditions and beyond all conditions, in being, Consciousness, Truth, and love, communing with the

Divine in all forms and formlessness. So, meditate, let go when you meditate, expect nothing, and all things will be given to you.

How to Meditate

Meditation is always a special occasion. So be prepared, because anything might happen. Begin with your posture; use a firm base, cushion, chair, or meditation stool. Allow your spine to be straight, neither leaning back nor forward. Let your head and neck align with the spine so your crown chakra is presented to the heavens. Tuck your chin slightly in. Let your tongue be on the roof of your mouth.

Relax the shoulders, fold your hands, one inside the other, comfortably in your lap. Your legs should be folded in the cross-legged position you are comfortable in, or if you're sitting in a chair (if you are, sit toward the front of it), plant your feet firmly on the ground with your knees parted to create a firm base.

Now allow your body to sway slightly backward and forward, side to side, round and round, gently balancing and aligning your body. When the swaying stops naturally you will be more aligned than if you try to sit straight… and become relaxed, alert, and still.

Take full breaths in at the nostrils and lips, filling your lungs, extend the diaphragm fully, and fill the abdomen and pelvis. Allow a space, a gap, before following with the out breath, until it is finally released at the nostrils. Remember to breathe out fully. Allow a gap, a space, and repeat.

Now, clear your mind. As thought, sensations, and emotions arise, simply let them go… through you. Become permeable, don't hold on to anything. Any condition that arises simply passes through you, and you return to your breath.

At the end of meditation, take your time to rise, remain aware, and re-enter the outside world with grace and gentleness.

In Summary

In the Last Spot on the Sun, we looked at the two essential elements for awakening, the final veil, and the nature of divine Truth. We tried to show that you cannot fathom or explain the Divine, with some help from the marvelous story of Rumi and his spiritual teacher Shams. We discussed ego as the activity of fear and desire leading to illusion. We talked about the gift of meditation as enjoyment of your eternal state (with instructions), and how we lost touch with the wise self-regulation of our early childhood. Finally, we recognized western psychology as the preeminent method of healing the psyche.

1. If you are serious about inner work—psychology and spirituality—you should have a teacher, mentor, or guide in your life. If you have one, all is well and good. If not however, you can inwardly prepare for them to appear in your life. Spend half an hour in an imaginal exercise. Close your eyes and imagine the meeting between you and your teacher. Witness your attitude, your expression, what you say and feel as closely as you can. Repeat this exercise and inwardly prepare for the meeting in the outer world.

2. Draw a picture that depicts the relinquishing of your self-identity, the dropping of the ego-states of resistance and protection, releasing yourself from the prison of your self-importance.

3. What is the difference between truth and Truth? Try writing down your thoughts on the practical truth of the relative world or truth as we usually understand it, for example as the opposite of lies, and spiritual Truth, the unchangeable verity of divine existence.

4. Divine voices in poetry like Rumi, Hafiz, and Hanshan convey directly to us the beauty and the miracle of life. These inspired mystics are sometime shockingly direct and always profoundly human in their utterances. Try writing a poem each day, whether you consider yourself a poet or not. Set the collection aside, give yourself a break for a few days, then read your collection of poems. You may hear, to paraphrase the great Rumi himself, "your voice echoing off the walls of the Divine."

5. Time to begin your meditation practice in earnest? If you are new to meditation, you can take your lead from the meditation instructions in this chapter. If you have already begun, does your practice discipline and commitment need refreshing?

6. What is your view about the ongoing controversy in spiritual circles about mental disorder being a sign of spiritual awakening?

9. A Resident in the Divine Realms: Numinous "Experiences"

Questioner: Who is the other?

Richard: The other is myself. This is the second radically important question for inner enquiry. The first is "Who am I?"

Q: Who are you?

R: ....

Q: What is God?

R: Reality.

Q: Who is God?

R: Everyone, everything, and all and nothing, and no one...

Q: Can I reach the enlightened state?

R: You are already here.

How do you have an experience of the Divine? What does it feel like and how does it appear in our consciousness?

You are not there when you have an "experience" of the Divine. One way of saying it is: God is present when I am not. The great potential to realize yourself, which is a human birth right, is like shedding skins. As the skins lay on the ground all around you, you don't think let's put one on again. You are going to slither off in a new skin and a new look—the old skin is dead. So when we have a genuine encounter with the Divine, we metaphorically shed the skin of identification and attachment to self— small self and the ego-processes; the false recognition of ourselves as a personality that is partial and stands off against other personalities and characters and appears to interact with them. When we succeed in doing that, we have no recall, no memory of the event. Both memory and anticipation are time-oriented conditions of the small self in the world of appearances which is bound to the relative state of space and time and changing circumstances, inner division, outward separation and suffering. The divine Self which we reach by spiritual means stands outside of time and space. This is why we cannot correctly refer to a divine meeting as an experience.

When the spiritual teacher Nisargadatta Maharaj, in translation, was credited with using the word *apperceiving*, it was an attempt to express how we consciously perceive or understand, since we neither perceive nor miss the encounter, because no idea comes between us and the Divine. If it did, we wouldn't be able to "experience" the Divine. We would be stuck against the idea of it only, just like we are with everything else in the relative world. The thought always intervenes.

So our apprehension of the Divine is only intuited and felt *after the event* because when we return to our usual outward form and identify with it we have come back to ourselves. We know that something exceptional has taken place, and yet we also know we missed it, necessarily, because if we had been there it would never have happened!

Here are three metaphors—soaking in nectar, the distant resonance, and the waterfall's roar—for describing this numinous "phenomenon." First, it can feel as if we are soaking in nectar, a vivid, transpersonal, precious spiritual energy is running over and through us which is almost physical. Second, it may feel like a distant resonance. As if a gong or a huge bell has been struck and now all we hear is the aftermath, the deep swinging resonance of disturbed air or thrumming. Third, it can feel like being at a distance from a waterfall when you can hear the mighty roaring without having any direct connection to the source or cause itself, the waterfall. You cannot bring it back with you. In fact, you may disturb a very deep longing, divine longing itself, if you try. Many people in their first divine encounter have been passionately inspired to pursue a monastic life, a life of renunciation, when they see that is how they can realize the only thing that is of any real value… and that is Reality, Consciousness itself—taking up residence in the divine realms.

The Travel Brochure and the Holiday

When the Searching Stops...

A time comes in your spiritual search when you no longer need input or further outward stimulation. Some people get annoyed when I don't express any interest in learning about their teacher, therapist, or guru. But then after talking to them, they tend to calm down and understand. It is not that I am showing disrespect for their teacher's practices or approach. It is simply that we are looking through different windows at the same view, and I have looked through many. Now, I look through my own.

When the searching stops and you're not looking ahead to the next book, workshop, or retreat, how does it feel? How do you know when it's right to stop searching and looking outward?

At the beginning of the psycho-spiritual search, at the outset of the process of self-discovery, you can be dazzled by the options. Therapy and healing approaches, philosophies, methodologies, spiritual practices, psychological exercises, devotion, karma, the mind defeating the mind, Taoist practices, Zen, opening to emotions, meeting the body-mind, the role of the psyche, character and personality structures, and ego-processes—it is a maelstrom of delicious possibility, a spiritual hypermarket. Somewhere among this teeming variety, you have to choose and eventually apply yourself. While you're engaged with a practice or method you look to the one side and your mind says, "Hey, that looks better than what I'm doing." So you jump ship and go along with the new method. You practice for a bit and then you hop again and so on. Even if you don't hop, you'd be less than human if you didn't at least look!

Let Loose in the Sweet Shop
Now hopefully you have some wise guide or someone in your growth field who advises you. You are allowed to be let loose in the sweet shop *for a while*. But the wise advice, at the right time, is that you should choose a way and stick with it. If you don't, you are in danger of working yourself into the ground and getting nowhere, because inner work is fraught with those kinds of dangers. So much so that when I was writing my book *Your Essential Self*, as I charted the process of inner awakening, intermittently I introduced passages about the drawbacks, dangers, and mistakes. I called the first of these passages "Short Cuts and Dead-Ends." Next came "Short Cuts and Dead Ends 2," then "More Short Cuts and Dead-Ends." You're beginning to get it aren't you? By the time I arrived at the transcendent and spiritual realms, I was getting desperate for a good title, "Spiritual Drawbacks and Dead-ends," "Transcendent Pile-ups and Falling off the Edge of the Cliff"—it became very silly indeed!

This book was going to put any sane person off the process of self-discovery! The way I portrayed it was a minefield, a cesspool of despair, despondency, and failure; defeat and disaster were guaranteed. I had to reinforce the positive somehow, so reluctantly I played the negative material down, withdrew whole passages, and generally made the material more balanced. So please remember, the primary danger is playing around, dilettante fashion, at the crucial moment of potential commitment, instead of choosing and committing to the route that gets you somewhere.

Now, which path should you choose?

Your Inner Resource of Great Wisdom
The simple answer is the one most often given: the path with heart, because it is the only one worth choosing. Presuming that you have negotiated those first hurdles

effectively and you are on the path with heart, you make your way along past the signposts of self-discovery: revealing and healing character and defenses, deepening in awareness, through the stages of deep forgiveness, healing of the original wound, and attaining wholeness and finally transformation.

The transformational threshold marks the end of your primary concern with personality and character. It marks your growing attention to greater matters, the matters of heart, compassion, real relationship, love, and consistency, growing through more advanced stages of ego-processes and non-attachment, and heart-centering peace and purpose.

To engage sincerely with awareness and genuine openness, the screen of thought must be removed. There is no real relationship in relating through the obstacle of conceptualizing and which leads to assumptions, preconceptions, and illusion, followed by delusion, not to mention projection and transference of inner states onto the outside world and the events and people in it. At this middle stage of human development, you are drawing directly on the inner resource of great wisdom, insight, and aspiring toward at the very least spiritual vision depending on the tendencies of your true nature.

Transforming the World

Your true nature is not your True Self. I use the term "true nature" to denote the flowering of your individual personality without defensiveness, pollution, or inhibition. It is who you truly are and though it is strictly speaking merely the wrapper, even the wrapper is a temporary modification of the Divine, or the Divine in the realm of appearances, so you need to honor it if you aspire to the sacred life, just like anything else in the world of manifestation.

The manifest world is the ordinary world, relative time and space, the realm of duality—day and night, right and wrong, near and far, all of that; the place in which you find yourself before you really awaken. When you awaken you find that you are in the real world. And when you are in the real world, the relative world is transformed. You have found what you were looking for.

How does it feel when the searching stops?

Reaching the Heart
The spiritual search and journey are heroic. When the hero returns he brings a boon that is of benefit to the whole community, to the collective.

The way in which this manifests is in the desire to speak of spirituality, to share with others the fruits of your labors, the experience of the ordeal, and particularly to offer illumination and insights. You take pleasure in sharing, or in some cases teaching, the spiritual. In time this compelling impulse to speak spiritually is transcended.

What happens is this: it all starts to look the same really. You penetrate the truth of a scripture or a poem or a book of wisdom all the way and then the next one says basically the same thing, just using different images and symbols, nuances, cultural inflection, and so on. A place inside you in the heart has been reached, attained. What's the use in looking at the travel brochure after you've been on the holiday? Who is interested in the menu after the lunch? Yesterday's papers? Or last year's personal schedule? It's rather like that.

Sacred Calling

Your sacred calling is a divine gift; it is divinely-given. Usually only after the heart-opening life of transformation, authenticity, and compassion can we begin to "see," intuit, and open our spiritual vision to the content, role, and fulfillment of this calling. Usually we are only able to begin to hear after the heart's silence has replaced the ego-mind's spectacles of distraction.

Sacred calling is not for everyone. So let us start from this basis. The basic fact is that by no means does everyone, spiritual in their core-nature though they may be, experience or possess a sacred calling. Usually this is not problematic. If you are a secular person, orientated to the relative world, physicality, and the basic urges of human nature and feeling, with no sense of lack, then you get on with your life without any spiritual curiosity or disturbance. The problem only comes when you hear about sacred-spiritual calling through New Age, MBS, traditional religious teachings, or New Religious Movements (NRMs) ideas and, desiring some of the pleasures of apparent spiritual life you conceptualize and orient yourself falsely through thought to the spiritual—or "think" yourself spiritual.

Thought represents the veil of darkness, the appearance of illusion, and the creation of delusion. Thought is technology, creative processes, inspiration and formulating, bringing ideas and visions into form. At the other end of the spectrum, thought is idle, unconscious, automatic, a procession of randomness and arbitrary concerns, fantasies and nonsense. Choose how to use the gifts of your mind, but remember that spirituality is beyond and prior to not only mere thought, but also experience, materialism, and the relative world of space and time.

If you have peered deeply into your soul and your inner world and you intuit or know that you have a spiritual destiny, you need to discover exactly what it is. Either through inward consideration, experiential work, psycho-spiritual practices or some other means you must find out who you are…then you must live it.

If your calling is greater than you imagined or if it's lesser, you surrender to it. It is not a matter of individual will or self-aggrandizement; it is a matter of Divine will and the celebration of existence. Your sacred calling places you in the realms of Truth even as you stand in the Mystery at the meeting of the worlds.

Awakening in This Lifetime: Initiatory Experiences

The higher purpose and sacred meaning of human beings is: to spiritually awaken in this lifetime and discover for themselves their true nature, to live from that nature, to be loyal and true to themselves by resonating with their deepest truth, to know that to deviate from it is to lose themselves in the most despairing and crazy way, and that to die to the dream of the false nature and awaken to the Truth in this lifetime is to achieve human fulfillment. No other experience of apparent joy, happiness, fulfillment, or satisfaction is anything other than a deviation, a distraction, an avoidance of the Truth, of the real human condition. That human fulfillment leads ultimately to human liberation, the condition-less condition of real freedom, and deliverance from delusion, hallucination, fantasy, and the assumption of the attitudes that lead to despair and downward spiraling into ignorance.

The way is through psychological enquiry to understand our humanness, spiritual practice to illuminate our souls and develop sacred practices and realize heart and spirit. But as well as these, the world teaches us through direct experience, by offering opportunities and teachings experientially, so long as we are prepared, alert, and ready to receive them and the initiation they offer us. Let us look now at these initiatory experiences.

ɔʒ

The ordinary world is also the extraordinary one. Every day we are surrounded by significance, meaning, and depth. Through practicing awareness, we become increasingly sensitive and deepen in our sense of reverence, of wonder, of the miraculous. The extraordinary becomes commonplace and each moment is blessed. We are steeped in ritual in our daily routines—

sleeping, waking, eating, and walking can all be everyday sacred acts. Each moment is an opportunity for experience that connects us to a deeper reality and initiates us into the mysteries of life.

Initiatory experiences can also be spectacular. They teach us to see death in life, inspire new inner strength and courage, and lead us to truth and awakening. Through challenge, trial, or ordeal, we are led to renewal and rebirth.

A young man in his early twenties has a dream of initiation. In the dream, he is dressed in a primitive's loincloth, standing on a log which floats in murky water. All around is primeval jungle. His arms are raised directly over his head and he is clutching a primitive spear with both hands, poised to strike. The water swells and heaves with the slippery backs of submerged serpentine creatures. At any moment one of them may spring out of the water to attack him. But he is ready. His knees are bent and flexible to maintain his balance on the log. He is sweating with terror and exertion, waiting but strangely exhilarated. He continues to wait, perfectly balanced, supremely alert. The young man wakes in fear and mental turmoil. The dream feels so real for him, so significant and vivid that it stays with him as an underlying current, a compelling atmosphere in his waking life.

He shares the dream in a therapy workshop and enacts the dream up to the point at which he woke up. But then, at the therapist's suggestion, he takes it further. The creatures seem to appear in the group room and he vigorously fends them off with fatal thrusts and blows of his spear. He maintains perfect poise, faultless balance. His movements are graceful and flowing like Tai Chi. When the fight is over, he stands in the middle of the room sweating and smiling. He is streaming with energy, experiencing the fullness of the exhilaration his dream had only hinted at.

This ritual represents a male rite of passage that was offered to this young man from the deep unconscious and fulfilled in the workshop. It symbolizes an exploration of phallic energies, male maturity, and the transmutation of fear into self-responsibility. By the end he had undergone an initiation into manhood through a primitive ritual that has contemporary significance for his life.

Modern Western society ignores the need for entry points and transitional stages in life, so outward rituals are not passed down through wise tradition. But human transitions are insistent and natural. Rites of passage reside in the inner world and arise out of the unconscious. They appear in dreams and invite us to live them out in dreaming or waking life. When we accept their invitation, we are invariably enriched. We pass through a threshold of development by ritualizing the inner images which signify deep changes in our inner world.

Women's initiation rites have different structures and narratives to men's. This is Anna's initiation dream, which features the female qualities of surrender, fructification, and concord with nature:

> I am walking beside a lovely lake. The water is sparkling in the sunshine and reflecting a beautiful blue sky with patches of wispy cloud. Then I am in the water up to my waist and, before I know it, I am walking *under* the water! I am able to breathe and take in the magical landscape inside the lake. There are beautiful underwater flora, waving ferns, and incredible animal life. I approach a circle of large rocks and standing right in the center is a woman wearing black. She turns to me, and I feel overwhelming love from her. She is holding something for me and I step forward to see what it is. Just then I wake up.

Working on this dream, Anna discovered that the "woman wearing black" symbolized the wise female aspect of her psyche. In subsequent dreams her inner wise woman appeared as a black cat, a priestess, and a dark moon, always black and mysterious, beckoning to her to make the descent into her soul's mysteries. As in this dream the wise woman always bore her a gift and the gift was the symbol of her next step to initiation.

We can choose to respond to initiatory rituals with openness and enthusiasm or ignore them. When we ignore them, we allow priceless opportunities to pass us by and we diminish ourselves. Through indifference or aversion, we deny life and stunt our growth and development. Life becomes bland, tasteless, and colorless, and leads to numbness. But when we respond positively to initiatory events, we receive some of life's greatest treasures.

This is one of my experiences of initiation. It took place over three days and nights in waking life. The insights I gained stayed with me and guided my life for a long time afterward.

ɞ

One summer morning in 1983 I left home with a small pack, a sleeping bag, and a walking stick. I was a young man of 30, confused, afraid, and deeply troubled in my heart. I had many questions about love, human relationships, and existence, and a pressing need for answers. A friend had told me about a witch, a wise woman whom she had met in north Wales in a house set into the side of a mountain. The witch's revelations had comforted my friend and given her a sense of direction in her life when she most needed it. The chance of an encounter with some greater wisdom seemed to be just what I needed, so I decided to look for the witch with only an inadequate map and meager directions to her house.

I hitchhiked to north Wales and made my way to the hills in mounting winds. The dark atmosphere, the agitated flurries of wind, the creaking trees, and the sense of haunting presence intensified and reflected my inner turbulence.

My initiation began on the very first day with an experience that acted as a fierce jolt on my consciousness. Looking back, it seemed designed to disturb me into opening towards what was to come. I was strolling down a leafy lane in blazing sunshine when I noticed an assortment of caravans in a small field. A group of gypsy women appeared and beckoned to me to come into their field. As I entered through the broken gate, I was surrounded by a swarm of grimy-looking children pawing at my shirt and trousers. A large Irish woman aged about sixty introduced herself as Molly, saved me with a sharp reprimand and invited me to have tea.

We sat together around the ashes of a camp-fire and a charred kettle was placed on a rusty, gas-fueled ring. The gypsy women asked me where I came from, where I was going, if I lived on my own, and what I did. They pried into my life with a jarring mixture of pious pleas to the Virgin Mary and colorful curses. I noticed a chubby young girl of about twenty wearing a short cotton dress leaning against the doorframe of a caravan. With her eyes fixed on me, she seductively stroked her bare legs.

Unexpectedly the atmosphere changed. Molly began to extol the girl's virtues. "Don't you like her? Isn't she beautiful?" she demanded. I began to feel uneasy. Bizarrely, Molly invited me to stay and live with them. She told me their husbands were laying tarmac on the roads and would be returning shortly and that I could work with them and live with the chubby girl. The situation was becoming increasingly strange and threatening. One of the women asked me to give her my shoes. I stood up and backed away, walking increasingly rapidly as the children and the old women pressed toward me. But they stopped as I fled through the broken gate, as if it was an invisible barrier. Hurrying down the lane, I turned for a last look at the field. The women were engaged in their respective tasks as before, and it was as if I had never been there.

That night I lay in my sleeping-bag on a hillside under the stars. The lights of Liverpool glittered across the moonlit estuary and the raucous sounds of drunken singing floated up from the village hall below. Exhausted, I fell into a deep, dreamless sleep.

In the early hours I woke in almost total darkness, feeling instantly alert—and *terrified*. Drunken revelers from the village hall were swarming all around me on the hillside, fighting each other in an orgy of screaming and violence. I could just make out the flash of black leather jackets in the starlight. They seemed to be divided into two rival groups: bikers and farmers perhaps. I couldn't make out whether their cries were of pleasure or pain, or both. I lay completely still and prayed I would be safe. Miraculously, although some of them fought within a few meters of where I lay, I went unnoticed. The whole nightmare must have lasted about an hour.

When they had gone I got out of my sleeping-bag and set off. Whenever I met someone, I enquired after the witch's house, without success. Later in the morning I found myself in a beautiful little valley. As I began climbing a small hill I looked down and read the words, "He falls for the first time." The words were carved and painted in faded color on a small board of old wood. A few footsteps later I found another wooden board bearing the words, "Jesus meets His sorrowful mother." The boards were part of a series of steps set into the side of the hill. I recalled the Stations of the Cross, the stages of Christ's suffering on his final journey, the *Via Dolorosa*, the path of sorrows.

I fought briefly with my youthful antipathy to Christianity. This antipathy was balanced by attraction and now the attraction won out. I became identified with the suffering described by the words on the steps. My climb represented my life, and each step filled me with a sense of reverence and devotion.

At the top of the hill was a beautiful miniature chapel, barely furnished with four wooden chairs and a tiny altar. I sat down in one of the chairs. A little black cat wandered in and began playing among the chair legs. In the profound silence I fell into a meditative reverie of deep stillness and unexpected peace.

On the second morning, I rose at dawn. Striking off the path, I became embroiled in a thorny area of brambles and wild briars. Eventually I freed myself, and battling against strong winds, I cut across a field of grazing cows. In the distance I could make out the curious sight of the solitary figure of a man who appeared to have stepped out of the nineteenth century. He wore a battered old brown hat, a long leather jerkin, and thick grey wool trousers tucked into black boots, and he carried a three-pronged wooden fork.

I was straddling the gate of the field when he caught sight of me. I hailed him though he was still some distance away. Tremendous gusts of wind burst through the air between us. Suddenly he fell backwards. As I began to run towards him, his legs shot straight up in the air and his entire body shook. By the time I reached him, he was dead.

I began performing CPR. But looking down on this ancient man with his deeply-lined, parched, brown skin and his frail body, limp and lifeless like an oversized ragdoll, I eventually gave up trying to resuscitate him. I ran up the small track from which I had seen him emerge to try and get help. Just visible at the end of the track was an ancient farmhouse. Two guard dogs were chained up, one on each side of the gate in front of the house, like mythical gatekeepers. Straining against their chains, the dogs snapped and slavered at my ankles, as I dashed between them.

I knocked at the door and an old woman answered. She was plain, plump, wearing an apron and drying her hands on a tea towel. She looked like a character out of a fairy tale.

"There's a man lying on the road. We need to call an ambulance," I said, becoming conscious of my agitation in the breathless tone of my voice. She asked if the man was her husband, and all I could say was that I didn't know.

I left her so she could make the phone call. Stepping back into the windswept lane where I had left the body, I felt a presence, a mood of mystery and reverence. I found myself approaching cautiously and attentively. I sat down beside the body and began to settle into the momentous atmosphere. The old woman approached from behind me, and as I stood up, she saw the old man.

"Oh, it's him," she cried. Then she uttered some words I will never forget: "What will I do now… I will have to leave the farm," and she burst into tears. She began to tell me about her husband. He was eighty-five years old. His name was Jones. They had a son called Owen. They had moved to this mountain in 1919 (thirty-three years before I was born, I calculated) to raise cattle and sheep as tenant farmers. Since then they had never left the area.

"Every time I asked," she said, "if we could go for a holiday, he would say, 'What for? We have all we need and there's the farm to look after.' For sixty-four years, he had left his bed at 6.15am, eaten breakfast, donned his hat and jerkin, reached for his fork and left the house to start the day's work.

"I must phone Owen," she said suddenly and turned back towards the house. Like his father, Owen was a tenant farmer on a neighboring mountain. I turned back towards Mr Jones and gradually re-entered the atmosphere again. Quite spontaneously, my body began to sway and I sang in a language unknown to me, while feeling profoundly peaceful and connected. I felt that I was singing the spirit out of his body, easing the personality of Mr Jones out of worldly life and conducting his soul's release into the afterlife. I sang and swayed for nearly an hour, feeling deeply intimate with the process of death.

A mud-spattered Land Rover drew to an abrupt halt in the lane and a thick-set man in his mid-forties sprang out.

"Hello," I said, "Owen?"

He nodded. I had just started to explain what had happened when an ambulance pulled up. Two uniformed ambulancemen alighted, zipped Mr Jones into a long black bag, and carried him away on a stretcher with practiced speed and efficiency.

And he was gone.

I spent the rest of the day with Mrs Jones in her antiquated farmhouse. In between phoning relatives, funeral directors, the police, and the doctor, she told me about her life. We formed the kind of immediate closeness that comes from a shared trauma.

A young police officer arrived, eyed me suspiciously, and took down my statement.

I left Mrs Jones in the early evening. I had done all I could. Oblivious to the mounting storm, I wandered the winding lanes, absorbed in my thoughts and emotions. By nightfall the rain fell in icy sheets on the furious spiraling wind. I got caught in an expanse of deserted countryside between two villages. Struggling against the deluge, I sought shelter in a dilapidated caravan filled with sacks of manure in the middle of a waterlogged field. I lay down exhausted and fell asleep in my wet clothes. In the early hours of the morning I awoke. I was completely drenched with water lapping over my sleeping bag. The dilapidated roof had caved in and the caravan was knee-deep in water, rocking like a ship in a storm in the relentless winds and the impossibly dark night.

I abandoned my sodden sleeping bag and struck out for the road with angry squalls of rain beating down on my head and the wind tearing my eyes. An hour later, I reached the next village. Wet-through and freezing cold, I hammered desperately on several doors, but no one answered. The place was like a ghost town. The occupants may not have heard me in the din of the crashing wind. The wind bit through my clothes and froze my soaking skin. My teeth started to chatter, and my limbs felt numb. I began to fear that I might die. I collapsed in a bus shelter and listened to the wind play eerie tunes blowing through the gaps between the panels. I could feel myself giving in to tiredness, cold, and exhaustion and I fell into a dreamy, hypnotic half-sleep.

Suddenly, I felt a physical blow. It was as if someone had psychically hit me. Abruptly, I came to, leapt up, and walked briskly down the road. The rain was pelting down vertically with renewed force. Litter bins, tree branches, sheets of paper, and plastic bags flew around in the air and the freezing wind howled at my back and pushed me onward. I felt guided by self-preservation, a sense of hope, and the instinct to survive. When I reached the outskirts of the village I saw a light glowing in the very last building and I could smell bread baking. As I passed through a door into the blinding light, the dry warmth of several large baker's ovens enveloped me in a welcoming, life-giving embrace. Mercifully, a man dressed in white approached me and offered me a mug of hot tea and a tray of warm cakes. I slept beneath the ovens until midmorning when the baker drove me in his van to the nearest large town where I caught a train home.

It wasn't until later the next day that I read in the newspaper how a mini-tornado had hit the west coast of Wales. It had torn across the Atlantic at high speed causing force nine gales, freak waves, storms, and several fatalities. People were swept into the sea, wooden beach huts were smashed into kindling, roofs were ripped off houses, trees were uprooted, trucks toppled over, and fishermen were drowned.

Feeling the rhythmic rocking of the train and gazing into the blurry colors of the Welsh countryside, visions of witches, whirling winds, Mr Jones, the waterlogged caravan, and the sleeping village, Christ's Stations of the Cross, the little chapel, the battle on the hillside and the gypsy women drifted through my mind. I felt exhausted, exhilarated, and strangely satisfied. I was speechless and glad to be alone and quiet at last with my thoughts and feelings.

Initiation often comes unexpectedly. Although my search for the witch had been thwarted, my quest had been successful. I had received everything I could have wished for from the journey. When I arrived home, I looked up "witch" and the definitions seemed to evoke the qualities of my journey: "... to conjure away... one who is in harmony with the rhythms of the universe... Shape-shifter... powers of aversion and attraction... averting disaster..." I recalled the four sights of Siddhartha Gautama, the initiatory experiences that propelled him into his spiritual search: disease, old-age, death, and the wandering holy man. My memories of the last three days had evoked them all.

My initiation had begun with disorientation in the gypsy camp. I had faced my long-held fear of physical violence on the hill amid the fighting drunks. Walking the Via Dolorosa, I had experienced humility and reverence.

The saga of Mr and Mrs Jones showed me a life in all its completeness and the inevitability of death. Human fragility and the presence of death became raw fact for me on the night I spent in the mini-tornado. The episode with the baker represented a symbol of hope, faith, and a reminder that help can appear when you least expect it and most need it.

My journey in Wales left me with new expansive questions rather than answers. Sometimes wordless answers led to new expansive questions. They gave me a deeper, more expanded vessel to journey in, a larger capacity for enquiry. The initiatory experiences had enabled me to confront my fears and the new questions pointed past fear towards new courage. They informed my life for the next few years. They were the questions that I most needed to ask. What is fear? What is a life? How should I live? What is death? However much I quantify or describe these experiences, they will always be more than I can speak of.

Into Life's Mysteries

In initiatory experiences matters that we cannot speak of, insights that we cannot give words to, understanding that we cannot describe urge us onward to more profound levels of experience and understanding.

Enrichment and nourishment often grow out of challenges and difficulties. Life and mystery are always our teachers, seeking to initiate us. The heart is enriched through an ordeal or challenging passage. We awake to a deeper inner knowing, insight, and communion with our spirit. We reinforce our trust, expand our sense of self, and immerse ourselves in profound wisdom and a deeper love. In the ongoing journey of our personal unfolding, initiation can also be gentle and wise as it nurtures the inner strength and courage we need to face further challenges in our development.

This chapter concludes Part 3 in which we have tried to offer some spiritual truths and guidance for creating a new vision, following the gentle demolition. In Part 4 we look at the dawning of a revolution of spirit.

In Summary

In this chapter we discussed experiences of the Divine. We asked what happens when the searching stops after the initial stages of shopping around in the spiritual hypermarket. We looked briefly at the dangers of the psycho-spiritual path, reviewed the stages of personal and spiritual growth and development, from choosing your path to transformation. We distinguished your true nature from the True Self and considered the destiny of having a spiritual sacred calling. Finally, in some detail we examined awakening and initiatory experiences with some illustrative examples. The following exercises are designed to help you assimilate the material in this chapter through personal exploration.

1. Here are three questions for you to meditate on. I suggest you take them one at a time and devote at least two weeks, or more, to each one: Who am I? Who is the other? Who or what is God (or the Divine)?

2. What have been your "experiences" of the Divine? Record these events in writing and drawing, and if you have a friend or co-journeyer in inner work, verbally share your experiences with them and invite them to do the same.

3. In the section of this chapter entitled "The Travel Brochure and the Holiday," I have summarized the journey of personal and spiritual growth from initial to quite advanced stages of development. Consider where you see yourself in this schema and give some thought to the stages you have passed through and your preparation for the stages ahead. Record your musings in your inner work notebook.

4. Sacred calling is a divine gift. Although you discover it with certainty in what I call the second stage of awakening, it may also be apparent in your early life as an invitation to fulfill some task or as an intuitive sense of "rightness" in participation in the sacred-spiritual life. Do you think you have a sacred calling from the Divine? If so, do you know what it is? As before, express and record your discoveries in your inner work notebook.

5. What are your own experiences of initiation and awakening?

6. In this chapter, I mentioned briefly the difference between the initiation rites of men and women. This is a big subject, and one that is beyond the scope of this book to address fully. However, as a man or a woman and in discussion with your friends of the same and the opposite gender try to set down some initial thoughts and feelings about quite how initiatory rites differ between the sexes.

PART 4: REVOLUTION: THAT GLIMMER COULD BE THE DAWN LIGHT!

10. The Ocean of Consciousness—the Form of Formlessness

The ocean pitches and swells, tossing and spiraling with the force of water currents, tides and the magnetic pull of the moon. Inspecting the ocean surface we see a myriad of multi-faceted, endlessly changing patterns and forms, interrelated, some similar, some remarkable, others pedestrian, but together somehow a mesmeric panoply, a tapestry-like abstract of mingling realities, structures, and unknown narratives of mystery and the unknown.

From the ocean's surface we begin by noticing the details, the minutiae. These minutiae are extremely significant, fascinating, and crucial in our estimation. To our eyes their beauty is unparalleled, beyond fiction, as we move into the stage where we are stunned and enchanted by the world we are awakening into. Next, some pattern emerges from the accruing minutiae. Essentially, because we have an innate impulse to organize and experience, and because all things are really one, patterns and relationships and associations emerge between any two, three, four or more arbitrarily occurring incidents.

Some of these patterns over time, through scrutiny and discernment, are discredited and abandoned. We move beyond their seemingly inexact, superficial appeal and progress into newer and deeper areas of insight and exploration. We seriously consider our maturity at this early stage of inner development and awakening in a precocious but nonetheless necessary way. Precocious because there is still a very long way to go to transcendental understanding and necessary because in the inner journey we must validate and nourish ourselves essentially from stage to stage.

In one single moment I see in this maelstrom of the ocean, my mother's face, the form of an animal, a staring eye, a graceful line, three swans in mid-flight. The longer I gaze, the more the ocean surface fashions and yields up to my eyes and my perception. I recall a line of adolescent poetry, a portentous and precocious phrase I wrote once long ago: "All things have pattern." Yet, it seems to me now that they do; I *know* now that they do and I see that the patterns in the outside world are merely extrapolations of my thoughts, fantasies, imagination, and spiritual vision. Here, now, gazing intently but calmly into the ocean surface, the most profound of insights is possible, imminent, approaching... but it doesn't come and this somehow is the magic, because if it came it would be over and finished. But with this looming immanence, this pregnant pausing, I find myself relaxing beyond pressure and expectation, flying away beyond anticipation, assuming absolutely nothing.

Within this looming immanence, the spiritual teacher presumes to speak of Truth, the Truth exactly as he or she sees it at that time. The teacher fashions the teaching on the pattern of the waves, the whirls and flurries, the white crowning crescents and the swells. He or she records as faithfully as possible the form of formlessness for the instruction of the seeker. And this seeker has no understanding of the formless, doesn't know that the formless is simultaneously in form or the great compassion that is inherent in the teaching.

While the seeker clings to the form of the formless, the teacher takes it all very seriously, outwardly. But inside he holds the form of reality and inspiration lightly, knowing that it could crumble in his hands, knowing that to hold tightly is to introduce doctrine, law, and limitation. To believe in it is anathema to the Truth, because the Truth is only in the silence and in the formless form when we can detect the Mystery within. This is how the teacher guides the seeker: by example, by showing the way, by lighting the truth to a great burning fire that scalds and scorches and destroys the ego-personality until, fully unformed, the seeker steps into the spiritual fire.

Teacher or Teaching?

The question that seems to be commonly asked at this time is: Is it the power and efficacy of the teacher or is it the teaching itself that is most important? The objection to the teacher taking precedence is redolent of the lack of trust in both the modern era and ancient times. If the teaching is to take precedence then the self-help, un-surrendered aspect of the ego-drive is accommodated with disastrous results. So which is it? The intermediate but nonetheless deep answer is that the teaching is vivified and the transmission made possible out of love for the teacher. The reverse, of course, is unthinkable as it represents an act of spiritual salesmanship (the teacher peddling the method). But the genuine answer is that the teacher and the teaching are inseparable, because they are the same and completely identical.

And now we have come full circle. For the notion of personality as impression, which we explored in chapter 5, has been replaced by personality (the teacher's) as Truth. The teaching is only as true as the teacher.

The Apparent Difference between Spiritual Teachings

All spiritual teachings are attempts through the use of symbol, metaphor, and myth to describe and explain spiritual truth. As such, they are never to be taken literally but always symbolically and as representational and sometimes poetical portrayals. Because people are inclined to literalness, spiritual direction has tended to be nailed into a coffin of fixity and deadness.

Spiritual teaching should really be looked on as a way or a tool. Exalted, transcendent, and ultimate as these teachings may be, and infinitely worthy of our reverence and gratitude, they are nonetheless a means. Once the job is done and the journey is over, you should have no need of them.

Comparing spiritual approaches, religions, psychologies from a critical, competitive point of view, asking which one is better than another and which one is best, is a futile but compulsory practice for the judgmental mind.

In psycho-spiritual therapy in both groups and individual sessions spiritual questions should be encouraged. They signify the ability of the mind to think and engage with truly important issues, which the outward material concerns of the outer world are ultimately a reflection. Clear the thinking mind; move it to vividness and clarity and the world does indeed change, though not always in the way we want it to.

The Therapist-Guide
A worthy therapist receives spiritual questions and facilitates spiritual exploration in the role of spiritual guide. Providing the questions are not merely masked psychological impasses or dilemmas, the therapist responds out of the function of spiritual teacher. Now

since all expressions, including the verbal, of spiritual truth are metaphorical, symbolic, and mythical in nature, the spiritual teacher can agree or not agree. The literal truth of the client-aspirant's question is irrelevant: what matters is the living truth in the exchange.

Those who have trouble with this aspect of the spiritual teaching function tend to be logical, rational, intellectual-based individuals whose physical and emotional survival has depended on retreating and centering the attention in the mind. In fact, logic itself dictates that, if spiritual truths and physical truths are separate, then we can only represent (but never literally) spiritual facts in the relative world. Even what I am writing here in this paragraph is merely an evolved way of speaking about that which cannot be expressed here. Rather like the sun, we can walk underneath it, never look directly at it, but it is certain that if it were not there then we would not be here.

Spiritual questions are important because they represent the seeker's deep desire to transcend the mind state, to enter the heart, to surrender to the transcendent and the Divine. This cannot be done without a great struggle and part of that struggle is to lay bare one's thoughts, objections, fantasies, theories, and beliefs. All of these must go. They must be relinquished and to do that you must understand their uselessness, as well as the futility of holding on to them.

The teaching function of the therapist is here indispensable. Since you are most likely by far to have put yourself in the middle of a social group who, like your family, will tend to hold very similar views of life to your own, even when they appear to be dissimilar, it is unlikely that you can liberate yourself or even become aware of the subtle and gross influences of your belief system. To change it you must have contact and a relationship with someone who transcends the individual character function and acts from a higher level of awareness: that is the therapist-guide.

The Dynamics of Truth

Levels of Consciousness: Destruction and Rebirth
There is an attitude in contemporary spiritual circles that says that awakening is not subject to individual will and therefore whatever you do will not change the event of your spiritual awakening. Several other schools of thought advocate discipline and strong application to meditation or some spiritual practice, methodology, and philosophy. Which is right?

They are both right. But to understand this, first, you need to be familiar with the levels of consciousness that a human being can inhabit and participate in. Second, you need the humility to understand that everything you think inside one level of consciousness is destroyed in the next—destroyed and reborn really—as something else, something entirely different.

Three Levels of Consciousness
These three levels of consciousness give you the key to understanding different spiritual schools, their approaches, and diverse practices. It helps you to see what level of consciousness they operate in and what level they are relevant to.

In the first level of consciousness which is the egocentric field of me, myself, mine, I, and so forth, the application of effortful spiritual practices for awakening is appropriate. This is because you are engaged in beginning the process of self-witnessing. Nothing you do—apart from when you are successfully self-witnessing—will be anything other than egocentric. As you practice awareness everything that you see will be ego, whether you, the other, or the numinous. So you have to behave appropriately and appropriateness here means practicing attention to the small self and all its ramifications in your life—the life you are obsessed, held, and absorbed in, the definition of yourself, and your clinging and attachments, fear and desire.

In the second level of consciousness which is the heart field, the life of transformation and compassion, all is heart, compassion, and authenticity. The embracing of the other in "I" is a given, almost an assumption, and a motivation and aspiration. This brings about the flowering of your true nature in the fulfillment of your authentic purpose.

In the third level your spiritual practice and discipline (*sadhana*) toward perpetual consciousness and merging with the Divine is paramount. Self and other are transcended as you might walk away from a mirror. The gift of devotion in whatever approach you have received it manifests in your life, your body, and your spirit in never-ceasing spontaneity, freedom, and surrender.

These three levels of consciousness may be summarized as self, other, and God. Level one is the ego-I, level two is the other as yourself and no separation, and level three is the living insight that all is the Divine. Now we have a firm basis for understanding truth, both relative and absolute.

Five Stages of Truth

Truth can be understood in different ways, which creates confusion and miscommunication. Truth beyond the usual meaning of relative truth and verity used to be considered and practiced in a rarefied space, such as the monastery or ashram. How can we practice and avoid confusion for the seeker in the secular world? Here are the five stages of truth (or Truth) that we can experience and communicate.

Personal Truth
First is the most commonly understood meaning of truth. It is based on infantile and adolescent assumptions and is exclusively reactive in tone and content. It is likely to incite disagreement and conflict. The reason for this is that as adolescents and in childhood we are struggling to establish a sense of ourselves—first within and for ourselves and second as an identity which we can hold on to, believe in, and interact through with others. The identity becomes more important than the characteristics of the identity. That is why a child, adolescent, or "adult" clings so tightly to identity even when it does not bring him what he wants and even when it brings him what he doesn't want.

Truth in this first level is fluid in the sense that since it is reactionary it depends almost totally on what is being reacted against. But it is also fixed in the sense that the individual maintains a stubborn, set, un-thought out, and unreasoned internal image of the self for the purposes of individual survival in a perceived hostile environment.

So, truth in the first level is fundamentally subjective, defensive, and personal. Its main function is to support the image, the persona, and the personality, as well as an outer expression of inward character. We could paraphrase it like this: "The truth is what I think it is" or "If I think it strongly enough then it is the truth."

Heart Truth
Second is truth as it is manifested and understood in the intermediate psycho-spiritual stage of *individual authenticity*. This level of truth is firmly and steadily attached to the core of the person who has reached the level of individual authentic behavior in response (as opposed to reaction) to his fellow human. The sense of truth here grows from, is relevant to, and constellates around the core or center of the authentic person. Insofar as this stage involves the flowering of the individual, his holding to truth (in the personal authentic sense) is naturally paramount, of supreme importance. Only if an individual possesses this sense of truth may he be sure that he has become authentic and likewise only when he has become personally authentic can he possess this sense of core truth or the certainty of a genuine connection to his inner true nature, his core or essence.

So, truth in the second level is primarily authentic, both subjective (but in a deeper sense than the first stage truth) and objective (inasmuch as it perceives the reality of the other as self), and genuinely responsive. We could paraphrase it like this: "Then truth arises in my heart and I always trust it, or the truth is my constant companion. I live it and breathe it."

Spiritual Truth
Third is the level of truth which, after the core, responsive truth has been dissolved and relinquished (in a transformative act of individual annihilation, sacrifice, and renunciation) may rightly be called spiritual and impersonal. Before this, all truth has been relative and individual regardless of whether it was reactionary or responsive. This third and more advanced level of truth has a spiritual vividness bearing no necessary relation to any other spiritually perceived truth, either in content,

style, or approach. This is one reason why there are so many valid (as well as invalid) spiritual approaches, ways, and methods today. It is like the dictum that all roads lead to Rome. Although in this case it is not so much that *all* ways lead to a spiritual goal, so much as that all genuinely spiritual ways (although we should bear in mind that all such ways and means should be applied by an enlightened mind) lead to a spiritual outcome or advancement.

This is why spiritual teachers always sound so certain, why they tend not to refer to other paths and means; why arguably we have the excuse for holy wars and the persecution of heretics. In a sense the perspective of the spiritual teacher or guru is the truth with no need of comparison, of consulting other points of view, since all views of the Absolute, unlike perspectives on relative phenomena, are themselves absolute. In fact, if we consider the question deeply, all views of the Absolute, of God, are equally valid (providing of course that they are genuine), therefore there is no real need for a distinction. The rule should be that if you encounter such a genuine view of the Absolute, either directly yourself or through another who is "ahead" of you on the spiritual path, you should devote yourself to it, since this is the view you have been shown. This is the gift you are given. Your objections to it (and there are often many: the teacher is not as I expected him to be, the country where it appears is not where I want to live, the spiritual revelation does not conform to my beliefs) are spiritual "tests," opportunities to test faith and strengthen commitment in the pursuit of devotion.

So, in this stage reality is transcendental, a window onto the Absolute, a perspective on the Divine. We could paraphrase it like this: "Having arrived at a direct apprehension of the truth, I have developed a mode of seeing and expressing the way of truth that is aligned with the absolute. The glass is unblemished."

Absolute Truth

Fourth is the stage of Truth. Absolute Truth is represented with a capital "T" for the simple reason that it possesses no opposite. It has leapt a divide of relativity—time, space, opinion, individuality, perspective, and so on; it is no longer partisan. When you are in the realm of Truth you can only communicate it directly to others who are also in the realm of Truth. Otherwise you are likely to be misunderstood. The other will almost certainly filter Truth as a notion through one of the first three levels, thus reducing its meaning and significance.

It is as well to consider here the roles or functions of, respectively, the spiritual aspirant and the spiritual teacher. An enlightened function is not necessarily a teaching one. They are different functions. Obvious though it sounds, the assumption is often made by aspirants and arrivers alike that one inevitably follows from the other—but it doesn't. Therefore, we have many spiritual realizers who have assumed the teaching function and spread great confusion and uncertainty.

Absolute truth has to be handled differently to all the other levels of truth. The best way to describe this is to turn it on its head and say that it handles you or you must surrender to it handling you. Truth comes through you and whereas before with the successive levels of relative truth you were a component of the dynamic interaction of you-truth-the world or another, here you are entirely out of the way, annihilated. For Truth has a condition, a demand to make of you: get out of the way and manifest me.

Convincing someone of Truth is mostly futile, so I wouldn't try. An encounter with Truth however may leave even the most cynical person in no doubt whatsoever of its existence. We might paraphrase it like this: 'Absolute Truth is uncompromising and does not rely on anything beyond itself. It may only be uttered by those who have direct apprehension of it through divine "experience."'

Transcendental Truth
Fifth is the transcendence of all concepts—individual, essential, spiritual, absolute—of truth or Truth, as the bliss of unawareness engulfs the manifestation of individual consciousness in the fire of the Divine. To manifest the divine personality in an individual lifetime is the greatest and most transcendent attainment of a human life. Some of us will believe it, some of us will glimpse it, others of us will doubt it, and still others will desire to manifest it.

Only when all of these aspirations and attachments are shed and dissolved can the impossible human displace the possible, can the unbelievable be believed. What is real is manifested in your renunciation of all that is bogus, unreal, and inauthentic. As long as your motivation is toward Truth, you will attain the highest levels of spiritual transcendence which is the divine person residing within.

Transcendental truth is called *Turiyatita* in Sanskrit. It is the beyond and past the beyond. It is the most sublime Truth. Only when all even relative and absolute concepts are shed may it appear as Reality itself. We can paraphrase it like this: "Transcendental Truth is the ultimate illumination, the light of Consciousness that manifests in the relative world as awareness."

In Summary

At the beginning of this chapter in "The Ocean of Consciousness" we discussed how the spiritual teacher speaks the Truth. We asked which is the most important—the teacher or the teaching? We considered the apparent conflict between spiritual teachings, the therapist as spiritual guide, levels of consciousness, and, finally, the five stages of truth. Work through the following exercises to deepen in these subjects and enquiries.

1. Spiritual teaching is a spiritual teacher's reflection of Truth. In the first section of this chapter I offered a passage beginning, "The ocean pitches and swells..." You too can do this, so long as you deeply trust that the Truth is everywhere in everything. Do not discriminate, choose, or evaluate, rather bring your attention to this present moment, exactly where and how you find yourself in this moment and now record your witnessing of the Divine in the world.

2. With regard to the section in this chapter entitled "Teacher or Teaching?" what experience of the teacher being coincident with the teachings of Truth do you have or what thoughts do you have about this topic. Write about them in your inner work notebook.

3. Some spiritual teachings seem to contradict others, while still others may embellish or clarify other teachings. How should we deal with the conflicts and the confluences? Why today do we have so many spiritual teachers and spiritual teachings, offering such a diverse range of spiritual approaches and philosophies? Is it a good thing or not?

4. What are your spiritual questions? Examine the themes of your present life, see what arises persistently and what questions are inherent in the lessons that are appearing in your life.

5. What do you think your spiritual practice and discipline contribute to your spiritual attainment? If you are simply destined to awaken when you awaken, is there any point in spiritual practice at all? What is the role of spiritual practice in your understanding?

6. Write in your inner work notebook about the five stages of truth with some personal reflections and perhaps anecdotes from your life to illustrate your understanding and insight into the contrasts and unfolding of truth from your own experience.

11. Sincere Third-Stage Practice

The Gates of the Sun

The following is a partial account of an inner journey extracted from my personal inner-work notebooks:

> And I appeared at the Gates of the Sun. Blinded absolutely by the glare. Within me (except I had no form) I felt a vibrant uprush from the souls of my "feet" and the exhilaration of incredible energies. From above (in my "body") I felt an inhuman weight, an oppression of titanic dimension. As it "pushed" me into an inevitable annihilation, I "stood" against it, and this tension of opposite forces gave me existence or form. "I" stood between heaven and earth, between contradictory impulses, and the tension centered me in my chest and my heart. And in this perfect balance point, this pivotal border, a numinous fire raged and crackled and destroyed everything. This source-less, Self-sourcing fire was the fire of the soul and spirit and mystery, the initiating ritual that brings us into the presence of the Divine.

In every movement, nuance, and impulse the persona, your character, and small self seeks and longs for the light, the emergence into truth and illumination, to be subsumed in the Divine. You are intent on dying to your ego as the cause of misery and the endless resource of suffering.

Following the full flowering of the personality, the border or threshold between the ego condition and the spiritual path appears before us.

Four Signs that You Have Found Your Spiritual Teacher

The spiritual teacher (or guru, sheikh, roshi, lama, or spiritual director, depending on the tradition) is an ambiguous figure. He or she is inner and outer, human and divine, wise and foolish, consistent and inconsistent. What are the signs that you have found the spiritual teacher or teaching that is right for you?

1. Positive Engagement

Other than in rare cases, the effects of spiritual teaching are not instantaneous. This means you are in it for the long haul. You don't resign yourself however. You embrace it willingly and joyfully. If you can't, don't do it. Attitude is everything. When you enter a spiritual practice, a spiritual dimension, be positive or, if you are not, ask yourself what convoluted suffering prevents you feeling positive. Negativity can entirely sabotage your spiritual effort.

So that's first, *positive engagement*. It's like anything else: when you go on a long-awaited holiday you feel positive, when you go to work in a job you like you are ready and happy to work, when you see someone you love your heart goes out before you. Your attitude always portrays accurately not only what's happening now, but how it will develop and what the outcome will be.

But now you have decided on a course of action, you're attracted by a teacher, a method, a philosophy, and you are engaged positively.

2. Ego-Challenge

Second, remember that your ego may not agree with what you have chosen and that's alright. After all you might expect ego to resist, argue, and disagree with a course of action which leads to its demise. The real thing may not be Indian sitar music, wafting incense, and a man with a white beard and long flowing robes. Neither may the person you fall in love with match the picture you have of your preferred mate as you might describe him or her in a dating ad. The challenges, the differences, and the incompatibilities are what make relationships vibrant, dynamic, and worth having, and validates them because this is how you are tested to grow in interpersonal love. The spiritual milieu, teacher, and philosophy are attractive to a deeper part of you than your ego-preferences. The spiritual teacher, particularly, may be unlike anything you ever imagined.

The mystic teacher and author Caroline Myss is quite comical in her self-reflections on this, resembling as she does a publishing executive (her previous employment) or corporate motivational speaker. She is at pains to reveal that she doesn't have the image of a spiritual teacher, but resembles more closely a school teacher. A friend's small child who was in the room when some friends and I were watching a Myss video remarked, "She sounds like she's telling you off!" Or how about the psychotherapist and author Mariana Caplan who after doing the round of the "right" kinds of eastern yogis wound up following a blues harmonica-playing, Jewish singer with dreadlocks in San Francisco, the modern crazy-wisdom Baul, Lee Lozowick. And this is the whole point of the teacher, the teaching and the method: it should challenge your ego. So that's the second sign: *ego challenge*.

3. Self-Revelation

Now, the third sign. Because attitude here applies to commitment, choice, application, and readiness to practice in the genuine encounter, with the emphasis on the limitations of character, all your weaknesses are exaggerated and intensified. I remember this in the Ram Dass stories about his initial encounters with Neem Karoli Baba, which eventually climaxed in his realization that the teacher knew everything about him. Character is revealed, seen, and no longer hidden. Finally, it is exaggerated to prepare the way for healing, for lancing, for purifying.

When I met my first spiritual teacher, certain significant events took place, which reflected and demonstrated these basic aspects of my character, surprisingly quickly. First, I didn't want help. And underneath this I desperately wanted help. But I was too proud, too seemingly self-sufficient, too self-centered, and too self-deluded to accept it. Second, I couldn't hear because my heart was closed. One of the reasons we do not listen and hear is that we do not have the inner capacity to receive, to take in, because we are so full up with stuff—memories, unfinished business, regrets, imaginings, anxieties, anger, fears, and fantasies. Third, I was scared and scarred. Fear for me was double-edged: I was drawn to it and I abhorred it at the same time. That's how it was for me with him also; I was afraid and drawn to him.

When I was a child, I saw a cartoon strip that I have always remembered. I knew it said something profound though I was too young to know what it was. A boy is sitting on a bus and a great big guy, who is gruff-looking and overweight, is moving down the bus looking for a seat. The seat beside the little guy is empty and as the big guy moves toward him the little guy is thinking, "*Please* don't sit here next to me. *Please* sit somewhere else." The big guy moves past the boy and down the aisle and the think bubble changes as the little guy thinks, "OK what's wrong with me? What's wrong with *this* seat?"

Years later, sitting in a group with my teacher, the cartoon came back to me. He was talking about the night-time pursuits of us younger men—the sensual life of testosterone we all enjoyed or felt guilty about or relished or were conflicted about. We all knew that at some point he would draw attention to someone individually to drive his point home or perhaps that was what the whole teaching discussion was about. It must turn out to be about one individual, only you didn't know. Anyway I was sitting there thinking I really hope he doesn't settle on me, single me out, and start to shine the spotlight over here. I really hope he doesn't do that! Then when he had entirely ignored me and settled his attention on someone else, my inner monologue turned into: Why didn't he single me out? Am I not worthy of his individual, undivided attention? What's wrong with me? Attention equals love equals existence; the comfort of knowing that I exist, that I am here, that I am.

So you feel seen by your teacher, understood and empathized with, but more than anything else, *seen*. And accompanying that seeing-ness is the marvelous hint of acceptance, because if he or she can truly see you, then you must to some degree be acceptable to them. Your character is exaggerated and stretched to the point it becomes transparent, revealing the self that was previously concealed. So the third sign is character-revelation or self-revelation.

4. Profound Relief
The fourth sign is relief and it stems from the experience of being seen. But it includes something else: the affirmation that you are alright, that there is truth in the world, someone to speak it and someone to hear it and that it is enormously joyful to sit in the same room as that person and share breathing, speaking, listening, feeling, vibrating, harmonizing, and learning. A wonderful process begins to take place as you surrender to this extraordinary relief and liberation, the purification of your soul, your mind and your physical form. Emotionally, physically, intellectually, and energetically you clear out until you occupy an entirely clear, transformed place. This

state of open awareness is enormously relieving. And it does not increase gradually, that's to say you don't have a little bit and then it progresses or accrues or intensifies into more and more. It is there *immediately*.

So, this is a sign of the genuine spiritual encounter and in time it leads to spiritual initiation. It only need happen once to activate, stimulate, and meet the deep longing of your soul's journey to its eternal state. Take your time; don't begin until these initial experiences have taken place. Be aware and vigilant. Remember it is better to wait ten years for the right teacher, than practice for ten years with the wrong teacher. But a sign that you have it right is this feeling: *profound relief.*

These four experiential signs characterize, define, and herald the genuine spiritual encounter—positive engagement, ego challenge, self-revelation, and profound relief. Once these four experiences are in place and you feel everything is unfolding with a sense of rightness, expect further tests. The test usually strikes at the heart of your material attachment: money, time, power, relationship, or some other seduction which serves to test you. If it is to be a valid test it must be a powerful enough distraction that you move closer into your center. It must affect you energetically and it must be real, because the spiritual test brings about a real effect in the psycho-biological-energetic organism. It realigns you. It awakens your heart. It re-kindles divine love in you.

The spiritual teacher is one who awakens your heart, who you respond to, and in that response you feel the outcome and the realization of the Self. It is a relationship about life, for life, life-long, and beyond. The spiritual teacher is a reflection of you and can be anybody or anything, but in the formal traditional, psycho-physically refreshing, and thoroughly transforming sense, he or she is your greatest fear and your greatest desire. He or she is like no one else and ultimately indefinable. No sooner do you fix a perspective on him than you lose him again. Most important is your sense of gratitude that they are here.

The Heart of All-Embracing Love

The spiritual teacher has nothing to offer. This is the vacancy, the quandary, and the bounty of the spiritual teacher. The spiritual teacher is not the modern self-help guru, selling yourself back to you by having you be "the best you" you can be, realize your true happiness, or live your most egocentric dream. The spiritual teacher is the one who gives nothing, asks for nothing, and, through the process of profound emptiness that you enter into with him, you realize the silence in you, the inner space, the complete lack of any kind of event or experience, and the total lack of hungering for any kind of event or experience. At that point you make a choice and the choice is not made from your petty, small mind, the mind of egoic self-thought, self-creation, and self-thinking that creates separation. It is made from the heart, the realm of wholeness, acceptance, compassion, and all-embracing love.

Find this in yourself. And do not be reluctant or resistant to finding it outside yourself too. The discovery of the guru is not a trip through time and space. If you have become caught up with that, then stop now! It is not like looking for a lover or perfect mate. Like all searches, that search is doomed. This search for the spiritual teacher is definitely doomed to fail, because it doesn't work that way. You wouldn't seek a dolphin in the sky any more than you would look for a bird in the ocean, so understand just as well spiritual location and orientation: if you are seeking the eternal then enter the eternal and enter it on its terms when it beckons to you.

Renunciation or Celebration?

The history of organized, institutionalized spirituality has tended to have something to say about the relationship of human beings to the world in general and to pleasure in the world in particular. One of the prevailing notions has been that the world as we know and experience it is somehow dirty, sinful, or meager and to transcend this mortal plane with its suffering and sinfulness is spiritually virtuous and advanced. The companion notion is that there will be a more wonderful, ideal, and love-filled place beyond in the future to which we will go, ascend, or rise to (it tends to be "up") that will vindicate us and make sense of our travail here on Earth.

The other principle notion has been to enjoy and indulge, have fun and do what you want to celebrate the human experience and connect to the spiritual or transcendence in this lifetime. Participation and indulgence may in time bring you to a place which resembles the renunciate point of view, but in the meantime enjoyment of the transient realms is seen as a legitimate course.

So which is correct?

First, always look carefully at paradox when it appears in conflicting or even complementary ideas, because paradox is a clue. It is the scent of the spiritual. It indicates that you are approaching a threshold, a border between the worlds and if you choose you may take the opportunity to slip through. Paradox also implies a separation of parts that rightly belong together. In this case, two worldly, rather than truly spiritual, concerns. The first, the renunciate position, is the attachment to the world whereby you desire and seek to be released from it and the second is the attachment to the world whereby you seek freedom through immersing in it. The first is "out" the second is "in." They are complementary; neither one is separate from the other. They are really two halves of a whole concept. This is the creativity of the ego-processes, the artistry of the mind. It takes a single idea, turns it to face in the opposite direction, divides it into two and—voila!—it has created another concept. Ego is truly God-like!

Both apparently different points of view are forms of attachment to the world. They are forms of relationship, enslavement, or bondage to the fleeting world of time and space, of relativity, and appearing and disappearing phenomena. Neither one of them is necessarily a way through to the transpersonal, spiritual realms.

We should understand this. A practice, a path, or a method should contain within it our means to liberation. But if it doesn't, then it is a means of attachment. Institutionalized, organized religion tends toward attachment, because it is not in and of itself anything but a systematized set of beliefs and accompanying rituals, either esoteric or exoteric. Religion is reminiscent of drug rehabilitation or serial relationships. In the first an alcoholic may be considered a successfully reformed junkie; in the second a person in a failed relationship seeks solace in a new one without actually changing anything inside them, so guaranteeing that the same, or at least a similar, drama plays out as before.

Religion is a legitimate bondage. It is the acceptable "spiritual" appearance of bondage for those who don't wish to appear to be imprisoned in life, but seek to adorn their prison bars and paint the chains. Not even the founders of world religions were "religious" in the institutionalized sense. They were the very opposite. Lao Tzu was famously in disagreement with Confucius, Buddha rebelled against the contemporary condition of Hinduism, Christ argued with the Pharisees and actively opposed the Judaism of his time.

We may be positively or negatively attached; attachment is attachment either way. Neither is true spirituality a matter of mere belief. It is a spiritual reality. This reality is consonant with our very nature; it is the essence of who we are. It is precisely because of this intimacy, this closeness, that searching is futile and absurd. For the truly spiritual seeker, the search is abandoned. The way—the true way—is sought and sought alone.

The Three Levels of Loss

What binds and links the psycho-spiritual journey together is the process of loss. Our lack or deficiency, sense of worthlessness, and lack of self-esteem is based on a thought and that thought is that I am insufficient in some way. This thought, this sense of lack, leads us and motivates us potentially in all we do. So, as young men and women, we ask what job we want to do, what sort of relationship we want. As we "mature" into adulthood, the question gets more refined, based on the disappointments we have experienced. We may then modify, adapt, or change completely what we think will lead us to human fulfillment.

There is a point of departure here for inwardly-inclined people and outwardly-orientated people. So what I have to say now applies to the inner seekers, spiritually-inclined people who have some deep inner allegiance to the esoteric aspects of spiritual life, transcendence, and the Divine. *Sooner or later it occurs to us that nothing in the outer world is going to satisfy us.* It is painful to go through—the despair, the dejection, and the disenchantment of the experience of seeing our goals, desires, and aims, one after another, disintegrate before our eyes, but that's the way it is. This process of loss—loss of enchantment, loss of gullibility, loss of unawareness, loss of being "asleep"—leads us to our true nature and in time to the Truth.

So what exactly do we have to give up and lose? It all depends on your present challenge, which depends on which stage of your life you are in. I don't mean psycho-biologically, but spiritually. The psycho-biological stages of life I have written about at some length in *Your*

Essential Self.[19] They describe the appropriate conditions and challenges for the different stages of life from the chronological, developmental perspective. But the stages I am talking about here are different, and they can be entered into at any stage in the developmental model. All that means is that you can awaken any time!

Loss of Attachments to Self-Identity

My three stage model of human unfolding concerns the processes of awakening, liberation, and realization. In the first level, we are obsessed with personality, character, and defenses. It's all to do with the past and survival and protection. So the challenge at this level is to let go of or lose your attachment to all of this. Character defenses, personality defenses, emotional-behavioral patterns, assumptions, opinions, the whole character perspective, lack of forgiveness, the axis of painful character traits that leads to anger, hurt, sadness and reaction—there's lots, of course! And it all has to go.

Unless you let go of it all you cannot discover your true nature, so you won't know who you really are. The whole point is that you have sealed the doors, put the defenses in place in a most sophisticated way; you have imprisoned yourself and thrown away the key. You think that it's really you, but you are a long way inside, protected, numbed, suppressed, and hidden. In the first level you have to surrender your attachment to everything that up to now appears to have been your protection, everything you consider to be "you." It amounts to identification, separation, and division… everything you have marginalized or thrown out of your psyche and projected must be brought home to you, brought back, reclaimed, re-loved, so that you are made whole.

---

[19] See chapter 5 "Stages of Transition" in *Your Essential Self,* 97.

Loss of Attachment to True Nature
Now this state of wholeness does not bring you to the spiritual threshold as is popularly supposed; it brings you to the threshold of authenticity and transformation. In an amazing unselfconscious leap or act of transformation, you allow yourself to center in your authentic heart, your genuine self. It is a second birth, a staggering act of real compassion for yourself and everybody and everything else. This is your true nature. For the first time you embrace your true nature in genuine response to the world, both inner and outer, and now begins a mighty journey of love, compassion, forgiveness, expansion, and deeper happiness than you have ever known before. If you have a spiritual guide or psycho-spiritual therapist who has brought you to the threshold then he or she now functions in an entirely different way, guiding you through the demonstration, the expression of yourself in your transformation and authenticity in the relative world of duality. You will encounter all sorts of trials, resistances, challenges, and tests, but they are easier than when you were holding on to a false self, a persona or mask, like in the first level. The time comes however when, as I said before, you are asked to release even this, to relinquish the self-nature, the truth of your individual soul for a transcendent reality, a truth beyond the individual self, even in its true nature, and that is a great loss.

Loss of Attachments to Non-Attachment
Do you know the lovely story of the elderly sadhu who came to see the Buddha? He came, as was customary, with gifts. In each hand he carried a gourd to present to the Buddha. As he approached, the Buddha cried out, "Drop

it!" and the elderly sadhu dropped the gourd in his right hand and carried on approaching. Then the Buddha cried out, "Drop it!" and the sadhu dropped the gourd in his left hand. Somewhat bewildered he continued to approach and the Buddha cried out, "Drop it!" At this point, according to the story, he enters enlightenment. This is the same as the three stages I am talking about. The first stage is dropping what you are carrying in the right, active hand. It is how you are approaching the world, meeting people in the world and events in the world, with animosity, with hate, with anger, defensiveness, and reaction. All of these are expressions of fear, symptoms of feeling threatened.

That is why most people are essentially intimidating; in whatever form, if you observe closely, people are essentially intimidating each other. The second stage is dropping the true nature that you have always had beneath the personality and character, that which is now precious to you, because you have discovered it and it is authentic. So it is a worthy sacrifice and you have something to put into the spiritual fire and that something now is really everything you have.

In the ancient stories when a student approached a teacher, a student who was intent on being a real adept, who wanted to really learn and realize the Self, he approached with "fuel." This is written in the ancient Upanishads. Today people think that if they pay money, they get to receive the spiritual teaching, but that is merely an aspect of ubiquitous spiritual materialism. When you approach a teacher for spiritual teaching authentically, you must carry fuel, which means that not only are you bringing an offering, but the quality of that offering is as strong as your aspiration to learn to receive.

What can loss possibly mean at the third level? In the Buddha and the sadhu story, what has he got left to drop! What have you got left to drop when you have let go of your false self and your true self? First you must let go of attachment to spiritual progress or to the illusion that anywhere you wind up is *the* place and from there you construct a spiritual reality. Sometimes that is so subtle that you believe in it absolutely and no one can budge you. In any case you are by this time so way ahead of most everyone else there are very few people who can challenge you. Then you must let go of the last vestiges, the subtle holdings to the ego-processes. Even after all you have been through you still have great attachment to the last traces of ego-forces and they must be finally relinquished. It is a spiritual fact that the ego and its accompanying behaviors and attachments are with you right up the final stages.

Behind the Veils

Do you know that experience you can have with another human being when you look at them deeply? You look straight into their eyes, into the soul of the person, as if to say, "Hello are you in there?" And they look out a little shyly at first and then with increasing confidence they meet you? This is exposing the lie of the ego directly. Personality and character are the direct descendants of the ego; the ego in living demonstrative form and, charming as you may be, it's really all for show, either deliberately and consciously, or unknowingly and unconsciously. But it doesn't make any difference; in the end you are concealing yourself out of fear, playing the game of lack out of a deficit of self-esteem. You are simply disempowered and playing small.

Whenever a psycho-spiritual thought has led to a means to spiritual progress or awakening it has come from this basic motivation: you look into the face of love or spontaneity or reality and feel overwhelmingly that your present life is *not that*. As a result of that insight and conviction, you feel determined to follow a path to what is real. That path has never been followed before; it is utterly unique. But it has to be constantly informed by the purity of that first basic insight. This insight is known in various ways as faith, trust, dissatisfaction, shock, seeking, or the search for the impossible. You have in effect understood that the present condition of three-dimensional space-time contains nothing but misery and suffering. This is because everything here is based on desire and fear and you know where that leads; it leads to dissatisfaction, frustration, and sadness.

We must begin to shed our attachments to the individual "dark" trinity of character, personality, and ego if we are to practice or progress spiritually, because this ego-based realm is the shadow land, the world of grey shapes and indistinct forms passing endlessly away into the fog. Once the clarion call of "shock" has seized you, you are possessed with a single thought. This thought is to awaken at any cost. So you move into the upper realms of the heart of compassion, authenticity, and understanding, which characterize the lives of the saints and the mystics who have been gripped with the love divine. This is to peek behind the veils. It is the beginning of the spiritual path and the great adventure of growing a human life flows from these insights and understanding.

The fear of making the commitment to one's true Self manifests in our resistance to spiritual endeavor. Fear always leads to contraction and contraction to resistance. Out of complacency and a false sense of endless opportunities, we think we have forever to become enlightened, whereas the truth is that we have only now or we have eternity, but now and eternity are only available to us when we use fear as a signpost and find the way through it to the other side.

Enlightenment is not merely for others, for Orientals, told to us in ancient stories from distant cultures, romanticized and fetishized. Enlightenment develops in stages through levels of letting go, as we have seen in the previous section. While the guru or spiritual teacher may suit many seekers around the world, in the west we have our own precious and profound psycho-spiritual tradition. May it be ripened, blossom, and come to fruit in this present century. In the next section we will look at the excruciatingly painful condition of a therapy client poised on the edge of a psycho-spiritual breakthrough in a personal letter.

A Letter to Emma

Some of the complexities of the healing relationship with the therapist-healer-guide are expressed in the following letter to a client called Emma (name changed). This is an actual letter, reproduced here with her permission. It was written when she was experiencing excruciating difficulties and was blindly lashing out in anger and disappointment, knowing somewhere deep inside her that this was the transference of her own anger and torment, her despair at ever being able to love, her inability to truly relate, and her meanness of soul and spirit fighting in despair from the corner up against the wall of her own making.

Please read it as inspiration, a *mantra*, a commitment, a *mudra* of the soul, a prayer, an evocation, and a profound encouragement to ascend to the heart. Emma had been working in therapy with me for an extended length of time, so some of what may appear to be assumptions in the letter come from a deep familiarity and wouldn't be appropriate for clients seen over a lesser time period.

૭ઝ

Dear Emma

I do not shepherd you through the veils, if I am merely a commodity you pay for. The therapeutic relationship is both complex and simple. First, it is complex because it is outside most people's experience. The purpose of the healing relationship is to heal you initially of the limitations and the contractions of the past. Everything you experience within this relationship is your *past* life. That's how complex it is. The only way to be with you effectively is to accept it all, the whole thing, and to remain present and receptive and to consistently and relentlessly allow you to bring this material that is so sad, painful, hurtful, and angry-making into the sacrificial fire of therapy.

Second, it is simple because it embodies and expresses great acceptance and love. When you haven't experienced these qualities, you may find it hard to recognize them when they are present. You may simply feel that there is something faintly attractive, or even repulsive, about them. You want and don't want to have them and this ambivalence is projected onto the therapy and the therapist.

The therapist is a spiritual teacher. He or she must be. If not, then he is merely a symptomatic counselor, rather like a motor mechanic. As a motor mechanic fixes your car, the therapist who is only a symptomatic counselor deals with symptoms and affects and fixes you. Then you feel better, you get on with your life, your relationships, and your work.

But people are not mechanical. They might pretend to be machines and their behavior is very often machine-like (*mechan* means tricky from Greek the "mekhanikos," meaning resourceful, inventive, ingenious), but people are not machines, because they have souls and because they are spirit and ultimately because they are consciousness arising in temporary individuated forms. People are really modifications of the Divine and not even pieces of the Divine. Human beings *are* divine—that is what we are!

So a psychology of humanity and a psychotherapist who practices authentic human psychology must express the required depth, so he can meet you on all levels of your spirituality and humanness.

He does not do that by being partisan, biased, or by bringing his personality into his contact with you. In fact, he can only be of any use at all when he has realized that his personality is comprised of defensive, aggressive, protective forms of ego-processes. The therapist is not really interested in his own small self or ego-processes anymore and he is certainly not interested in yours! What he is interested in is what will cause you to awaken, to become liberated, and to finally merge with your True Self.

That Self is so magnificent, so splendid, and so brilliant that you can only get an indirect hint of it through transference and projection—the loved one, your image of the Lord, of the Goddess, some splendid sight or experience. Now take all of these and multiply them by a thousand. This will not come close to who you are in reality.

Not only is the goal (your True Self) inconceivable to you, but so also is the means, the way, and the method. That is where the teacher or guide or therapist comes in. The therapist doesn't know either, but he has clues and he knows more than you do (or he is confident about knowing less—it amounts to the same thing!). He knows that your personal journey is reflected in the relationship you have with him. That's because he is closer than you (if he's not, then you should be his therapist!) to who you really are. In effect he has a closer relationship to your True Self than you do! And that's why you can trust him… with your life, because he knows and understands and stands in true relationship to life in all its forms.

The relationship between the therapist and you is an accurate gauge and the process and the healing takes place *within* it. Don't be fooled, the real therapist does not bring a toolbox; he does not appear with methods and ideas, strategies and philosophies—you have enough of them already. He appears as himself before you, open, available, intelligent, and wise.

Now what about when none of this appears to be how it is for you in your relationship to your therapist?

The first possible explanation is that he is not the therapist you thought he was; he's just a symptomatic counselor, a fix-it sort of therapist. The second possible explanation is that you have missed him, fallen out of relationship to him, because some big breakthrough is on the horizon and rather than deepen in your healing relationship to the teacher-therapist-guide you are going to sabotage it and mess it up completely, so that you don't change.

The therapist is patient. He takes everything that's thrown at him. Sometimes he responds; he never reacts. When he appears to react, it is for a reason and that reason originates in the heart. It is a heart-reason which is totally different from strategy. It is intelligent and wise, rather than knowledgeable and clever. He is not trying to manipulate you; he is trying to shepherd you to the other side by whatever means he can, by whatever means you allow him to use. Your resistance is unconscious and it is destructive. It is a sort of addiction to remain as you think you are and to become all that you truly are appears to you to be such a burden, such a great responsibility, even an impossibility.

So you struggle against the healing, against the therapist, against the whole process. Cynicism enters in: he is only after your money, he wants to cause you harm, he wants to take his own stuff out on you, he's even more screwed up than you are. The doubt sets in: you can't or won't change, who wants to anyhow? Who do you know who has experienced lasting change through therapy, counseling, meditation, or spirituality? It's all nonsense, garbage. You've had enough anyway, you've paid enough in time and energy and money and engagement and particularly relationship! You're tired, exhausted, you want to be "normal" and if you stop now you can be "normal." No one you know is in such a bad state as you are and you do therapy, so therapy is probably the cause.

Therapy is no good for you—it doesn't work and it causes harm. You're better off without it.

And so you have scapegoated your own process of self-discovery and instead of using it to allow yourself to go through to the other side, to awaken, to transform and become authentic. You relent, you backslide, you give in... *tragically*, just at the moment when something of immense significance is about to happen: the transformation of your habitual sleep, of your unconscious body-mind into consciousness, into the life of the heart, into awakening.

You cannot do this on your own. Along the way there are so many pitfalls, so many wrong turns and false paths, seductions, illusions, deliriums, chimeras. The therapist warns you off and gently guides you through, past, and around these obstacles. He uses his skill in timing and evaluation, intuition, higher instinct, trust and faith, acceptance and challenge. When you look back it appears tremendously complicated, like a dance that must have been conceived, produced and choreographed by a great artist. But it is all you; one individual, unique process of self-discovery in which the therapist has participated, sometimes like a mirror, a friend, a savior, an archetypal parent, a divine being, a flawed human, a confidante, a trusted companion. In reality he has practiced profound friendliness; he has wished the very best for you. But not content to leave it at that, he has practiced and made all the right moves that would bring you home to yourself.

Struggle less, arrive sooner. Talk less, listen more. Try to understand. Bring attention to the things of importance over all the rest; and there is so much! More than anything, remember what you are here for, who you are, why you're here, and what your purpose is. To meet and be with someone who knows that already rubs off in the most instinctive and powerful way. You become affected deeply by his authenticity, but you must be receptive, you must allow yourself to take it in... and you must trust deeply and completely.

Will he challenge you? Well, yes, of course, he must. Will he offend you? Definitely! You are already deeply offensive to yourself. He will highlight this, he will show you what you are doing to yourself, how you don't love yourself. Will he hurt you? No, never intentionally. Sometimes when you are working together you will feel hurt and at certain times you will feel that he has hurt you. Try to remember that this is never the case, because you are hurt already. This painful hurt is the revisiting, the re-feeling, perhaps the first experience of full emotion—it is the doorway you have had the courage to open, it is the beginning of release, integration, and change. Does he have a right to comment on you? Of course, when he intuitively sees that it is the right time. This will challenge, test, expose, even hurt at times, but it is absolutely necessary, and never done without reason.

Is the therapist working *for* you? No, he is definitely not working for you. He is working *with* you. This is a joint practice, a sharing, a meeting. He is not the expert; you are the expert. He is not authoritative, although he may speak with authority. He does not ever tell you what you *must* do, although you may hear it that way, but he may give encouragements, guidance, direction. And yes, at times he will tell you when behavior—yours or another's—is not alright, is unacceptable, or inappropriate.

Here is a further challenge. This sharing, this relationship, is unequal. As your guide, the therapist necessarily knows more than you. He has traversed the terrain, stood naked and humiliated, felt the inside of the dragon's mouth, crawled over the cut-glass, been washed away in a tidal wave of emotions. He has been there. He will hold and contain you; he will provide the presence and the essential emptiness in which you are received, recognized, acknowledged, and at last "seen." You will feel amazing relief from this contact, from this connection but, don't forget what I said before, you will struggle and fight against it. Sometimes you and he are polarized, sometimes it is easy between you, sometimes it's casual, at other times formal. You experience the therapist-guide as distant and close, but you go on regardless. Faith and trust triumph. You will get there, *never doubt it*.

According to your tendency, the therapist-guide may be a temporary relationship for you. That's alright. Remember though that if you have a tendency toward serial relationships or if you have a tendency toward single-minded monogamy and loyalty this will be reflected in the therapeutic relationship, because *everything* is reflected in it. This relationship is like no other; it is the mirror of your soul. And, like everything... it will end.

When it ends you will feel overwhelming gratitude and respect, honor and reverence. You will look back on it as the way, the path, the means by which you have arrived at the authentic human existence and you will wonder why everyone doesn't do it! Be accepting of everyone in their limitations, in their ignorance. While you don't want to become a boring evangelist, you will want to find a way to express, to give back, to represent what you have discovered and to bring the sacred treasure of illumination into the community of souls you number among your friends, family, and wider networks. Surrender to the artistic impulse to express through your life, in your creative expressions, in your home, your relationships, work, and family. Bring it in, be proud of it and yourself, and share it generously.

You find yourself now on the peaks of wisdom, on the precipice of intuition, on the mountain-tops of compassion. Knowledge and cleverness mean less to you—much less—than wisdom and direct, inner knowing. Quoting, referring to others' wisdom, scholarship and knowledge mean less to you now. Poised on the edge of a breakthrough I am sure you feel scared... and beneath that, terrified. You want to hold on and you want to let go. You want to argue and you want to accept. You want to fight and you want to surrender. Trust. All will be well.

Let go of illusion, transcend conditioning, and rise to the heart-level of awareness, live the life of transformation and authenticity. Now you stand at the threshold. You have a steep learning curve ahead of you. Many people enter therapy and never change, never transform their lives irreversibly and permanently. This is because it is so difficult to do. It is difficult to find a practitioner who can facilitate this, difficult to find one who has experienced this and we are so enormously, unconsciously resistant to taking self-responsibility for our lives, our emotions, our relationships, and our human foibles. Unconsciously we prefer to blame someone, something, anything, rather than take responsibility for ourselves. Take total responsibility for yourself now. Only then can we go on. Not because I say so, but because anything else is merely going over old ground.

Old ground and repetition are the materials of the habitual life—everyone does it all the time. Life doesn't change, it just mixes round and round, so the same patterns of emotion, feeling, and behavior arise repeatedly. If you can work with a therapist who witnesses, sees you, is not invested in the outcome, stands somewhat apart yet involved, and possesses sense, intelligence, and most of all heart, and symbolizes these attributes in your life and in your healing, then it *is* possible. This relationship is very rare and it is the first necessary requisite for inner transformation.

The second necessity of transformation is that you do what you don't want to do. This may sound innocent enough, but it is nearly impossible. What will happen is your ego will present two sides and you will vacillate between the two, until you decide which one is the one you don't want to do and then you will do it, but it will always be your decision and so it will not be what you don't want to do. The therapist-guide has to give this challenge, this test. He may only offer it if he has received it in his own personal travail.

From some time ago in many different ways I have offered this to you. Your ego-processes are so strong, as is your sense of survival—the two are the same—that you haven't been able to accept the challenge. Now you can, and must, if you want to go further. The form of these challenges can never be known beforehand, so it would be useless of me to tell you what guise they will appear in, but when you feel great resistance to your deepest guidance, that is the time! Do it anyway!

The reason this is so important, so crucial, is that you cannot erode the ego-processes wholesale, and you cannot defeat the ego by fighting it. You defeat it by seeing through it, by loosening its hold on your life piece by piece, a little bit at a time, until gradually you're free. Any other way, for almost all people, is too much. They fall into shock and the ego strengthens to revive and return them to their habitual lives (and the madness of repetitively going over old ground again).

These two elements—the therapeutic healing relationship and doing what you don't want to do—are what separates the people who dabble in inner work from the ones who attain.

No one else can decide for you. In some senses not even you can decide for you! You see, always in therapy work, in psycho-spiritual work, there are two beings; the small self trying to keep everything in place just as it always was, not wanting to rock the boat, and the rebel, the subversive one who stands *against* the status quo.

Which one is which is sometimes very difficult to discern. The small self can pretend to be all sorts of things it is not or it may act as a deceptive controller or a seducer pretending to care and give you what you want, so long as you don't do anything too risky. In a multitude of ways, you fool and deceive yourself for the sake of your survival. But you no longer need to be in survival mode. Life is much more—more expansive, more exciting, more fulfilling, more loving— than that!

Awakening is being yourself, without apologies or compromise. You take responsibility for yourself and your life like never before. Jeanne de Salzmann, a disciple of Gurdjieff, said: "You receive exactly what you give... you take all, you accept all without any sense of obligation. Your attitude toward life is the attitude of one who has the right to make demands and to take—who has no need to pay or earn. You behave that all things are your due—simply because it is you. None of this strikes your attention, yet this is precisely what keeps one world separate from another."[20] Let these transformative words revise your thoughts and revive your spirit!

It will be very hard for you to believe what I just said. You will think that I am acting out of self-preservation, self-pride, and wanting to be liked. But I am not. That is because my center is whole now. It didn't use to be and when it wasn't, I needed other people, like you do now, to confirm that it was alright or not alright. Now I don't turn to others. Others actually are not at all reliable, because they will confirm almost anything you want. They will take sides or collude because they want to be liked, because they are stuck in the limitations of conditioning and defensive character. Collusion gives them some

---

[20]Jeanne de Salzmann, *The Reality of Being: The Fourth Way of Gurdjieff*, Shambhala Publications 2011.

temporary relief from their own inner conflict. They are trying desperately to survive.

Where your therapy has brought you to now is a real choice. Do you want to go on living as you always have done? Or do you want to change—radically? Do you want to be free or do you want to be chained?

The precise step you find yourself at is the decision to let go of anger once and for all. This does not mean that you will never get angry ever again. It means that you will not be chained to anger (and sadness, resentment, frustration, anxiety, and so on). It means that when you are angry the anger will be spontaneous and appropriate, never personal and defensive, never merely a justification for your character.

I have traveled with you this far. I have been your therapist, guide, and teacher. You have done some incredible work. If you turn away now (and you may choose to) you will know yourself, be far more aware, see yourself fall in the dark pit of personality and character and see yourself climb out. But if you carry on, by dropping anger you will open your heart in a way you have never done before. With your open heart leading you, you will be able to live a courageous life, a compassionate life, a life such as you would have wished for when you were young. This is what you have always wanted and always longed for, and now it is within reach. How do you cross the threshold to it?

You need to *practice*; practice heart-centering, listening, and compassion. The choice is made from the heart. The therapeutic, healing relationship between therapist-teacher-guide and client-adept-seeker is a manifestation of divine energy. It is very significant, because it goes beyond itself. In fact, all relationships should do this. For example, take marriage partners; if the relationship is to survive and flourish it must embody something *beyond* itself, in this case the unity of soul and spirit, of the divine and the human, of human love and transcendent love. It represents the divine marriage, the inner ceremony of unity and spirituality. The same is true of friendship, family relationships, and all other kinds of relationships; they represent and symbolize the essence of love and connectedness in all their varied aspects.

The therapeutic relationship is peculiar in this regard, because it is the symbol of healing. It stands for the two becoming one. The great saying in Matthew 18:20: "For where two or three are gathered together in My name, there am I in the midst of them,"[21] is the most cogent expression of this. The symbolic act of collaborating for the purpose of healing is a staggeringly powerful symbol that goes beyond itself and stands for healing—*all* authentic healing.

Therefore, when it is truly entered into, the bond between therapist and client is extraordinary.

I am aware that you have heard much of this before, aware that you have worked with me for a substantial period, and that you have done good work, work that gives me a lot of faith in you, and this faith you should have in yourself too. Now is the time for much of what you have heard to sink in, to become a part of you. Approach this inner work now with increased respect and honor. From now on, please don't be flippant in any way about this archetypal process. I am not a "shrink"; I am your psychotherapist, sometimes your teacher (particularly where in the groups you have been a student) and potentially, if you choose, even your spiritual teacher. None of this is possible if you are flippant. Flippancy is an expression of disrespect to yourself. And it does you dishonor; it is an irreverence you cannot withstand at this

---

[21] The Holy Bible: Authorized King James Version, New Ed edition, Collins 2011.

crucial juncture. The stakes are too high; the crucial importance of attitude is central.

I wish you well. I have always wished you well. I will always continue to wish you well, whatever you decide.

୦ଃ

This may seem a strange place to finish our reconstruction and glimmer of revolution, which has been the subject of the last two parts. But actually it is entirely appropriate. Many or most people at this present time of human evolution falter or refuse to jump. Instead they become entrenched in their character and personality, which swells to prevent and protect them against transformation. Some courageous souls make the jump anyway… but for the body of humanity to transform as a whole we must rise individually and then collectively into the heart center. This is where we begin in Part 5.

In Summary

This chapter spoke of the spiritual gateway, our longing for the Divine, dying to the ego, and ending suffering. We asked how you know that you have found your spiritual teacher and gave four signs. We discussed the futility of searching for a spiritual teacher, of paradox and the attachments to the acceptance or rejection of worldliness and pleasure. We discussed the deepening levels of loss in the spiritual journey, relinquishing defensive character and personality for authentic awakening and we ended with a letter to Emma, a seeker poised on the brink of breakthrough. This chapter ends our examination of the dawning revolution of spirit. In Part 5 we set about proposing a new paradigm for future living. In the meantime, work with the exercises that follow to ground yourself in the subjects we have discussed in the previous chapter.

1. Meditate on your longing for the Divine, your transcendent desire for wisdom and illumination, your impulse toward healing and seeking the end of suffering.

2. The four signs that you have found your spiritual teacher are: positive engagement, ego-challenge, self-revelation, and profound relief. You may have experienced all of these and found your true guide and teacher or perhaps you have met spiritual teachers who have not felt quite right because one or more of these signs were missing. Write your story as clearly and honestly as you can. It may be instructive, inspirational, revealing or perhaps all three. Consider how you might share it with others.

3. Whether you have found your spiritual teacher or not, events and figures of significance have influenced

your spiritual journey. For some you feel gratitude, honor, reverence. Compose an altar in a quiet, private space in your home. Make this altar beautiful and adorn it symbolically with objects that remind you and recognize the important events in your journey so far.

4. Contemplate the three levels of loss. Contemplation differs from meditation. Whereas in meditation you tend to allow thoughts to pass through your consciousness and deepen into the being-state, in contemplation you actively allow thought and follow it in an intentional inner exploration. Thus, contemplation and meditation comprise a harmonious, balanced complement. Take some time now to contemplate the three levels of loss which we discussed in this chapter

5. How could you depict the relationship between character, personality, ego, and the core, essential self in a picture?

6. With regard to "A Letter to Emma" and my letter to myself (in "Death and Resurrection," Chapter 3), write a letter of inner guidance to yourself from your wiser self.

PART 5: A CRITICAL NEW INNOVATIVE PARADIGM

12. The Spiritual Revolution: Ascending into the Heart

Today there is a collective intuition that we have to change. Much is wrong with the world. We sense that we should care more, love more, sacrifice more for each other, but we don't really know how to do it.

People are sad, angry, fearful, and complacent. People are out of touch with themselves and their inner essence. The way back is also the way through and it is a big event. The spiritual revolution that has been spoken of so much over the last 100 years must come about if we are to change in a way that is positive, enriching, intelligent, and heartening for us individually, collectively, and globally, and of course spiritually.

But before this spiritual revolution can happen, people have to learn to care. They have to be encouraged to ascend into the heart energies that are intrinsic and natural to humanity. They must accept the challenge to love without exception. To love not only what is easy to love, but also what is hard. In time they will discover that what's hard to love is the deeper, more revealing, spiritual challenge that expands their hearts and they will discover their inner essence, which they have been separated from for so long.

Without this spiritual revolution and the heart-opening that must precede it, humanity is in danger. Both from within and without, humanity is threatened with the inevitable fallout of anger, hate, and lack of kindness to themselves, to others, and to their environment. The sacred life must return.

Our sacredness must be our central reality... and we must live it, because if the unsacred, secular, a-spiritual life persists there is only one possible outcome: the dehumanizing of humanity and the descent into a less than human condition. This process has in fact begun, though few recognize it. The predominant concern of people today is with themselves and with the concerns of their lower animalistic centers.

So what needs to happen?

We must retrieve our essence, the central core of our deepest humanity. This is the source of human happiness, compassion, and Reality. Without it, we are unhappy, dissatisfied, lost, and that is how we feel today. Human beings feel lost and confused, questioning and not knowing, facing the simplest or the most complicated issues. From the point of view of ignorance, it seems that selfishness is the way, but people can be shown, they can be taught, they can be reminded, and they can be inspired... by example. Let the ones who know wisdom, therefore, live their deepest truth in the most intelligent, fundamentally enlightened life they are capable of living.

The Commitment to Live from the Heart

Ego-processes have brought humanity to the present day crisis of inhumanity and ignorance, so that we can no longer avoid the need to follow the deep impulse to transcend the ego. It is no longer choice, but necessity.

You may decide whether to follow self-centeredness and selfishness in your life or the inner divine forces that are calling to you to listen and live them. Let us make a commitment to live from the heart, from liberation and authenticity, and from the divine source to the best of our ability, as much as we are able, and as far as we possibly can, *now*.

You can cling to the conformist life and learn a little about spirituality or you can jump into the deep end and live it all the way. Then the sacred life takes root in you and you fly with the wings of the spirit. Today there is much information about spirituality—reading, courses, TV, film—but less popular are the strictures and demands of sadhana, the fruits of practice, direct and experienced. The former is reading the menu; the second is savoring the food.

We must heal the present situation, the one that is so taken for granted and which most people feel powerless to change. Yet the power to change is within each individual. It is a personal responsibility. Only make the decision to become empowered and allow yourself to work steadily toward it.

People today live almost exclusively in the lower chakras. This means that their concerns are lower energy concerns, instinctive preoccupations emanating from the animalistic centers. The rising generations of young people, late adolescents, and people in their twenties and thirties are concerned with marriage, creating families, having children, making money, buying a house, establishing a career, attaining promotion, and amassing wealth, prestige, and status. All these values and aims are supported unquestioningly by their parents, grandparents, and elders who consider these concerns of paramount importance.

Please understand me. I am not criticizing making money, raising children, and the great virtues of creating a healthy loving family. My point is that these overriding aims and concerns are overemphasized, out of balance, and supported by previous generations who seek tacit support and, to at least some degree, absolution for their perceived failings by supporting their own children in doing what they attempted to do better.

There is another more overt point which we really should not shy away from. The population explosion reveals that the world's population of over seven billion is increasing at an unsustainable rate. It is predicted that by 2025 it will top eight billion and by 2050 over ten billion. The increased global population's insatiable appetite for resources including food, housing, shelter, energy and power, health services, plus a large increase in waste, all have tremendous financial implications. The effects of such a rise are not only environmental, but economic and societal... and further, they are spiritual.

I live in the wilderness of Andalucía in southern Spain in the foothills of the Sierra Nevada. It is a biosphere reserve.[22] I was walking with my wife and our four dogs today and I looked at the mountains, the vast blue sky, and the views extending in all directions as far as the eye could see—no houses, no people, completely unspoiled—and I said we could be the last generation to experience this.

---

[22] A biosphere reserve is an area of land protected by law to support the conservation of ecosystems and the sustainability of human beings' impact on the environment, and to learn how to protect the world's plant and animal species while dealing with a swelling population and its growing needs.

People in fifty years will look back and this will seem as distant and impossible as we view Hardy's Wessex or Gurdjieff's South Caucasus. It will be gone, extinct, never to return.

Walking in the mountains is to connect with the Great Mystery; it is to fly into expansiveness, almost indiscernibly you grow in a strong internal elation—the experience never fails to make you feel happy.

Spirituality and the sacred life, among the many complexities of practice and intention, are the manifestation of the natural state of happiness. This happiness is not fleeting or vacillating, but rather it is complete since it is not dependent on outward circumstances, but rather it is sourced deeply from within. It is only possible in one who feels and feels deeply, in one whose life is profound rather than flippant or shallow, in one for whom life is a celebration of good fortune and inner treasure, in one who has realized that there is no one else, no others and that all is Consciousness.

This practice is so crucial we should start without delay. Happiness will erode your resistance and blind happiness will erase your reason and soothe all your inner conflicts. First you must *feel*, *balance*, and *energize* then…. let go!

How to Be Happy: The Three Principles of Happiness

Nothing *makes* you happy. Real happiness simply *is*.

Let us begin with a story—the story about how I forgot about happiness.

One summer long ago, I was one of the group facilitators at a personal growth holiday on a Greek island. In this collective community, people ate, socialized, and took group workshops and courses together. I was giving therapy workshops and running an early morning meditation.

One lunchtime we were sitting around digesting our delicious food and sipping tea when one of the group members asked me, "How do you become happy?" "Aw, you're not still trying to do that are you?" I remarked sardonically. The questioner withered and onlookers murmured their admiration. One or two told me later that they thought I was "spiritually advanced." But the truth was that I was jaded about happiness. So to defend myself, I acted as if it was beneath me. I took more pride in the struggle, the application of effort and the ordeal. In a way I had gone from wanting happiness to boycotting it and by a kind of emotional logic it seemed to be a real place that I had arrived in. What I didn't know was that it wasn't the end.

All my life I had made advances and arrived somewhere and thought to myself, "Oh, I get it, this is it; this *must* be it." But of course it never is, because there's always further to go. That's how it was with happiness, I found out later when, stumbling in the darkness where all the best discoveries are made, I encountered happiness in an entirely new way. This time it wasn't the focus, the goal, or even the intention. This time it was merely a side-effect, a perk that arose in an entirely unexpected manner, expansive and unassailable, when I *remembered* happiness.

Many of us have forgotten about happiness—genuine happiness. There are three rules or attitudes to remember and practice. Practice is the key element here. It is not and never is enough to know, to collect knowledge, and become clever. Real intelligence is recognizing the need to practice, what to practice, and how to practice it.

The First Principle: The Disposition of Love
We are usually unaware of our mood or temper, even less aware of our habitual state of mind and oblivious to our customary emotions and behavior. This principle begins with a new practice that doesn't even challenge the status quo. It begins where you want to be—happy. I want you to *cultivate the disposition of love*. You are used to a disposition of irritation, of frustration or hurt or anger or sadness or depression. Now whatever your previous disposition was, replace it with the disposition of love. This means that your prevailing tendency, your mood, and your temperamental makeup will from now on become one of warmth, kindness, and consideration, inclining toward your fellow human beings with tolerance and generosity. And not only to them, but to all other sentient beings as well as inanimate objects and all events and circumstances. You become gentler with yourself, more inclined toward reconciliation and forgiveness (which is the second principle).

Here is an exercise to start you off. First imagine love extending to those closest to you. The easiest ones for you to love may include: your family, children, husband, wife, partner, boyfriend or girlfriend, mother, father, relatives, work colleagues, and special friends. Then extend this loving feeling to your slightly more distant acquaintances. Using your life activities as a guide, bring more and more people to your heart and mind, as you extend the field further and further outward toward people to whom you are only tacitly connected, but who nonetheless feature in your life.

Now what you begin to see is that some people are harder for you to love than others, and it is these ones you are now going to concentrate on. Dismiss negative thoughts about them. These people are the real challenge for you. For they will enable you to increase the feeling of love that's inside you. Increasing your inner feeling-experience of love allows you to expand and extend your heart and the love you extend to them will return to you.

Now you are beginning to create a reciprocal circle of love, persist in the disposition of love, and everyday be mindful of the positive benefits to your well-being, your health, and your happiness.

The Second Principle: The Daily Practice of Forgiveness
Not forgiving hurts you the most. It causes you far more pain than it causes anyone else. You are suffering. Consider it; you harbor resentment, bitterness, blame, and unforgiveness in your heart the whole time, while the one you blame hardly thinks of you at all and gets off scot-free! While you suffer 24/7.

Why do you do it? As you work down through the layers you find the one absolutely clear and resonant reason shamefully, guiltily, reveals itself by crawling out of your unconsciousness. It is that resentment is the raw material of the self; to maintain the separate, divisive, unforgiving model of the individual entity you are creating and identifying with, you must feel angry about something or someone... all the time.

The simplest, most effective method to start forgiveness as a daily practice is to hold the person you want to forgive in your heart. Let them be there as often as you can and don't waver. The more reasons that are presented by your judgment, criticism, and blame for throwing them out of your heart, the more firmly you must keep them there. Let them simply melt in your heart, because they're not really what this is all about anyway. What this is really about is your need to suffer (remember?) and preserve your individual sense of self. And you have finished with this foolishness now... and forever. So hold all the life events, relationships, wrong-doings, resentful acts, and unfairness you can think of in your heart, and in time, you will not only release the unforgiven, you will find that you are free.

Now you are beginning to create a reciprocal circle of forgiveness, persist in holding people, events, and relationships in your heart and melting them with profound acceptance, and everyday be mindful of the positive benefits to your well-being, your health and your happiness.

The Third Principle: The Power of Acceptance

Acceptance is one of the most powerful principles for inner well-being. Acceptance in the psycho-spiritual sense is often misunderstood. It does not imply in any way condoning, approving, even tacitly, or supporting wrong-doing, immorality, or downright evil deeds. That is about libertarianism and giving license, a sort of "anything goes" mentality. No, acceptance in the sense in which it is meant in the third principle for happiness is the attitude that somehow everything fundamentally is unfolding as it should, in a way which we might be unable to understand just now. Also implied is our attitude and meeting of events in openness, receptivity, and an underlying wisdom which receives the mystery of life, our ability to be with the unknown, with uncertainty, to not have to prescribe and anticipate life events constantly. This wisdom tells us that life is fundamentally good. And it is; even the worst events turn out to reveal some beauty of soul and spirit in both individual and collective ordeals.

We only have to look at the very worst examples of human suffering to see that the light of truth shines, if anything, ever more brightly in troubled times of despair and darkness. The eclipse of love is only a period before the light bursts through and shines again.

Let us now turn to the all-essential practice. Start with your breath and relax. Then slowly and gradually become aware of everything in, out, and about you, emotionally, physically, mentally, energetically, spiritually, inwardly and outwardly—sounds, tastes, smells, touch, what you see with eyes open or shut—be aware of it all and accept it... and accepting it means not wishing it to be other than it is at present, right now, not regarding it with a sense of lack, progression, future orientation, criticism, evaluation, or judgment. Allowing everything inside and outside and around you and in your expanded field of concern and relationship to be alright *just as it is*.

Now you are beginning to create a reciprocal circle of acceptance, persist in holding people, events and relationships in your heart and melting them with profound acceptance, and every day be mindful of the positive benefits to your well-being, your health, and your happiness.

The practice of happiness is profound and crucial, and its worth is immeasurable. So, when you feel ready, devote fifteen minutes at the beginning and the end of your days to these three practices (five minutes each). After a month, you may decrease the time you spend practicing the three principles of happiness, if you wish. But you might find you enjoy them too much to stop. In any case the effects after a month will be significant and the practice will continue in your heart and mind even if you stop... with surprising results over time.

Community—When the Soul of the World Dances

The inner human wealth that we are discovering on our journey here—living from the heart, the call of the divine, sacred living, gratitude, respect, honor, interdependence, non-prejudice—create a firm basis for compassionately living together in mutual tolerance, cooperation and harmony.

Whatever we do affects the whole. When we see past our small self into the soul of the world, we experience everything as a single living organism. The small self tends to compartmentalize and we feel we are separate from the rest of existence. But we are all interconnected, so much so that no feeling, thought, or action is exclusively our own.

How would it be if this inner human wealth matched the material wealth we enjoy in the West? If the emotional, relational, intimate, and compassionate connection between human beings was every bit as opulent and lavish as the material lifestyles to which many of us have become accustomed? The rising into the heart that awaits humankind could bring about the most extraordinary revolution in heart, sincerity, empathy, and kindness humanity has ever seen. But what makes it so far-fetched? Why does it sound so impossible?

Human Wealth—Open Hearts
We have become cynical, and negative. We have become quick to believe the worst of people, slow to believe the best. This extends to the world at large and to people in general. If we think that an individual is likely to be selfish, shameful, selfish, greedy, and if by extension we see the human race in that likeness—a sophisticated, out-for-what-we-can-get species struggling for survival, tacitly entitled to perform dirty deeds, to act without integrity, without regard for relationship to others—then

we have every right, do we not, to be skeptical, distrustful, and contemptuous of the human race... of which we are a part? Doesn't our inner shame and our contempt for ourselves get projected and transferred outward? How can we trust others when we don't hold ourselves in the esteem that ensures we would act in the most scrupulous, ethical way to the utmost morality of our inner being?

Why is it so impossible to imagine human inner wealth matching outward material wealth and creating a world of peace and understanding based on tolerance and cooperation? And why is it so much harder for us than the present world which we seem to have no difficulty imaging at all?

Even now in the instances when we share our human wealth—the heart-felt qualities of expansiveness, generosity, and kindness—a transformation takes place. We can cultivate these qualities through inner work, therapy, meditation, and conscious maturing. As we get older, we may begin to see more clearly and realize that we are not as separated or isolated as we thought we were when we were younger. The compartments of our lives become less rigid as tidy conceptualization gives way to our untidy, open hearts.

We are All One
When I was in my thirties, I was a young and ambitious therapist. For some time, I had wanted to attend the training workshop of a world-renowned therapist and teacher who lived in the USA and traveled the world giving seminars, but every time the opportunity came I had been thwarted. Finally, all the circumstances were favorable, and I enrolled on a week-long residential training course.

The first morning began with introductions and an outline of what was to come. I returned after lunch, feeling excited and eager with anticipation. When we regrouped for the afternoon session, the teacher announced that the daughter of the couple who ran the center had had an accident and needed to be rushed to hospital. He encouraged us to do what we could for her parents and announced that he was canceling the afternoon session.

The other students were understanding and sympathetic, but I felt outraged. A ranting dialogue ran inside me: "No, no, no, I have paid for this course. I have wanted to work with this teacher for years. We only have a week. Why should we have to forfeit our teaching afternoon because of this accident? What have these people got to do with me?"

Much later I understood what was behind what this teacher was saying and my strong reaction to it. We are all part of a community. As therapists trying to help others to resolve their emotional issues and love themselves, we cannot separate ourselves from those around us. We so like to compartmentalize, to say I am a therapist on a training workshop: who cares what's happening next door to me? But it does matter and it *must* matter to us. In my youthful hubris, I was caught in a process of acquisition, to be better, to be more. This experience taught me that we are all connected; we are all One.

The Outward Projection of Our Inner State
Now I am in my middle years my sense of isolation and separation tends to be less. But I still get caught. Although I know now that we are not separate, fear and personal insecurity still challenge me to practice this knowledge. The sense of me, myself, and mine sometimes feels under threat from the outer world.

When this happens I stop and I breathe. I accept the circumstances just as they are and I deepen into the profound experience of *simply being*. Then I return to breath, the in and out breaths, the undulating rhythmic breath that sounds like OM, that is reminiscent of the universe itself and of all life.

Self-definition, competitiveness, insecurity, and fear prevent the building of genuine community. Our personal aspirations define us. If we aspire to goodness, we may only achieve this in relation to the projected immorality of others. If we need to excel, others must appear mediocre. The external enemy of our personal ambitions—our failure—is the necessary darkness that balances our light. It must be expressed in our rejection of others. In myths and stories, the hero must always be pitted against a worthy and equal adversary, because heroes and villains depend on each other for their definitions—Jesus and Judas, Gandalf and Saruman, Rama and Ravana, the Nazis and the Allies. In modern times the "War on Terror" provides a worthy nemesis and a projective screen for the USA's own doubtful agendas. In a less powerful country like the UK, where there are less grandiose opportunities for heroism to stir the nation, the faceless foes of drugs, street vandalism, and the inadequacies of the health service are trustworthy standbys around which to invent a conflict.

Worthy opponents justify anger and retribution. They confirm our separation and distract us from the real issue: we would rather remain self-absorbed and separate than connected and compassionate. But even a cursory examination of the human condition reveals our interdependence and interconnectedness. Our thoughts and acts of aggression are inadequate defenses against the obvious truth that we cannot afford to see ourselves exclusively as separate individuals, because we are a part of a larger whole. The larger whole may be family, friends, neighborhood, society, humanity, Earth or the cosmos: layer upon layer of community in which we participate in some way. The nemesis that carries our dark sides, which we delight in making a scapegoat to preserve our self-serving complacency, is necessary only when we reject the larger whole. And rejecting the larger whole is the outward projection of our rejection of our inner wholeness. Defining who we are only works in relation to others who we think are not us, those we have decided to discard.

Celebrating Diversity and Variety

Our sense of community begins with the community of selves within. As we become awake and responsive to the diverse tendencies and conflicting voices of our inner world, we develop inner harmony. We are more able to meet the needs and desires of those around us—our family, close friends, those we work with—and interact with in daily life. We can begin to see how our closest and most intimate community connects and relates with other communities with their diverse ways of thinking, feeling, and living. Celebrating diversity and variety; becoming curious to discover and understand the different forms and expressions of our shared humanity across the divides of race, class, and gender; rejecting the marginalization of minorities and cultures we don't understand; and cultivating openness, tolerance, and understanding over prejudice, intolerance, and ignorance, lead to a true understanding and experience of belonging, of community.

The psychoanalyst Alfred Adler gave us the concept of *Gemeinschaftsgefuhl*, which means *communal feeling*. It is the profound sense of caring for others and the world. He considered it the final goal of inner work. This is the experience of many. Inner work leads to a genuine concern for humanity. Rising into the heart allows us to feel authentic compassion as we discover that the other *is* ourself. The soul of the world dances and interpenetrates with our inner soul: we are not separate from ourselves or from each other.

The Foundations of Spiritual Life
Three essentials exist to complete an integrated, effective, authentic spiritual practice. They have been known and practiced for a long time. The following is merely a summary of the seemingly endless expressions of the three foundations of spiritual life. Once you have begun your psycho-spiritual practice in earnest they will appear in people, circumstances, objects, animals, nature, events, emotions, thoughts, until everything demonstrates, supports, and furthers your sacred life and spiritual practice.

First, the recognition of the Divine in the world. Nothing can happen without this knowledge or these stirrings of faith, the intuition of the Divine. Without it, you are condemned to the worldly, materialistic shadow life of superficial thinking and acting, of inauthentic feeling, of displacement from the eternal moment in the past and the future. You are lost, truly lost. So, this is the first point, the sighting of the Zen bull,[23] the beginning of the life quest, the excitement of the venture must be there. This makes you a spiritual person and a wise fool. You cannot explain it; you don't know if it exists or even if it is real, but you have no choice, it is decided for you; your life is dedicated to the impossible quest of spiritual enlightenment.

Second, the sharing of enlightenment, the teaching, the *dharma*, the ever-present insights of deep wisdom which characterize and typify the life spent in sacred pursuits. Everything is significant. Everything is powerful. Nothing is superficial or without spiritual meaning; experience is a full passionate intensity at the center of your life. You are never superficial, so neither is the world. From the most mundane to the most exalted,

---

[23] See Kakuan's "Ten Bulls" in Paul Reps's *Zen Flesh Zen Bones*, Tuttle Publishing 1998.

from the ordinary to the extraordinary, the circumstances, relationships, dynamics and story of your life unfold in profundity. All is teaching as long as you are listening, seeing, touching, and feeling life in its multi-dimensionality, in its endlessness, in its expressions of Truth. Life lessons fill you with excitement and inner knowledge. You learn from everything and everything learns from you. The sharing of enlightenment is inexhaustible.

Third, the help and support of sacred community. You yield to the help and support of the community. No human being stands alone; we are all interconnected and never more so than in our true spiritual nature. This nature, the very source and core of spiritual enlightenment, is one, a unity common to all. Our resistance to our divinity is expressed in our intolerance and prejudice of each other and in our unwillingness to combine together to attain the highest states of enlightenment.

Think for a moment: if the whole of humanity was to cease "doing" for only a short time and bring its collective powers to the spiritual endeavor, what could possibly prevent humanity from becoming spiritually enlightened, transcendent, and divine? Nothing could withstand this combining of efforts. Each person may be considered an expression of God, so with this combination of the Divine what could not be realized?

The power of the *sangha*, the community of like-minded souls, gathers in strength and power for the common good, to increase the great virtue of the impulse toward divinity. The act of surrender to the impulse to join together can be enough to accelerate your personal development through the layers of personality, character, and defense that comprise the ego-processes. Spiritual-divine celebration, ritual, ceremony, and discipline typify the community intent on spiritual practice and on manifesting the sacred.

Now is the time for us to act, to become inspired, and to be more than we could ever have imagined. The intention of psycho-spiritual community is to convey you further toward that exalted possibility that is your real life, your spiritual reality, and the transcendent heart-motivated intention of your soul.

In summary the intention of spiritual community is this: to be together without inner or outer separation or division, to practice tolerance and cooperation, to live in wisdom and peace, to live as One. Here is a story: A man came to his old friend's house and knocked on the door. The voice from within cried out, "Who is it?" The man replied, "It is I." The friend answered, "There is no admittance. There is no room for the raw at my well-cooked feast. Nothing but the fire of separation and absence can cook the raw and free him from hypocrisy. Since yourself has not yet left you, go, for you must burn in the fiery flames." The man left and wandered for a year burning with grief and his heart burned until it was cooked. When he returned to his friend's house he knocked at the door in fear and trepidation in case some careless words fell from his lips. The voice from within cried, "Who is that?" The man answered, "It is you, O beloved." The friend said, "Since it is I, let me come in. There is no room for two in this house."[24]

This story represents a human life. We are born and we learn to create a self. We wander through life with its experiences and trials. Finally, we return "home" and relinquish the self we have created. This cycle of birth, life, and death represents the psycho-spiritual process of human unfolding. The creation of a self in early life provides us with a vehicle for traveling through life. At the same time, it separates and divides. Defended from others and separated from God we make our way in the

---

[24] After Jalal al-Din Rumi.

world and if we are fortunate we feel the separation from our essence and our heart burns with passion, grief, and finally love and compassion. This is how we "return home" to our spiritual Self, to the reality of Consciousness and the divine Source where we are received in unity and acceptance.

Notice however that you must be fortunate enough to feel the heart sufficiently strongly. It is the divine call, the initiatory power of the authentic life-force. It is one of those spiritual rituals that is fading rapidly from our modern world view. It doesn't even have a name, so I have decided to name it and it is the subject of our next chapter. I call it the *Philozovo*.

In Summary

In chapter 12 we considered the event of human heart-opening as a preparation for a spiritual evolution and the need to retrieve the central core of humanity. We spoke of committing to the heart through rising above exclusive lower-chakra concerns. We told a story to introduce the three principles of happiness—love, forgiveness, and acceptance, and the possibility of world community. Last, we laid some foundations for leading a sacred-spiritual life. Work through these exercise in your inner work notebook to help the material from this chapter settle in you.

1. What does the spiritual revolution entail and why do *you* think is it necessary (if you do)?

2. How could we begin a collective movement of human beings living in the heart? What kinds of obstacles face humanity in achieving this?

3. What *is* happiness? Is there genuine happiness and counterfeit happiness? If so, what are they and what is the difference between them? What makes *you* happy?

4. How connected do you truly feel to others, to your community, to the world? Why has humanity succumbed to divisiveness and separation?

5. It seems as if, living in a world full of opposites, conflict inevitably arises. A thought conflicts with another thought, an outward force meets with resistance, someone's opinion clashes with someone else's opinion. Do you think that the principle of conflict is inherent in a world of opposites… or could there be a way out of this apparent impasse?

6. Examine the last section of this chapter entitled "The Foundations of Spiritual Life" and ask: are the foundations for spiritual living in place in my life or is there something I have to do to bring them about?

13. The *Philozovo*: The Call of the Divine

Defining the Philozovo

The word *Philozovo* is comprised of three parts. *Phil* is from the Greek, meaning "loving, tending, or dear."*Zovo* from Old Church Slavonic, meaning "to call," relates to the Sanskrit *huta*, meaning "invoked," or to the Proto-Indian-European *ghu-to* meaning "to pour," a word derived from *ghut* from which we get our word God. Thus the *Philozovo* means "the Love of the Divine Call."

Spiritual accounts of divine ecstasy have become very popular: Rumi, Kabir, Hafiz, plus the modern spiritual mystics who speak of celebration and life-affirming spirituality, like Osho and Paulo Coelho. Devotion is offered from among the spiritual fraternity to everyone from Einstein to Nisargadatta, from Meher Baba to Steve Jobs. No one of course really hears what the wise masters of India and others have been saying repeatedly: "Don't get stuck with a guru!"

When you hear the Philozovo, the practical may rise up with the inspirational and douse the exhilaration of the moment. When the call of the Divine, the call that your deepest Self is making to you says leave everything and devote yourself to me, when you feel the divine pleasure and love course through you, the great weight of worldly life may push down on your heart with its demands, duties, and responsibilities.

The divine call is always uncompromising, *always*—never sensible or restrained, never practical. When the Divine fills you, it plays on you like a musical instrument.

To stop it you must close down in an extreme way. But what right have you to deny the Divine?

On my desk I have the marvelous picture of the great Ramakrishna when he's filled with ecstatic spirit being held up by his followers who must be wishing him to stay and longing to go with him all at the same time. Other times I recall David in the *Tanakh* (Hebrew Bible) filled with the Holy Spirit with trumpets, lyres, cymbals, and surrounded by shouting, as he danced ecstatically in praise of God.

Ramakrishna and David were merely men. How were they different to you? Only in one regard: they welcomed the play of the Divine on them, in them, and through them.

If you are a spiritual seeker, a divine traveler, then why travel any longer, why contemplate your measured response to the Divine? What is it but resistance to Reality and Truth? So, if you know this now, what is stopping you giving your life to the divine Self? The freedom of complete surrender to the divine principle is the ecstatic revelation of divine liberation.

Meizumi Roshi said, "Die now and enjoy the rest of your life." Why is it that you say you are a spiritual seeker, that you have been one all your life, and yet when the opportunity arises to be close to God you refuse? Why is it that you yearn for the Divine and will not surrender? Why is it that you read about spirituality, admire spiritual practices, spend your time wishing you could be more spiritually advanced, and yet you won't make the one simple obvious sacrifice of self?

God-intoxicated souls known as *masts* experience a unique type of spiritual ecstasy. The spiritual master Meher Baba worked with masts for many years, maintaining that they were in such an advanced spiritual state that only divine love could reach them. Spiritual intoxication appears in the Biblical account of King David's ecstatic dance before the Ark of the Covenant as it was being brought into Jerusalem. In David's case, the dance[25] was a vehicle for him to access deeper recesses of his consciousness. Like other repetitive acts such as mantras, prayer and meditation, the dancing overrides analytical consciousness, opening a purer and deeper channel. In this regard, dancing and praying may be considered very closely related and this is the reason that many mystically inclined religious groups, such as Judaism's Hasidim, employ so much singing and dancing in their observance.

The intensity of David's dance provoked the wrath of his wife Michal, who was shocked at the raw emotionality he displayed in public, commenting that he had conducted himself "as one of the empty people." The King's retort defended his exuberance and suggested that his displays of ecstasy would intensify further in the future declaring, "I will continue to play before God!"

Like all genuine art, ecstatic dance reflects the desire of the inner self to transcend its limitations and merge with something greater; this is the root of its power. Most people find such a transcendent state to be uniquely blissful. Some, like Ramakrishna or the masts we mentioned previously, spend their entire lives in its pursuit; it is the soul's spontaneous desire to reach beyond its corporeal container and express its most sublime root in the highest realms.

There are two points to remember about the Philozovo that may help you. First, it is a central part of your ego's defensive processes to peddle the idea to you that at some point you will figure it out, attain some clarity, climb to some exalted position, or in some way through your great

---

[25] The word translated as "dance" in the Book of Samuel literally means springing round in half circles to music. It may refer to the *Malawiyeh* in which the dancer spun round in whole circles, while resting the heel of the left foot on the ground.

individual effort and applications get past yourself and enter a new spiritual realm of freedom and transcendence.

But you won't.

The ego is like a false lover who promises all kinds of great things that you never get. So let us make this clear once and for all, because in all likelihood you have been taken in by it for so long. The ego is not a way to the spiritual realms in any way. If you begin from the basis of the ego you will be starting from the point of view of lack, falsehood, and delusion, apparent or hidden fear and desire, defensiveness and aggression, competition and dissatisfaction. The only place you will get to from there is exactly the same as where you started. This will not work. Sooner or later you will realize this. And when you do you will be face to face with the Philozovo. The Divine is always present, always speaking to you, always calling.

Second, the word is transcendent, to transcend the ordinary conditions of your delusional, emotionally-obsessed, mind-dominated, controlled, fearful life no amount of thought-filled spiritual attainment will connect you to the absolute Divine. It is beyond thought, beyond rationalization, belief, objection, discussion, individual points of view, or even sense experience. It is only by responding from the Divine within yourself that you reach the Divine that has always been present. This is how you respond to the divine call.

The Passionate Response to the Call of the Divine

Not all that long ago people were prepared to suffer extreme torture rather than renounce their spiritual beliefs. Spirituality has always been intensely provocative and confrontational. Think also of the people who tortured their fellow men. And if you are bewildered by that, consider this: they both had the same stated motivations: to save the souls of, respectively, the tortured, mutilated, martyred heretic and themselves.

Today we live in superficial times. If someone approached you—à la an Eddie Izzard sketch—and proposed to hack you to death, unless you agreed with something you thought silly, you would be hard put to see the point in disagreeing. After all, you'd reason, it's only words and this guy wants to take my life.

But isn't there a deeper point here? Have we lost the spiritual sense totally? Today spirituality may be synonymous with pleasure, personal fulfillment, being the best you that you can be, having everything you want. It's sentimental, idealistic, unreal, and unchallenging. What's happened to the kind of spirituality where the spiritual teacher loved you so much that he was willing to lose your admiration just to teach you a spiritual lesson, or where the spiritual friend approached you to tell you something revealing and potentially hurtful about yourself, because he loved you more than he needed your friendship to survive the confrontation. Where is the modern day couple, married or otherwise, who are willing to live on the edge of revelation, emotional risk, and true love by consistently challenging their partner to awaken, remain open-hearted and be courageous, even more than kind sometimes, or at least to understand that kindness like beauty and compassion is not always a romantic vision in soft focus, because sometimes it must have teeth to really teach and be genuinely human, effective, and real!

Two stories come to mind to illustrate what I mean. The first is the monk and the samurai; perhaps you know it? The samurai comes to see the little monk. He's sitting quietly on the floor meditating and the samurai, huge and intimidating, towers over him and demands, "Teach me about heaven and hell!" The diminutive monk looks up and replies, "Tell you about heaven and hell! I couldn't teach you anything! You're dirty! You've got a rusty sword! You're unkempt! You're a disgrace to the samurai class!" The samurai becomes furious and draws his sword. He is about to chop off the monk's head when the little monk looks up and quietly says, "That's hell."

The samurai is stunned and amazed by the monk's extraordinary compassion. Realizing that this little man risked his life to teach him a spiritual lesson, he is so affected he bursts into tears of gratitude and wonder and he sheaths his sword. Just then the monk looks up and says, "And that's heaven."

The second is a somewhat peculiar story. It has personal significance to me, because my own spiritual teacher hated it. I don't think he really understood it like I did, partly because, as I mentioned before, he wasn't as literary or intellectual as me. This is something I often point out to my own clients, students, and seekers: because I am a would-be-scholar, i.e. not really a scholar at all, I have the tendency sometimes to dazzle the less-learned with volleys of impromptu literary, religious, or spiritual references, provoking the complaint that since I know so much and they can never know as much as me, they will never make it spiritually. This, of course, is rubbish. The lists of Zen, Sufi, Christian, Buddhist, and Hindu spiritual masters and adepts include many illiterate self-realizers. This is because wisdom is not knowledge. Knowledge is acquired, whereas wisdom is innate.

This story is about Ryonen, a beautiful Buddhist nun who provokes the prurient attention of the young monks in the monastery and threatens the stability of spiritual practice for the monks and herself in the process. She selflessly disfigures her face, making herself ugly, so that the members of the community are not distracted and she can apply herself to her Buddhist practices.

My teacher thought this a horrible story and taken literally it is life-negating, likely misogynistic, and very nasty. But surely it is symbolic of a spiritual truth. That truth is that we must turn away from the outward appearances, the dazzling play of consciousness, to become fully aware, engulfed, and overtaken by consciousness and incorporated into the Divine. This is not to say that the world of appearances and pleasure and so on are evil (we don't have to fall for that dichotomy), but simply that in the process of awakening and liberation we must turn from the outward life of appearances to enable us to see clearly with inner sight both the inner and the outer, which turn out to be one anyway, although we don't know that (in the wisdom sense) until we have gone through that stage of the spiritual process.

Spiritual practice takes us to our edge. There's always an edge, a dichotomy in spiritual practice, because you arrive in time at a meeting of worlds, at the border of time and eternity in a single moment. Inner and outer, earthly and heavenly, actual and ideal, human and divine—spirituality looks different from *here* in the world of time, space, and relativity, than it does from *there* in the world of purity, love, wisdom, *satchitananda* and reality.

We may not have to suffer extreme torture for our spiritual beliefs anymore, but for those of us who experience the Divine call, the invitation to unity, and respond passionately, it is like being painfully parted from our loved one. We ache, agonize, yearn, long for, and pray for unity with divinity.

Look up and See that Everything is the Divine

Every now and again it is important to stop... and *look up*. Then you will see the looming mystery that lays over all things, some constant, some eternal, some evanescence, the light of Truth. It is a divine glow.

When you experience the Philozovo, it is a call from Truth itself. You drop everything. It is the most urgent command you have ever heard. It is like the cry of a small child you must save from a speeding automobile or the plea of a kitten being savaged by a ferocious dog. Or the story where the cop risks his life to save a suicide and remarks that he couldn't have lived for one more day if he hadn't tried to save him.

You drop everything to respond to the call of the Philozovo. There is no time to waste, because time is merely relative and doesn't matter much beside the great resonance of eternity. But, more than that, you drop everything because you are compelled through passion, urgency, and complete distraction to abandon everything and be only together with and as the Divine. There are no words for this, no appendages or accompaniments, only Truth, only Reality.

Distraction is not something to resist. You have senses and thoughts and emotions. Therefore, distraction and engagement are bound to occur *toward something*. The question is: will you direct it toward what is sustaining, satisfying, and ultimately real, or will you direct it to something superficial, transient, and unreal?

In the world today it seems that people are interested in what is shallow, what is immediately rewarding and ultimately unreal. When a challenge is difficult, involving a struggle of some kind, loss or pain, they shy away from it and seek an easier option. But the easier option is not necessarily the best one. Knowing the Divine is not easy. You need to be involved. You need to go deeply into your innate wisdom, to practice and gain insights and eventually understanding. Familiarity with Truth is no easy matter. To live in Truth constantly and not merely part-time takes application, consistency, and discipline. These words are not in themselves necessarily attractive. The popular new paradigm is not to have to try too hard, not to have to necessarily question overmuch, perhaps not even to think. As for practice, well that may simply be asking too much; it may be too hard. But what else do you have to do? If you are involved in Truth, if you have heard the Philozovo and if you are filled with a divine longing, always, occasionally, or intermittently, there is only one real response, one genuine reply.

That reply is *yes* with all you heart, soul, body, and mind. All of your response must be gathered together in a single act of submission and surrender to the Divine and the act of submission is another unattractive notion to the modern mind. We have become a race of individuals. We humans have come to prize our individuality over all else. Our preferences, our opinions, likes and dislikes, prejudices, comfort, self-pride, aggrandizement, ego-feeding, relationships, personal ambitions, and desires have displaced all other concerns, even the concern for the Divine, real love, wisdom, compassion, selflessness, dignity, honor, reverence and peace... even happiness.

This realm in which we live and breathe and love is a realm of sadness, a realm of loss and heart-break. Everything is dying, everything is ultimately going, leaving, including ourselves and everything we hold dear, as well as everything we hate or are averse to, everything we notice or don't notice. Sometimes this awareness of the very transience of existence is enough to stimulate the Philozovo, the call to go beyond, the call of Truth. Look up now, just above your friend, your partner, your dog, a tree—anything in this manifest world. The looming light of the transcendent domain of Truth hovers brightly over all things and—here is the wonder!—this light connects all things and transcends all things and relates to the world of *maya, samsara*, of temporary arising forms as the Divine itself. This earth, the very heaven; this body, the sacrifice, these thoughts and emotions, the cloud of unknowing... just by looking up you see that everything is the Divine.

In Summary

We have introduced the Philozovo, the love of the divine call, in this short but important chapter and given examples of spiritual transport and divine ecstasy from different traditions. We discussed the futility of ego-based spirituality and the loss of spiritual sensibilities, illustrated with the two stories—the monk and the samurai, and the tale of Ryonen. Finally, in this chapter we examined the response to the call, its urgency and vividness and our surrender to the Divine.

1. What is you experience of the Philozovo? How has the divine call appeared in your life? What is your response?

2. This chapter referenced many examples of ecstatic lives and responses to the Philozovo. In order to deepen your familiarity with the divine call—and for sheer enjoyment too—read the accounts of the lives of Ramakrishna and David, the writings of Rumi and Kabir, Meher Baba and the masts, the ecstatic dance of the Hasidim, and so on.

3. I invite you to meditate on the Philozovo, the divine call, your response and how it is offered to you. Consider the themes of gratitude, patience, compassion, inevitability, Truth, and divine relationship with regard to the Philozovo.

4. Consider the futility of seeking and the ego's deception, offering the idea of cumulative spiritual practice and eventually reaching the Divine when the Divine is more present than yourself.

5. Devote one day, a single day, to the practice of looking up. Directing your attention above the bodily person, above a tree or a vista, an animal, a street. Try to keep an awareness of the physical presence, while still directing your attention above the physical appearance. Be open to perceiving the energy body, the etheric form, and the spiritual "appearance" of the physical world.

6. Spend a period of meditation, perhaps several daily meditation periods, contemplating the passage of time, the passing of lives, the endless procession of arising forms, death and life, birth and loss, the call of Truth in the very transience of existence.

14. How Eternity Looks in Time

Collective Resistance

Today there is a great collective resistance to genuine spiritual awakening. It's not necessarily negative because resistance is shaping and forming, in fact it is crucial for creation to occur. The pivotal question is: How will humanity as a whole respond to this resistance? If we support it, in itself, then we are lost. If we use it to create, we are liberated. This is the extraordinary timbre of the modern era. Egoic forces are so strong, dominant, and insidious that the stakes are high in the contemporary world of space and time.

The evolution of spiritual consciousness and the dawning of a new spiritual era is not subject to relative concerns, therefore any talk whatsoever of spiritual evolution, however appealing to the popular mind and supportive of spiritual materialism, is not only irrelevant, but misleading. Popular writers on spirituality must be aware that a diluted, shallow approach that teaches people to approach the spiritual, transcendent, and divine in a cheap McDonald's way is subversive in the most insidious way, cheapening and deceptive in the most psychopathic manner. Appearing to be spiritual to convey spiritual truths when you don't know what you are talking about is about as heinous as it gets, because you are weakening the very root of the plant as well as poisoning the atmosphere.

Spiritual evolution has provided a rallying point and cry to spokespeople who should know better, to philosophers and commentators who know more than they are willing to divulge but who are seduced by fame, material gain, and ambition. I am sure an internal justification exists from their sophisticated thinking but spiritual truths are timeless and not subject to the restraints and limitations of the relative world, transcendence is exactly what it sounds like, and divinity or God is self-sourcing and absolute, so it bears no relation whatsoever to the evolution of consciousness except that such evolution may in time with wise, profound, and brave guidance transform into the further dimension of Consciousness itself which is the True Self.

There can be no compromise for the ego in spiritual practice and endeavor. It is not the enemy, neither do we offer the ego nourishment through opposition. It is merely that it is a pretender, a falsehood, a fiction, expressed in the personal façade and character defense systems of the fearful survival-driven individual. Ego is mind, confinement, imprisonment. The individual can and should be free.

The Free Individual

The Individual is Entirely Free
The individual is entirely free. You are entirely free in truth. The ego-based individual, however, is entirely bound, un-liberated, not at all free. The problem is not with individuality per se. The trouble is with the individual who is ego-bound.

Today all individuals are bound. In this present era the only authentic model for spiritual development is one which revises the establishment, rebels against the anti-establishment movement that degenerated to become the new, now old, establishment. The great rebel-adepts of 2000 to 2500 years ago—Buddha, Lao Tzu, Chuang Tzu, Jesus of Nazareth—would never have subscribed to the religions that have been established in their names. They were true rebels. They were anti-establishment, counter-culture. To truly be a spiritual adept in this modern era the timeless truth of the rebel stance must be adhered to. The other positions are positions of fear. It doesn't matter what religion someone believes in, adheres to, or thinks worth following. It doesn't matter what spiritual book has entertained, amused, and stimulated you lately, or which "pop" spiritual teacher you admire or consider inspiring. The age-old wisdom remains true: read the book of your own heart; the Kingdom of Heaven or *Nirvana* is within; look to yourself; know who you are before anything else.

When you look firmly and deeply into the question, "Who am I?" you come eventually to the entirely free individual who is not bound, does not conform, and who is not chained to any thought, idea, assumption, expectation, or limitation—of any kind. He or she is entirely free.

The person who masquerades as an individual follows his own preferences, opinions, a rebel or conformist stance, but he is inevitably bound, because his total position is founded on the ego, on the small self, on the fear body, the pain body. He is merely the contraction of the ego that does violence to the spirit. Nothing could be further from the truth. *He* cannot be further from the truth

When you are truly spiritual, you yearn to become a free individual. This is the first requirement: you must really want to be liberated from your bound condition. Next you must understand a basic principle of spiritual life: all experience is passing, you are passing, everything is dying, but nothing that is dying is eternal and therefore ultimately divine. You must want—and you must *remember* to want—to be passionately and profoundly free, so you need to know that the process of freeing yourself is a process of loss; everything you think you are must be relinquished. This is extremely difficult, so you must practice potently, intensively, and intelligently.

There are two approaches that comprise the essential foundations of an intelligent, spiritual practice that results in illumination. One, you turn your face to the Divine, always, earnestly, fully, clearly, wisely, compassionately. You give it everything you've got! Practices exist for this and some of these will be incorporated into the exercises in my next book *Your Divine Being*. But the principle is simple: remember God, turn to God, be constantly aware of God, the divine Truth and Reality.

Two, your routine bodily, mental-emotional-energetic-based existence must be met squarely and bravely in a balanced way, so that your practice and priority can constantly be the enlightenment of the mind, body, soul, and spirit. You must free yourself first from your attachments to the material constraints of life. Your involvement in it must be minimal. This doesn't mean withdrawing from life. That is like expressing your attachment to material things by throwing everything away! You must meet life in a balanced, intelligent way that allows you maximum energy for practice. This also means that you are not lost or caught up in the vicissitudes of everyday life. You are free to watch, witness, contemplate, and meditate, but all of it should be passionate, free, full of peace, and tranquility. It doesn't matter what it looks like to others. You are not here to please or impress. You take everything seriously, while inside you are free from attachment to worldly concerns.

The individual is free. You are free. All of existence is fundamentally free. But you can only be free when you free yourself of ideas about freedom and reaction to other ideas that are imposed on you. There must be no veering, no imbalance, no yanking of your chain or pressure that makes you swerve to left or right. You are walking on the hair bridge over the chasm of fire, so the only way is to be balanced, unafraid, and poised between the opposites and impeccably centered in your being and consciousness.

The Free Individual has a Spiritual Identity

When the bound and imprisoned individual becomes liberated spiritually, there is no concern for egoic existence and self-serving behaviors. The free individual combines with others in mutual endeavor and enterprise with a spiritual motive, a transcendental divine goal.

Now everyone has a spiritual identity, a divine character. When you think of Ramana Maharshi, for example, there is a distinct individual present. He himself may have gone beyond his individuality, but for us, seeing photos of him, hearing the stories, reading the teachings and the conversational exchanges with him, someone is present, some personality is manifesting. Ramana would welcome you to the ashram. He cooked food for you and made sure you were comfortable for the night. All of this was an expression of his divine character.

Now think of another great spiritual adept: what about Neem Karoli Baba (known as Maharajji)? He would be mischievous, sly with his insights; he knows and he lets you know that he knows. You have to be on your toes around him, because you can't hide anything. He does not tuck you in at night. His compassion is expressed in altogether different ways from Ramana. Maharajji reads your mind; he humiliates you; he confronts you openly with your secret self. Ramakrishna's divine character is openly ecstatic, different from Vivekananda's scholarly, creative, beautiful, incisive manner and appearance. Then there is Gurdjieff (powerful, strong, challenging), Osho (formidable, endearing, urgent), Adi Da Samraj (uncompromising, absolute, lucid) or Nisargadatta (simply nails you to the wall!).

Spiritual, divine identity is worlds away from the defensive character-persona. Even when we have awakened, an appearance still exists, a presence in physical, mental, emotional, and energetic creation remains present as a form of existence in the world. Now what are you? Not the old history and emotional-behavioral patterns, biography, and endless forms of egoic suffering you used to be. Neither the formless drop returned to the ocean, the temporary, adaptive, arising, individual expression of consciousness you will be as you are re-assimilated into the supra-cosmic flow. But who are you now? At once a person, a character, but awakened, enlightened, and present here, functioning, and being exactly as you are without egoic limitations, without limiting thought, beyond fear and desire.

As spiritual companions, complements in life, we gravitate toward one another to perform some task. In the here and now the undertaking is non-egoic, the task is transcendent, for who wishes to be here in the world merely to fulfill the worldly material tasks of building up and releasing a life of drama and dust? The exalted task of which a human being is capable is the divine task which you may only know through your divine self. So stop and breathe now and ask: what is my divine task? Do not listen as another, but as that one—the divine self. The answer will be your life and let your life combine with others to bring about the success and completion of your transcendental task.

Let go into involvement and relationship with others selflessly, without thought of gain, even of giving and receiving. Without thought or investment in personal aggrandizement, act with utter selflessness, without others even knowing that you have acted, without others knowing that you were involved. Let these acts lay in your heart like a love letter unopened, like a precious stone, or an exciting secret. Let the brilliance of the expanded self, the divinity, glow and shine in and through you, as you become transparent to spirit.

An Exercise to Experience Your Spiritual Identity
When the heart has unloaded and all is still, your true nature shines through you. Spend a few minutes now in a relaxed, alert state, perhaps your favored meditation posture, allowing yourself to unload your heart. All concerns, worries, defeats, images, dramas, narratives, and content of your life that are filling your mind and heart… take as much time as you need to come to a point of stillness… spontaneously when you have emptied out the heart… when you have unloaded it… Now be the heart of Truth that you are, were and always will be… stay with it now and simply experience your heart… its purity… its silence… its profound emptiness… its peace. Resolve now to be in your heart and to allow your heart energies to be in you, to fill you and to shine through you… from within and outward into the world about you… Be yourself, be love, and don't let anything and anyone inhibit that or destroy that in you.

There can be no creation and destruction of what is only Truth, Reality, and wisdom, peace, bliss, and ecstatic fulfillment of the soul in this world... and the individual heart and spirit in the higher realms... all leading and spurring you on urgently, not to another place, another time, another circumstance... but to now, here, the present circumstance... exactly as it is, without any alteration, interruption, or interference whatsoever... climbing into this moment, inhabiting this eternal moment with all and everything... every expression of the Divine recognized as such... no ignorance, no assurance, no conditions, no mishaps, no mistakes for your being-ness, your "I am"... the well-spring of faith... the communication of Truth and Reality... your "I am" is the heart of all... "I am" is your very Self. Now contemplate your true spiritual identity.

The Murder of the Self
In the confused modern era, people believe that they are free. They think that if they can have, or at least strive for, what they desire and avoid, or minimize what they fear, that they are free to be themselves; to have, at least potentially, what they want, to do what they want, to possess, and achieve through their free will, the life they choose.

But this is untrue. People behaving like this are merely slaves to their desires and their fears. And furthermore, they don't know that they are ignorant *and* they don't know that they don't know. So there is a double foil of ignorance. If people in modern times were able to see how they really behave, they would be horrified. Everything they think they are avoiding has already happened; the murderer is already in the room, as they slip in and lock the door to avoid him! The murderer and the victim are the same person!

Many people today are murdering themselves and their lives by numbing themselves to emotions, by being unaware, by avoiding relationship, by not being present and rarely authentically responsive, by not valuing the precious gem of life while buying the plastic beads of cheap living. Their aspirations are reducing all the time, yet they do not know it. Many of the values, practices, and principles that enable sacred life are in imminent danger of being entirely lost, as the practice, words, and concepts, and the real present experience, slip away into oblivion through total neglect.

People are often out of touch with themselves, their true nature, their real feelings, their emotions, their ability to think freely and openly from a true inner morality and spirituality. Many people arecut off from the worlds, other than the material one, even when they consider themselves spiritual or religious, unable to be present, feel compassion, or act spontaneously.

They live almost exclusively through the mind which acts as a defense against real, unadorned experience. Everything they see, experience, do, and feel is interpreted through the mind functions until, rather like processed food, it is "experienced" as a genuine life event. Everything they think, do, and feel is sifted and filtered through a process of conformism (and rebellion), ambivalence, and ambiguity that precludes any free sense of knowing what they want or whether what they want is a viable possibility, a real aspiration. The forces of commercialism, mass media, the predominantly visual sense which has been accentuated to the detriment of the other senses dictate almost totally what we feel, how we live, how we behave, who and what we desire, what we fear, and who we are.

The Birth of the Soul
Before we can genuinely embark on the deep experience of life, we must awaken, and be born. Not born of the body, as in the very beginning of life, but born in the soul.

The present era is remedial. Time is needed to return to awareness, sincerity, and authenticity. People are not dissatisfied enough to want to change, let alone transform. By the time a person is 35 they begin to feel a hunger, a need to awaken to the real conditions of their life. If they have not acted on that urge—and many do not—by the time they are 42, they begin to enter early middle years in a childish state. Unable to truly engage with the psychological and soulful challenges of life, they are forced into repetition and a boring round of adolescent conflicts and aspirations for life. If, however, they rise to the challenge of the dissatisfaction that generally dawns in the mid-thirties (and occasionally before) they become available to, and may find a means to, wake up and by the time they enter their forties, they are ready to embrace true adulthood and to become self-referring, self-regulating, and inwardly wise. Then the spiritual life and sacred existence becomes a real possibility for them if they are spiritually inclined, because the soul has been born in the being.

The individual who is not free is also not a true individual. Because such a lot is unborn, unrealized, unformed, and uncreated in him or her, that they suffer pain from their sense of lack. This predominant feeling of lack expresses itself in low self-esteem, suffering from a negative self-image, little self-worth, feeling unconfident, an undeveloped sense of boundaries, and the tendency toward unsuccessful relationships. But most of all it expresses itself outwardly in the overwhelming need to combine with another human being to feel whole, fulfilled, lovable, and loved.

The failure of the connection to a partner who is also suffering from lack is highly predictable, although this obvious point seems to go largely unrecognized. The promise and the desire feed on themselves and support and re-create the sense of lack, which is re-affirmed by the failure of "relationships," which reflect on each partner as a personal failure indicating some further shortcoming.

Even if a relationship survives for any length of time merely temporarily, desire remains as an inner restlessness. This inner restlessness manifests in the need for a child, to start a family, to be conformist and prove one's worth, to deny feelings of deficiency by increasing the outward show of increase and rebuff the inner sense of lack, reinforcing the drive toward accruing money and wealth, serial lovers, or status and material ambition. But this simply makes the sense of lack even more acute as it is glossed over, avoided, and repressed.

From the spiritual point of view the individual who has realized themselves and expressed themselves through the freedom of their individuality is called to a deeper challenge. He or she has also to be able to set themselves aside. However exalted spiritually, the individual remains merely a shell, an envelope that can be set aside by the liberated self when called into the divine depths outside of time.

Every individual has to face this, everyone is making a choice, knowingly or unknowingly, concerning these matters, everyone has responsibility for the future of humanity. Everyone is directly affecting what will be expressed, manifested, and fulfilled.

Only when the individual fully assumes this responsibility is there a possibility that someday our night will come to an end and a new dawn, a new beginning, a new birth, a new ecstasy, a new dance, a new song will overwhelm us. That new dawn is very close, you just have to remember to be yourself, authentically, sincerely. Up to now humanity has lived as a crowd. From now on, if humanity wants to live at all it has to live as individuals, not as crowds. But that individual at its very depth, at its core, is *all* individuals for humanity is One, a unity, and one with all things and with all Life.

The Hope for Humanity

The identity with the individual self has grown in this present century to mammoth proportions, to giant size. This is a profound spiritual help to us in our endeavor to preserve the sacred-spiritual truths of divine realization in space and time for this reason: *All things tend toward their annihilation.* This is because all phenomena are strictly temporary, arising and falling, being born and dying. They are not eternal although they participate in the eternal through their inner essence which is eternity. As a thing reaches the crest of its evolution it atrophies and dies; when it becomes giant-size, all it can do then is wither and die. Whether the fruit, the blossom, the sea wave, the star, the symphony—everything must succumb to its own fulfillment by ending, by dying. Simply in facing its demise, it attains fulfillment.

As the river flows to the sea and dies in the ocean, the individual will die in this present century to the extreme development of its evolution. To paraphrase Nisargadatta's quote in the epigraph at the beginning of this book, flow begins when ebb is at its lowest.

All things tend toward death—this is the hope for the future, *our* future… and the future of humanity.

River of Compassion: Waters of Life

All my life the river has been *dharma*, teaching and instructing me. From stream to ocean, the river persists and overcomes in its course and represents my longing for the Divine. The river strives to reach the sea, waters trickle or gush in torrents, dam up to flow over obstacles, sparkle or threaten, beautiful and fierce. The river taught me when it flowed behind our house when I was small, when it moved down the estuary into the sea during my adolescence, and later when I meditated by it as a young Zen student and saw how each drop that detached from the cascading waterfall reflected the entire sphere of the totality within it, like an individual human life.

Now I am a spiritual teacher, I work to bring people back to themselves. I am simply selling water by the river. The years reverberate with the flowing torrent of my personal unfolding, the flowing waters of life that spoke to me repeatedly until I became still enough to hear—finally, the river has borne me into this eternal moment where arise all past, present, and future forms.

෬

As all good books should, let us end with a story, a teaching story. This is the story of the river. As we began with a story of a glass of water let us now end by entering the river.

One day Krishna Rau was walking along the banks of a sparkling river with his teacher Gurudev. They came across a rock baring their way. "Can you see that rock?" demanded Gurudev. "Do you see the miracle? Do you see the action of Universal Consciousness?" Here it is a rock, here it is a river, and here it is a human being. Whatever it becomes, it is only Consciousness."[26]

Do we see the miracle of Consciousness? Not only in the human being before us, not only in the magnificent flowing river of life, but in the obstacle, in the rock barring our way? Do we see that everything is Consciousness without exception... and now without any conflict or resistance Buddha speaks with Buddha, divinity confronts divinity, you and I are the same and *that* is the miracle.

---

[26]This story is derived from an account in Swami Muktananda Paramahamsa's book *Bhagavan Nityananda of Ganeshpuri*, SYDA Foundation 1996.

EPILOGUE

The End of our Journey Together

Here at the end of our journey together, let us look back at the terrain we have crossed.

- In Part 1 we made a statement about the contemporary human predicament of sacred-spiritual emergency.
- In Part 2 we proposed the demolition of what needs to be removed to promote healthy sacred-spiritual growth.
- In Part 3 we proposed a program for recovery and healing.
- In Part 4 we discussed the much-needed spiritual revolution to establish a new sacred-spiritual vision for the modern era.
- Last, in Part 5 we proposed a new, critical innovative paradigm for heart-opening and spiritual enlightenment.

Your Sacred Calling has focused on these five broad areas, often from a personal inner perspective. I believe that societal and global change *will* come about through each individual human being taking responsibility—deep responsibility—for their own life, growth, development, and, where appropriate, their spiritual awakening, self-realization, and our divine unity.

Remembering that We Are Divine

When we care, we care deeply, and we care for *all* things. You cannot care for some things and not for others. When you care for some things and not for others you separate God and you fragment your image of the Divine. This leads to delusion, because in the real world the Divine cannot be broken, it cannot even be wounded, because it is unassailable. The Divine is not only outward and objective; it is inward and subjective. It goes by other names—Truth, Reality, Wisdom, Love. It is *who you really are*.

Being who you really are means caring, caring for people, caring for actions and events, caring for the world... without any separation. Some people, things, and events are easy to care for, others are harder. These harder-to-care-for ones lead you to a choice—to forsake yourself and plunge into the negative, anti-life forces of ego, destruction, and lowering yourself to animalistic, reactionary, automatic, conditioned behavior or to carry on caring, knowing that this is your real nature and your spiritual awakening.

It is time for the world to awaken and that means that it is time for you to awaken. Awakening means embracing your spirituality, your transcendence, and your divinity. It doesn't mean working toward it, or putting it off for the time being, or justifying not doing it in any way. Awakening is remembering that you are divine. Awakening your soul and spirit is demonstrable; it means living a sacred life, a life of consideration and deep caring. Awakening means choosing life over death and higher spiritual tendencies and nature over lower and base tendencies, mechanical-ness and habit.

The world has been wounded by human beings. The sacred has been desecrated. Humanity has forgotten and forsaken its purpose; it has become complacent, lazy, negative anti-life, and fallen asleep. It is time to heal, time to renew, time to feel blessed for being born a human being; it is time to take your sacred journey.

Guidance for the Sacred Journey

Today we are immersed in ego—so much so to that a balanced life, let alone a sacred-spiritual life may seem almost impossible. The present era of individualism is so powerfully strong that our authentic, emotional, and energetic responses, mental clarity and understanding may be taken hostage by ego-processes.

We have to discern Truth amid the limitations of the present-day approaches to psycho-spirituality and sacredness. Each one of us must establish the basis for a balanced and responsible life. We must discover the teachings that clearly elucidate the genuine spiritual journey in contemporary times. They are in our hearts and minds as well as in the outer world and include the new, innovative, and radical confluence of counseling and depth psychotherapy with meditation and spiritual discipline, and represent guidance for the sacred journey in modern times.

The Future: A Vision of the New World

Before we finish, let's consider some summary sketches of life in the future—a future in which humanity has responded to the need to guard, protect, and treasure the sacred-spiritual truths in order to live from the heart and has awoken to the need to save and preserve the sacred principles for leading a truly spiritual life, the way to emotional and spiritual freedom.

Under the general headings that follow are short indications of how change and transformation could start in these respective areas of human concern. They comprise very brief sketches of future growth and development in the collective arena of humankind. I hope this section will inspire those with spiritual vision to expand and "flesh out" the material here in their own writings and discussions. Indeed, I consider it important to contribute to the discussion myself in my further publications and teaching courses. More than anything though, let us be active, enthused, inspired, and energetic in our application of these principles; we have no time to waste in the present circumstances of spiritual emergency… and sacred emergence.

Home and Society
The sanest way to live is in nature, in de-centralized, small-scale communities close to food sources, waste recycling, and using natural energy resources. These small societies should be ideally self-sufficient or involved in exchange with neighboring communities to supply their various needs and as far as possible self-governing in the supply of resources and communal subsistence.

Politically this will take some long-overdue revisioning and restructuring. The wise elders who oversee (formerly the governing role of politicians) the running of the community provide and educate people in rites of passage for natural life transitions. For example, natal birth, incarnating, puberty/adolescence, young adulthood, family duties, parenting, true adulthood, mid-life, spiritual gateways, wisdom maturation, and so on. This honors the sacred passage of developmental stages in a human life and has untold benefits for the community in terms of mental, physical, and emotional health and well-being. The society as a whole should be educated in the knowledge of the essential nature of rites of passage. These are conducted by societal elders who may have other roles in the community and who pass on their wisdom and knowledge to novices.

Each small-scale community reflects in everyday life, structuring and behavioral dynamics, a balance between the visible and the invisible worlds, the inner and the outer, the soul and spiritual forces, and the practical needs and necessities of life. Unless a community has a special function, for example, caring for the disabled, producing building materials, emotional education, or spiritual discipline, each day, month, and year reflects balanced involvement through occupying, respecting, and participation in mutual caring, cooperation, and the establishment of harmony, awareness, and the skills of mindfulness.

Each community is comprised of several biological families, single adults, different ethnic groups, people of varying ages, children in relationships of various kinds. The variety of each community reflects the diversity of the human family. For certain purposes associated with stages of life, separate houses or areas of the community are set aside for preparation for rites of passage, including all-women houses and all-men houses, pre-adolescent children's houses, areas for contemplative time, and retreat spaces for those about to enter into the marriage ceremony. Tolerance and cooperation, peace and compassion are reflected throughout every layer of society in the new vision—the sacred vision of the new world.

Nature is treated with great respect and reverence. Aesthetic areas, either unspoilt or fashioned with harmony between nature and human, are features of all communities. Farming and food production are considered a sacred opportunity for worship and compassion in providing the means to preserve life.

Animals are treated with utmost respect and accorded all the means to a happy life. Their relationships to individuals and the collective are considered meetings between arising forms of consciousness itself.

This is the basis of community: love, compassion and personal-psychological and impersonal-spiritual unfolding, the fundamental effort for the aspiration toward communal life. To accelerate and potentize the character and personality work, so that groups of people can live together practically and spiritually, balanced, heart-centered, and authentically motivated to transform and reach the spiritual, transcendent, and divine levels of profound human existence.

Education: Children and Early Years
Children are naturally self-regulating, self-healing, and self-governing—all these are natural processes inherent in babyhood, infancy, and childhood. Acknowledging and respecting these inherent processes make the education of children monumentally easier. Children are taught and inspired, guided and tutored, in the Mystery. The Divine is the prevailing context for their education; the overriding backdrop and theme of childhood is the source of compassion and the reality of Love. The education of children becomes a matter of divinely instilling the feeling and the experience of love, empathy, kindness, wholeness, and compassion.

Steiner education provides the most profound, inspired, spiritual basis for education at the present time. This approach coupled with the insights of western psychology enable us to respect the natural passage of child development and meet the educational needs of children in creative, enriching ways.

Traditionally, the tests and lessons of early childhood are dependency, trust, security, punishment, blame, possessiveness, jealousy, and attachment. The tests and lessons of adolescence are independence, betrayal, intimacy, philosophy, beliefs and opinions, making a stand, resistance, rebellion or conformism, self-worth, developing the "I," and creating an identity. In between the two are the tests and lessons of life from approximately seven to puberty—socialization, communication, mediating others' needs and desires, creating a sexual and power-based identity, intimacy, and relationship to individuals and the collective. However, the inherent struggles associated with traditional themes of childhood and adolescence should transform over two or three generations as the positive forces of heart and wisdom prevail.

Education takes place in a blessed, aware relationship with the teacher, in the home and community life, and through the experiences, events, and interactions of life itself. In this way education is not marginalized or segmented, but viewed as an ongoing reality of unfolding life.

Human Relationships
The romantic myth of love and quest, sadness, despair, and death is dislodged much easier with the new education of children. Since the romantic myth itself has arisen from the tribulations and frustrations of incomplete childhood transitions, the legacy of the romantic myth should fall away without too much wounding or leaving

too wide a scar. This natural healing will give rise to the new mythology or backdrop of inherent life guidance, one that is innately natural, transcendent, and intelligent in the holistic and deepest sense. The new myth is the myth of spiritual awakening, self-realization, and divine Translation—the furtherance of humankind into the body of light inherent in the psycho-physical form.

Relationships will be all about love, less about personal love or at least not personal love that resists or occludes impersonal love. Impersonal love is love that knows it is all-inclusive, all-giving, all-responsive, and beyond prejudice, patronizing, partisanship, or bigotry. Impersonal love is not divisive, preferential, separative, or ultimately involved in "specialness" or individual identity. The difficulty here is in the transition time. However, when begun from the Truth itself, great changes will be seen in the first generation, a transformation in the second, and, by the third, a metamorphosis into transcendental grounding and apparent, deep manifestation of spiritual, soulful, sacred vision and Truth.

Relationships are not only no longer orientated to romance, separation, possessiveness, loyalty/disloyalty, jealousy, and violence, they are orientated to the sharing and progression of love to all. Families are no longer exclusive or separative. Children are aware of their individual parents, but they are equally involved with other adults and each child feels the experience of being in relationship with several "parents." This may mean that adults gravitate toward children who are not "theirs" biologically but in a different kind of way—spiritually, emotionally, energetically, karmically, and so on—the two beings are drawn to each other through caring ties.

We must surely all be aware that we are living presently in extraordinary times for relationships between adults and children. Teachers not allowed to embrace pupils who are in distress, pedestrians afraid to go to the aid of the injured, therapists are intimidated into not following their natural caring instincts for fear of legal retribution—whatever the justification for these extreme conditions the fallout for these unnatural travesties is injurious and damaging. Also, many different kinds of inter-human relationships are being judged, ignored, and rejected in favor of conformist ideas of how we *should* relate to each other. Conventional forms of relationship marginalize and eclipse the richness of relationships and all the feeling, love, compassion, and caring of which humankind is capable. It is time to take these relationships—the ones that are not understood, recognized, or conventional and allow them and acknowledge their inherent richness in the variety of ways human beings have of caring for each other. The damage and the destruction we are doing in contemporary society by not recognizing, understanding, and supporting, but rather intimidating, persecuting, and criminalizing people for feeling, is immense. The results will never be understood and connected with this suppression, but will be revealed flagrantly, spectacularly, and negatively in the darkness of our future unless we act.

The principal trajectory for couples will be love and spiritual development and not raising children and creating nuclear family units. We are no longer principally concerned with the propagation of the species, less still with the propagation of the species as a cloak for reinforcing our sense of self-worth because it was stripped from us in childhood and adolescence. The approval that young couples seek from parents and grandparents for perpetuating the foolishness of propagating life to ensure approval is futile and widespread indeed. It is time for this utter stupidity to cease. People are worthy and estimable in themselves; indeed, people are embodiments of the

Divine. They do not have to perform or compromise, less still bow to ridiculous conventions and expectations.

Heart Teachers and Guides

The lower chakra concerns are on the ascendant for humanity, but they should be balanced and understood in the light—literally the elevated higher consciousness of the higher chakra concerns. This means that heart-opening, surrender, and acting as a conduit for the Divine becomes the life orientation for those who have the sacred calling to heal, guide, and awaken. Although everyone requires a mentor, a counselor, or a teacher to turn to for shared reflection and wise guidance, not all people are equal in regard to sacred-spiritual wisdom and the ability to teach and guide. However, all beings are equal in the sense that each one should allow, strive, and endeavor to allow their essence to radiate and be surrendered to the spiritual calling.

What has previously been known as the psychotherapist, counselor, or healer should increasingly be equated with spiritual teaching. All healing of mind, body, and soul should be based in the spiritual nature.

What was previously known as the psychotherapist, counselor and so on is renamed to release the associations with a medical model of psychological well-being (a contradiction in terms) and associated with and based on the spiritual teacher.

Not everyone is expected to awaken spiritually. All human beings are accorded equal respect in the fulfillment of their individual destinies. However, for those who are seen and understood by wise elders and guides to be ready, the age old tradition of transmission from teacher to pupil, from master to aspiring adept, directly through practice, ordeal, and inner transformation to attitude, orientation, and relationship applies. When the master sees that the disciple is ready, he transmits the teaching through esoteric ritual and clandestine means, in appropriate and effective ways.

Birth Process
The birth process is pivotal to the unfolding of a human life. In the present society birth is medicalized and pathologized. Interventions and fearful attitudes compromise natural deliveries and often traumatize both mother and baby. This is not an intelligent way to begin a human life!

Birth should be approached with sacredness and reverence as the gateway into the psycho-physical realms. The mother's inherent wisdom should be encouraged and respected with guidance and the wisdom from sage women.

The largely ignored wisdom of Frederick Leboyer and Michel Odent, and the pioneering work of Sheila Kitzinger comprise the basis for a fresh, compassionate, intelligent approach to childbirth, pre- and post-natal periods.

In the new society birth is a consecrated ceremony of reverence and gentleness, consisting of loving presences, calm, a complete absence of anxiety and fear, dimmed lights in a comfortable room with an optimum temperature, delivery into water should at least be considered, as far as possible no intervention from professionals with (unless there is genuine cause for concern) the new-born laid on the mother's stomach and allowed to bond through skin-to-skin contact.

Heart Opening: Authenticity and Compassion
The means to personal healing should be appropriately made available to all. Rising into the heart chakra and living a life of authenticity and genuine compassion should become increasingly common in society. In the small-scale community heightened awareness and the

condition of love and compassion for all should become the new consensus.

In the event of immoral (in the spiritual sense), corrupted, or unnatural behavior in any individual or group of individuals, the whole collective or the "family" of involved individuals congregating around that individual are involved in the process of ritual cleansing and purifying the emotional and relational context of the individual who has highlighted through adverse behavior some lapse in light-filled behavior in relationship to others, to the community, or to the sacred environment in which the collective lives and exists.

Whenever the new society faces an impasse, conflict or uncertainty on matters of decision-making, direction, or policy the default position is compassion; the voice of the heart is the ultimate reference point in the meeting between God and humanity.

The Biological Family

It is intelligent and responsive to the stages of human development that the biological family gets left behind or transcended. Since inner work becomes the common pursuit of humanity, this will happen quite naturally. The primary reason for retaining attachment to the biological family as a whole and to family members individually is overwhelmingly the inability to complete or transcend the dilemma of dependence/independence and the creation of identity.

The new form and idea is that once you have been mothered and fathered, brothered and sistered you grow into adulthood. Adulthood in the present conditions of contemporary human life occurs (when it occurs at all) on or around the age of 42 (and occasionally earlier). In the new future vision this may well change as more and more people are less delayed with remedial psychological work aimed at freeing them from emotional, energetic, and mental confusion, and dilemmas about human relationships.

Transition Time
In the intermediate stages of personal and collective healing and transformation—the transition time—through compromise, establishing strong structures based on truth and inner wisdom, collective meetings of wise elders to guide and give sage guidance and advice, the reduction in power-based leadership, its replacement with tolerant, cooperative, peace-based, harmonious-based release from family ties and outmoded loyalties, change will come about.

When our human relationships strive toward interconnected individuals living in tolerance and cooperation, living the dream of humanity, the vision that is attainable when we turn our faces toward sanity, heartfelt existence, and collective wholeness, the sacred-spiritual life has much to contend with, much to overcome. Genocide, misogyny, infanticide, slavery, political tyranny and corruption, religious indoctrination, scapegoating, torture, homicide, racism, sexual-orientation phobias, persecution—and this list is hardly exhaustive! It represents enormous opposition to love, acceptance, understanding, and mutual tolerance. I invite you and I invite others to write a companion list that speaks of the positive, prolife forces that represent the richness of the heart's love for humanity, the soul's deep engagement with human travails, the expansiveness of the spirit's transcendental wisdom for healing, and developing the human being to higher and higher degrees of sublimity, forgiveness, and wonder.

To live in the light of divine truth has nowhere near been spoken of enough. The details are every bit as formidable as is the list of life-negating and degrading human hatred and violence. Darkness has been an addiction and a compulsion of humanity's for too long now; it is time for us to speak of light, of consciousness and love and freedom! So let us join together as one human family now and celebrate in peace and joy the wonder of what it means to be gloriously human; let us prepare the way for human awakening and transformation.

Embracing Your Sacred Calling: Living a Spiritual-Divine Life

Now I invite you to start. What you can do *now* is work sincerely with your inner process, develop your heartfeltness, and progress into a deeper spiritual practice of devotion to obtain liberation. My books include copious exercises and encouragements about how to set up and conduct an effective inner work practice. Try to connect with others to combine in a collective effort of transformation. The group should start from the right basis of sacredness, spirituality, liberation, and divine fulfillment. The way is through the false strategies and complexities of character and personality into the life of authenticity.

If you become involved with authentic awakening, you will face your very deepest challenges and you will go further in your inner exploration, and beyond, than you have ever imagined. You will be set free and *only you* will be the decision-maker of this fate. You will come to a place where nothing and no one stands between you and happiness, bliss, and peace.

So if this meets your deeper aspiration for your life, act now and prepare and gather all you require to enable you to begin your sacred-spiritual practice. I encourage and inspire your sincere efforts toward living a sacred-spiritual life and embracing your sacred calling.

APPENDICES

The Sacred Space Meditation

Follow these instructions by either having a friend read them to you or record them yourself. After a few times of doing the meditation, you should be able to remember the steps.

Step 1: Preparing your Body
Make sure you will not be disturbed. Turn off your handheld devices, the telephone, and your PC. Make sure there are no electronic devices on or in standby mode in the room where you will be sitting, as this interferes with your energy field. Tell anyone in the house that you will be occupied for a while.

Sit quietly and alert in a meditation posture that is comfortable and perhaps familiar to you. Your back, head and neck should be straight, the crown of your head tending toward heaven, your sacrum and base chakra tending toward earth. Sit comfortable, erect and yet loose and flexible. Breathe and allow the breath to find its way gently and naturally down through your chest and solar plexus to fill your abdomen and infuse your pelvis. In time the breath should connect to the very base of your physical form at the perineum. Your eyes may be open or closed or you may prefer to partially close them. Relax your shoulders, your abdomen, your legs, then your neck, your jaw, and your facial muscles. Breathe steadily and naturally through your nose and follow the breath with your awareness through your body.

Now allow the body to sway or rotate gently forward, backward, from side to side, back and forth just subtly. When you allow this swaying or circling of the upper body to come to a still point on its own, you will find you are balanced, erect, and centered in your body. Don't be concerned if you feel your body is lop-sided. Trust that the swaying will correct physiological and anatomical leanings and imbalances and bring you to a sitting position which requires the least tension and effort, while also aligning your body and your energy system.

Bring all your attention now to posture and breathing. Take several breaths until you are comfort-table, aware, alert, and easy in your sitting meditation position.

This is the physical basis of meditation practice. But you may still practice when you are in a practical situation that prohibits some or most of these steps. Simply enter into the spirit of the steps described here and do what you can in the temporal, spatial conditions that exist. Now when you are ready, continue to the next step.

Step 2: Emptying Your Mind
Allow your mind to empty. Do this by becoming aware of your thoughts, the tone of your thoughts, the content and the feelings attached to your thoughts. Becoming aware of the energy of thoughts and your attitude to them, ask: Am I absorbed, fascinated, interested? After you have brought this awareness to your thinking process, release it and allow emptiness, allow inner space, allow the mind to relax. Be aware of the emotions attached to letting go of thought, but let go anyway and cultivate and tolerate the inner emptiness—empty, but still nonetheless alert, available, and present.

Now, deepen in the emptiness and sacred space of your mind, body, and heart. Be in the stillness and relax into the sacred space. As thoughts or distractions arise, simply let go of them and return to your practice of emptiness.

From time to time, check your posture, breathing, and balance. Maintain an alert, relaxed state. Practice for ten, twenty, or thirty minutes and when you finish take several deep breaths, gently shake your body, return to the room with each of the senses and rise in gratitude and reverence for the time you have spent in sacred space.

The Consciousness Exercise: a spiritual Method for the 21st Century

As before, follow these instructions by either having a friend read them to you or record them yourself. After a few times of doing this exercise you should be able to remember the steps.

Take a few minutes to prepare yourself and your space. Turn your phone off and make sure that you won't be interrupted for 15-20 minutes. Sit or lie down (so long as you are not tired) with a straight back. Your feet should be flat on the floor or ground if you are sitting in a chair or lying down with your knees bent, unless you are sitting in a meditation posture, for example, cross-legged—in any case the point is to have a firm base and contact with the ground. Relax your shoulders, your torso, your pelvis, and feel the support of the chair or the floor beneath you. Relax your abdomen and begin breathing deeply, down through your chest and solar plexus, fill your belly and lower abdomen with air and follow the breath all the way down to the base of your torso, the center point on which your balance and physical grounding rely, and all the way down to the perineum. After taking several deep breaths and exhaling fully, return to normal breathing.

Preparation
Gently close your eyes and allow your body to be loose and find a place of balance and alignment through not holding it too rigidly or too tightly. Relax the unnecessary tensions and contractions in your body. Your breath should stimulate and invigorate your total energy system. Allow this through your awareness of breathing and through feeling awareness. Bring both feeling, in the sense of emotion and sensation, to the location of your breath and be aware of the effects of conscious breathing

in your body enhancing your inner state of relaxation and alertness. Begin when you are ready.

Step 1: Withdraw from the Five Senses

Become aware of sound, the sounds around you. Bring awareness to them individually and then collectively, like distinguishing a violin playing in the orchestra and then listening to the whole orchestra. Pay attention to sound... then let it go... and take your attention back from it. Now concentrate your attention on touch, feeling the tactile sensations of clothes on your body, the air on your skin, the sensation of a breeze, the pressure of your posterior on the floor or the cushion. Allow your attention to dwell on each... then gently withdraw it entirely... and leave sensation behind. Do the same now for the olfactory sense, your sense of smell. Linger briefly with the fragrances in the room, allow your attention to rest with them... and withdraw your attention completely. Similarly, with taste, attend to the tastes you can experience in this present moment, acknowledge and honor them... and withdraw from that experience also. Finally, become aware of your sight impression, visual images that you retain from before you closed your eyes. Be aware of them... and release them, let them go... and now begin to bring your awareness *in*—inside your skin, so you completely bring your attention inward to the interior of your body and away from the outer world.

Step 2: Withdraw from the Physical Body

Become aware of the bodily systems in turn—the respiratory system, the flow of the in-breath and the out-breath, filling your body with life-giving air. Now withdraw from this awareness, respectfully and entirely.... become aware of the digestive system, your stomach and bowels and the processes that are occurring there... withdraw from this also. This process is like shining a beam of light, it is the light of your awareness and after you move the light away you move on to the next focus of attention.

Now the circulatory system—become aware of the flow of blood throughout your body, your pulse, and the pumping of your heart... and withdraw the light of your attention now... and focus your awareness on the skeletal, muscular, reproductive systems, and the whole of the interior, physical body, just for a few minutes......... and withdraw your attention now fully, retrieve it completely... and take a deep breath.

Step 3: Withdraw from Thought
Become aware of thinking now, the stream of thoughts... of worry and planning... and anxiety and creativity. Be aware of your thoughts and the kind of thoughts you are having. If there are any particular worries, just put them on hold for now and assure yourself that you will return to them in time. For now, you are taking a break from thinking, so bring your awareness away from thought... and withdraw deeper... deeper inside yourself.

Step 4: Withdraw from Emotions
Become aware now of the emotions in your body—some flowing, some static, some frozen or blocked, others streaming through you. Become aware of this varied emotional flow, the movement of sadness, excitation, stimulation, aggression, fear, pain, joy, and pleasure through the internal organs and systems and etheric spaces in your body... and withdraw your attention... and pull back, withdraw... and go further in... and further in.

Step 5: Withdraw from your Energy System

Become aware now of your energy system: its vibrancy or depression, its invigorating, strengthening excitement or dullness and apathy, movement or inertia, indifference or enthusiasm… embryonic and contained within you. Be aware of your energy, just as it is—without judgment — and gently withdraw your attention from it.

Step 6: Rest in Consciousness
All the time, as you withdraw your attention and retrieve your awareness, direct yourself steadily *in*… in toward your center, in toward a point that may or may not be physical for you, a central point, a dimensionless point that represents your core. Now relinquish your attention altogether and rest… in this core place. It is still and peaceful, transcendent and empty, entirely receptive with no content whatsoever. It is unhampered by drama, eventfulness, or restlessness of any kind. There is not a ripple, not a flurry or movement, no event, no thought or emotion, no sound, no happening, nothing going on… just peace… and profound inner silence.

Rest in this place—it is the home of your soul, the resting place of Consciousness itself. Transcendent of the world and its events and appearances, here, now, this is essence, stillness, and the fount of Love itself. Rest here easily and fully… for as long as you need. Then when you feel ready to return to the world, do so with great awareness. Bring your attention solely and thoroughly to your engagement with life, with the body and the senses, your thoughts and emotions.

When you are ready then, very slowly and gently open your eyes… and return to the room. Take a deep breath and stretch and shake your body into vibrancy and wakefulness. Take a look around you and engage your senses with the world… gently and lovingly.

Practicing the Consciousness Exercise
When you practice the Consciousness Exercise regularly and consistently, you will find that you can reach the place of core stillness increasingly quickly. Adapt this exercise to your circumstances and you will find that you can rapidly reach Step 6 in a short time in even adverse circumstances or equally you can extend it into an hour-long guided meditation. You may want to share the exercise with friends or practice it in a group, taking turns to facilitate going through the steps. Once you have familiarized yourself with the sequence of steps, you can practice the entire exercise in almost any circumstances.

The Consciousness Exercise is the very essence of meditation. All meditation techniques are a means to connect us back to our source, to the inner reality, to the Divine within. This exercise centers you and cultivates your inner stillness, so supporting your positive attributes. You may also teach it to others when they show a tendency to spiritual inner work and are ready to develop their awareness and deepen in stillness and emptiness.

BIBLIOGRAPHY

Some of these books and authors are mentioned in this book, some are quoted, and others are simply of relevance to the subject matter.

American Psychiatric Association, *Diagnostic and Statistical Manual of Mental Disorders, 5th Edition: DSM-5*, American Psychiatric Publishing 2013

Balsekar, Ramesh S and Dikshit, Sudhakar S, *Pointers from Nisargadatta Maharaj*, The Acorn Press 1990

Campbell, Joseph and Moyers, Bill, *The Power of Myth*, Anchor 1991

Caplan, Mariana, *Do You Need a Guru?: Understanding the Student-Teacher Relationship in an Era of False Prophets*, Thorsons 2002

Dass, Ram and Gorman, Paul, *How Can I Help?: Stories and Reflections on Service*, Alfred A Knopf 1985

Deldon, Anne McNeely, *Becoming: An Introduction to Jung's Concept of Individuation*, Fisher King Press 2010

Easwaran, Eknath, *The Upanishads: A Classic of Indian Spirituality*, Nilgiri Press 2007

Harvey, Richard, *Your Essential Self: The Inner Journey to Authenticity and Spiritual Enlightenment*, Llewellyn Publications 2013 and *The Flight of Consciousness: A Contemporary Map for the Spiritual Journey*, Ashgrove Publishing 2002

Holy Bible, King James Version, Zondervan 2010

Mitchell, David, *Cloud Atlas: A Novel*, Random House 2004

Reps, Paul, *Zen Flesh Zen Bones*, Tuttle Publishing 1998

Rilke, Rainer Maria and Mitchell, Stephen, *Duino Elegies and the Sonnets to Orpheus,* Vintage 2009

Salzmann, Jeanne de, *The Reality of Being: The Fourth Way of Gurdjieff*, Shambhala Publications 2011
Tabrizi, Shams-I and Chittick, William C, *Me and Rumi: The Autobiography of Shams-I Tabrizi*, Fons Vitae 2004
Vernon, Roland, *Star in the East: Krishnamurti – the Invention of a Messiah*, Sentient Publications 2002
Waite, Dennis, *Advaita Made Easy*, Mantra Books 2012
Zimmer, Heinrich, *Myths and Symbols in Indian Art and Civilization*, Princeton University Press 1972

INDEX

A

Absolute, 84, 107, 131, 132, 152, 229, 230
acceptance, 19, 33, 48, 56, 80, 82, 86, 137, 182, 238, 241, 253, 256, 265, 275, 276, 286, 287, 328
Advaita Vedanta, 19, 78, 131, 132, 136
aging, 58, 66
ahimsa, 72
archetypal, 76, 158, 176, 256, 263
ashram, 64, 151, 152, 170, 180, 227, 305
ataraxia, 52
attachment, 89, 111, 113, 119, 131, 157, 175, 176, 189, 195, 199, 239, 242, 243, 244, 246, 249, 304, 322, 327
authenticity, 18, 19, 33, 36, 45, 126, 135, 140, 144, 157, 160, 165, 169, 201, 226, 228, 247, 251, 256, 259, 269, 310, 326, 329
awakening, 17, 19, 34, 61, 82, 84, 85, 104, 119, 126, 150, 160, 174, 181, 182, 187, 192, 193, 198, 204, 216, 217, 218, 219, 225, 246, 250, 256, 265, 295, 301, 315, 316, 323, 329
awareness, 20, 29, 36, 43, 53, 55, 60, 63, 64, 81, 86, 103, 107, 131, 137, 142, 152, 155, 157, 172, 187, 189, 199, 203, 224, 225, 231, 239, 259, 297, 300, 310, 320, 326, 330, 331, 333, 334, 335, 336, 337

B

being, 19, 25, 29, 30, 34, 36, 39, 45, 47, 49, 56, 58, 60, 61, 64, 65, 68, 72, 73, 76, 81, 82, 94, 99, 103, 105, 106, 107, 111, 112, 117, 118, 119, 122, 132, 144, 145, 147, 151, 152, 154, 155, 157, 159, 160, 164, 165, 166, 168, 172, 182, 189, 193, 196, 225, 227, 232, 238, 245, 248, 250, 252, 253, 256, 261, 266, 274, 275, 276, 278, 279, 284, 290, 291, 293, 295, 296, 305, 306, 308, 310, 312, 314, 315, 316, 317, 320, 323, 324, 325, 328
belief, 117, 127, 152, 164, 169, 182, 223, 244, 292
Bhagavad Gita, 84
blessing, 66, 162, 166, 187
Buddhism, 42, 72, 149

C

Campbell, Joseph, 338
chakra, 102, 109, 190, 287, 325, 326, 330
character, 60, 76, 110, 115, 118, 119, 122, 126, 128, 135, 143, 147, 151, 157, 162, 165, 174, 175, 197,

199, 210, 223, 227, 234, 236, 237, 238, 246, 248, 250, 261, 262, 264, 265, 266, 284, 302, 305, 306, 321, 329
charlatans, 44
childhood, 34, 96, 110, 113, 116, 124, 135, 152, 179, 187, 192, 227, 321, 322, 324
Christianity, 42, 146, 209
commitment, 139, 181, 193, 198, 229, 236, 251, 252, 269
compassion, 17, 23, 37, 52, 54, 56, 63, 80, 83, 84, 86, 109, 121, 134, 140, 144, 153, 160, 165, 199, 201, 220, 226, 241, 247, 251, 258, 262, 268, 281, 286, 293, 294, 297, 299, 306, 309, 321, 324, 326, 327
consciousness, 17, 19, 26, 34, 35, 36, 80, 82, 98, 102, 135, 148, 150, 155, 158, 159, 160, 177, 187, 189, 194, 207, 225, 226, 231, 232, 253, 256, 266, 291, 295, 301, 302, 305, 306, 321, 325, 329
Consciousness, 85, 87, 106, 146, 154, 186, 189, 196, 218, 225, 231, 232, 271, 286, 302, 313, 314, 333, 336, 337, 338
control, 53, 96, 140, 164
counseling, 29, 32, 33, 45, 255, 318
couples, 324

D

death, 27, 60, 61, 72, 73, 75, 101, 106, 144, 145, 177, 179, 204, 211, 213, 214, 285, 293, 300, 312, 316, 322
defense, 143, 164, 284, 302, 309
delusion, 48, 52, 68, 81, 103, 106, 109, 115, 117, 141, 152, 153, 182, 199, 201, 203, 292, 316
depression, 52, 187, 273, 336
desire, 27, 36, 52, 58, 60, 73, 78, 81, 83, 89, 90, 108, 118, 119, 120, 121, 122, 123, 125, 126, 129, 132, 140, 143, 151, 153, 160, 177, 179, 187, 188, 192, 200, 223, 226, 231, 239, 242, 250, 265, 291, 292, 306, 308, 309, 310, 311
destruction, 17, 71, 73, 75, 77, 80, 82, 109, 144, 308, 316, 324
disciple, 25, 28, 46, 104, 181, 182, 261, 325
Divine, 18, 19, 24, 26, 36, 37, 38, 64, 65, 76, 82, 84, 87, 89, 100, 106, 109, 114, 121, 145, 151, 152, 153, 155, 156, 165, 172, 179, 184, 186, 187, 188, 189, 192, 193, 194, 195, 199, 202, 216, 217, 223, 226, 229, 231, 232, 234, 245, 253, 265, 283, 284, 289, 290, 292, 293, 295, 296, 297, 298, 299, 304, 308, 313, 316, 321, 325, 329, 337
divine psychology, 53
divinity, 24, 32, 56, 87, 284, 295, 302, 307, 314, 316
doubt, 52, 84, 100, 121, 230, 231, 255, 258

E

ego, 28, 40, 49, 50, 52, 53, 54, 61, 62, 69, 100, 101, 102, 103, 110, 111, 112, 114, 115, 118, 120, 122, 123, 124, 126, 127, 128, 130, 134, 135, 145, 152, 157, 158, 160, 162, 171, 175, 182, 184, 187, 188, 192, 195, 197, 199, 201, 220, 221, 225, 226, 234, 235, 236, 239, 243, 249, 250, 254, 260, 265, 266, 269, 284, 291, 292, 297, 299, 302, 303, 304, 316, 318

ego-processes, 28, 54, 103, 124, 135, 175, 195, 197, 199, 243, 249, 254, 260, 284, 318

ego-self, 40, 111, 122, 123, 152, 160, 162, 175, 182

enlightenment, 23, 52, 53, 65, 78, 82, 84, 87, 98, 100, 104, 105, 108, 109, 111, 114, 115, 117, 118, 126, 128, 132, 153, 162, 248, 283, 284, 304, 315

entertainment, 78, 96, 114, 121, 122, 123

existence, 23, 60, 66, 78, 80, 82, 101, 137, 154, 155, 162, 166, 192, 202, 206, 230, 234, 238, 258, 277, 297, 300, 304, 305, 306, 310, 321, 328

F

father, 25, 34, 47, 66, 74, 76, 96, 110, 148, 150, 152, 160, 211, 273

fear, 30, 36, 52, 60, 83, 87, 118, 119, 125, 126, 129, 140, 143, 151, 153, 160, 177, 179, 182, 187, 188, 192, 204, 205, 212, 213, 214, 226, 239, 248, 250, 251, 279, 280, 285, 292, 303, 304, 306, 308, 309, 324, 326, 335

focus, 32, 64, 91, 112, 272, 293, 335

food, 101, 114, 143, 152, 153, 154, 269, 270, 272, 305, 309, 319, 321

forgiveness, 36, 56, 157, 163, 165, 199, 246, 247, 273, 274, 275, 287, 328

fulfillment, 3, 28, 43, 82, 89, 90, 101, 114, 159, 178, 201, 203, 226, 245, 293, 308, 312, 325, 329

G

God, 25, 26, 84, 110, 113, 130, 132, 136, 145, 151, 152, 153, 166, 176, 184, 186, 194, 216, 226, 229, 243, 284, 285, 289, 290, 291, 302, 304, 316, 327

gratitude, 9, 36, 37, 222, 240, 258, 266, 277, 294, 299, 332

ground of being, 17, 151

grounded spirituality, 19, 175, 179

guide, 32, 33, 46, 48, 58, 63, 91, 117, 133, 149, 181, 189, 192, 198, 222, 224, 232, 247, 252, 254, 255, 257, 258, 260, 262, 265, 273, 325, 328

guilt, 22, 36, 56, 100, 163, 169

Gurdjieff, 42, 104, 115, 146, 261, 271, 306, 339

H

happiness, 17, 27, 53, 56, 68, 121, 123, 124, 128, 144, 182, 203, 241, 247, 268, 271, 272, 273, 274, 275, 276, 287, 297, 329
healing, 23, 31, 32, 33, 36, 37, 44, 45, 86, 91, 118, 130, 135, 149, 157, 158, 168, 174, 192, 197, 199, 237, 252, 254, 255, 259, 260, 262, 263, 265, 315, 321, 323, 325, 326, 328
healing relationship, 32, 33, 252, 255, 260, 262
heart, 19, 23, 36, 42, 45, 52, 56, 60, 61, 63, 64, 68, 74, 80, 82, 109, 121, 134, 135, 140, 144, 150, 151, 152, 154, 155, 160, 163, 165, 175, 178, 185, 198, 199, 200, 201, 203, 206, 215, 223, 226, 228, 234, 235, 237, 239, 241, 247, 251, 252, 255, 256, 259, 262,264, 267, 268, 269, 273, 274, 275, 276, 277, 278, 281, 285, 286, 287, 289, 297, 303, 307, 308, 315, 319, 321, 322, 325, 326, 327, 328, 332, 335
Hindu, 26, 72, 294
Hollywood, 58, 59, 184
human awakening, 23, 134, 160, 329
humanity, 17, 18, 22, 24, 28, 29, 33, 34, 35, 36, 39, 43, 45, 52, 54, 64, 68, 70, 78, 96, 134, 145, 162, 172, 253, 264, 267, 268, 269, 277, 280, 281, 284, 287, 301, 311, 312, 319, 325, 327, 328, 329

I

ignorance, 17, 29, 33, 52, 53, 54, 100, 101, 107, 109, 114, 150, 203, 258, 268, 269, 281, 308
illusion, 38, 53, 103, 114, 128, 153, 162, 164, 182, 187, 188, 192, 199, 201, 249, 259
impersonal, 87, 89, 118, 130, 228, 321, 323
individualism, 18, 28, 32, 39, 48, 50, 52, 53, 54, 318
initiation, 70, 78, 104, 155, 158, 203, 204, 205, 206, 207, 213, 215, 217, 239
inner ecology, 29, 31, 39
inner work, 21, 32, 39, 40, 45, 58, 59, 62, 68, 69, 85, 106, 114, 135, 136, 139, 140, 142, 143, 151, 164, 166, 175, 179, 182, 187, 192, 198, 216, 217, 232, 233, 260, 263, 278, 281, 287, 327, 329, 337
inner world, 29, 35, 36, 38, 81, 83, 89, 92, 142, 143, 145, 148, 168, 171, 172, 202, 205, 281

J

Jung, 86, 157, 158, 160, 179, 338

K

King Kong, 58

knowledge, 17, 28, 39, 44, 90, 91, 115, 121, 136, 168, 259, 273, 279, 283, 284, 294, 320

L

lethargy, 72
Love, 17, 18, 84, 241, 273, 289, 316, 321, 336

M

Maslow, 157, 159, 160, 179
maya, 107, 187, 298
meditation, 21, 64, 107, 142, 147, 153, 155, 174, 182, 189, 190, 191, 192, 193, 225, 255, 266, 272, 278, 291, 300, 307, 318, 330, 331, 333, 337
mind-body-spirit, 37, 115, 121
mouna, 118
mystery, 18, 70, 75, 182, 210, 215, 218, 234, 275, 296

N

New Age, 37, 42, 44, 49, 85, 99, 106, 121, 201
Nicky, 9, 88, 89
Nirvana, 66, 303
Nisargadatta, 10, 72, 76, 131, 132, 134, 135, 136, 195, 289, 306, 312, 338
numinous, 56, 64, 166, 184, 195, 225, 234

P

path, 50, 76, 82, 89, 110, 111, 113, 117, 118, 120, 121, 122, 123, 126, 128, 136, 145, 146, 151, 160, 165, 198, 208, 209, 216, 229, 234, 243, 250, 251, 258
peace, 3, 17, 42, 108, 151, 160, 189, 199, 209, 278, 285, 297, 305, 307, 308, 320, 328, 329, 336
personal growth, 29, 32, 42, 43, 85, 99, 157, 160, 181, 272
personality, 36, 49, 64, 76, 82, 92, 104, 110, 111, 113, 118, 119, 122, 125, 126, 127, 128, 130, 136, 139, 140, 142, 143, 150, 151, 152, 155, 157, 158, 160, 162, 164, 165, 174, 179, 195, 197, 199, 211, 220, 221, 227, 231, 234, 246, 248, 250, 253, 262, 264, 265, 266, 284, 305, 321, 329
Picasso, 133
pleasure, 27, 37, 114, 143, 147, 148, 200, 208, 242, 265, 289, 293, 295, 335
power, 53, 54, 64, 66, 76, 85, 92, 96, 106, 114, 135, 136, 148, 150, 163, 166, 221, 239, 269, 270, 284, 286, 291, 322, 328
pride, 54, 261, 272, 297
projections, 128, 146, 157
psycho-spiritual, 3, 23, 37, 39, 44, 48, 70, 89, 142, 157, 170, 174, 175, 187, 197, 202, 216, 222, 228, 245, 247, 250, 251, 260, 275, 283, 285, 318

R

Reality, 24, 61, 64, 70, 71, 83, 87, 89, 90, 102, 115, 176, 189, 194, 196, 231, 261, 268, 290, 296, 304, 308, 316, 339

relationships, 34, 35, 92, 102, 106, 142, 143, 206, 218, 236, 243, 253, 258, 259, 262, 275, 276, 284, 297, 310, 311, 320, 321, 323, 328

religion, 22, 32, 34, 36, 42, 43, 49, 87, 169, 243, 303

renunciation, 196, 228, 231

S

sacred, 18, 19, 20, 21, 23, 24, 26, 27, 28, 31, 36, 39, 54, 62, 63, 64, 65, 66, 68, 69, 71, 101, 102, 106, 112, 124, 152, 180, 181, 187, 199, 201, 202, 203, 204, 216, 217, 258, 268, 269, 271, 277, 283, 284, 287, 309, 310, 312, 315, 316, 318, 319, 320, 321, 323, 325, 327, 328, 329, 332

Sacred Attention Therapy, 3, 31, 34, 175

sadhana, 152, 180, 226, 269

salvation, 50, 87

seeker, 32, 80, 90, 220, 223, 227, 244, 262, 265, 290

seeking, 60, 110, 111, 114, 145, 215, 241, 250, 265, 299

Self, 32, 46, 85, 87, 107, 111, 117, 118, 126, 158, 159, 177, 178, 195, 199, 216, 226, 234, 236, 239, 246, 248, 251, 254, 280, 286, 289, 290, 302, 308

self-discovery, 48, 58, 149, 157, 159, 174, 182, 197, 198, 199, 256

self-help, 48, 115, 174, 221, 241

Self-realization, 118

separation, 38, 40, 98, 103, 113, 124, 135, 162, 169, 182, 187, 195, 226, 241, 242, 246, 279, 280, 285, 286, 287, 316, 323

sex, 93, 143, 152

soul, 22, 31, 32, 36, 58, 72, 77, 78, 134, 145, 154, 158, 160, 171, 182, 202, 206, 211, 234, 238, 239, 247, 250, 252, 258, 262, 275, 277, 281, 285, 291, 297, 304, 308, 309, 316, 320, 325, 328, 336

spiritual, 3, 17, 18, 19, 21, 22, 23, 26, 28, 31, 32, 34, 35, 36, 37, 38, 39, 42, 43, 44, 46, 48, 49, 50, 51, 52, 53, 54, 62, 63, 64, 65, 70, 72, 74, 76, 78, 80, 81, 82, 83, 84, 85, 86, 87, 89, 90, 91, 98, 99, 100, 102, 103, 104, 105, 108, 109, 110, 111, 112, 113, 114, 115, 116, 117, 118, 119, 121, 122, 123, 124, 125, 126, 128, 130, 131, 132, 133, 134, 135, 136, 138, 139, 144, 145, 146, 150, 151, 153, 157, 158, 159, 160, 163, 164, 165, 166, 168, 169, 171, 172, 174, 175, 176, 177, 178, 179, 180, 181, 182, 184, 185, 189, 192, 193, 195, 196, 197, 198, 199, 200, 201, 202,

203, 213, 215, 216, 217,
219, 220, 221, 222, 223,
225, 226, 228, 229, 230,
231, 232, 233, 234, 235,
236, 237, 239, 241, 242,
243, 244, 245, 247, 248,
249, 250, 251, 253, 263,
265, 267, 268, 270, 283,
284, 285, 286, 287, 288,
289, 290, 292, 293, 294,
295, 299, 300, 301, 302,
303, 304, 305, 306, 308,
309, 310, 311, 312, 313,
315, 316, 318, 319, 320,
321, 322, 323, 324, 325,
327, 328, 329, 333, 337
spiritual celebrity, 78, 114,
115, 116, 128
spiritual liberation, 17, 18
spiritual master, 42, 76, 100,
105, 136, 290, 294
spiritual practice, 19, 21, 39,
78, 102, 111, 113, 117,
121, 128, 132, 153, 164,
168, 170, 174, 175, 176,
197, 203, 225, 226, 233,
235, 283, 284, 290, 295,
299, 302, 304, 329
spiritual revolution, 23, 34,
53, 54, 109, 113, 267, 268,
287, 315
spiritual teacher, 3, 19, 44,
49, 63, 72, 99, 104, 110,
113, 115, 116, 117, 121,
181, 184, 192, 195, 219,
222, 229, 230, 232, 235,
236, 237, 239, 241, 251,
253, 263, 265, 293, 294,
303, 313, 325
spirituality, 18, 19, 20, 22,
24, 28, 31, 32, 36, 37, 39,
41, 52, 78, 89, 96, 98, 99,
100, 101, 102, 103, 106,
110, 111, 113, 115, 117,
121, 122, 133, 134, 138,
139, 144, 145, 150, 160,
168, 169, 175, 178, 192,
200, 201, 242, 244, 253,
255, 263, 269, 289, 290,
293, 295, 299, 301, 309,
316, 329
suffering, 48, 52, 77, 88, 123,
126, 195, 208, 209, 234,
235, 242, 250, 265, 274,
276, 306, 310
surrender, 82, 89, 123, 150,
160, 165, 168, 181, 189,
202, 205, 223, 226, 230,
238, 246, 259, 284, 290,
297, 299, 325
survival, 17, 18, 30, 34, 35,
102, 114, 122, 151, 162,
164, 187, 223, 227, 246,
260, 261, 277, 302

T

Tao, 84, 184
Thanatos, 74
therapy, 29, 31, 32, 33, 35,
74, 132, 153, 155, 182,
204, 222, 251, 252, 253,
255, 259, 260, 262, 272,
278
three *gunas*, 106, 107
time, 10, 19, 21, 22, 25, 28,
35, 37, 39, 46, 47, 52, 53,
56, 59, 61, 68, 70, 74, 76,
78, 80, 81, 82, 83, 84, 87,
89, 92, 94, 95, 96, 98, 102,
103, 104, 105, 106, 107,
113, 122, 126, 128, 133,
134, 137, 139, 140, 142,
144, 145, 147, 148, 150,
152, 154, 160, 162, 170,
171, 179, 181, 182, 191,
195, 197, 198, 200, 201,
206, 208, 209, 210, 216,

219, 221, 230, 237, 239,
241, 242, 243, 245, 246,
247, 249, 250, 252, 255,
257, 259, 260, 263, 264,
266, 267, 272, 274, 275,
276, 278, 283, 284, 285,
290, 295, 296, 297, 300,
301, 302, 307, 308, 309,
310, 311, 312, 316, 317,
319, 320, 322, 323, 324,
328, 329, 330, 332, 335,
336, 337
transcendence, 52, 82, 100,
101, 111, 115, 159, 165,
231, 242, 245, 292, 302,
316
transformation, 23, 28, 34,
58, 59, 60, 82, 89, 98, 105,
106, 150, 160, 164, 199,
201, 216, 226, 247, 256,
259, 264, 278, 319, 323,
325, 328, 329
transmission, 65, 104, 118,
132, 221, 325
truth, 17, 24, 26, 28, 33, 35,
36, 42, 48, 49, 51, 53, 60,
61, 65, 82, 86, 89, 100,
103, 110, 117, 118, 119,
121, 127, 132, 134, 135,
138, 139, 150, 165, 168,
169, 170, 171, 174, 184,
192, 200, 203, 204, 220,
222, 223, 226, 227, 228,
229, 230, 231, 232, 233,
234, 238, 247, 251, 268,
272, 276, 280, 295, 303,
304, 328
Truth, 24, 61, 68, 84, 85, 87,
89, 114, 178, 183, 184,
186, 189, 192, 202, 203,
219, 220, 221, 225, 227,
228, 230, 231, 232, 245,
284, 290, 296, 297, 299,
300, 304, 307, 308, 316,
318, 323

U

Upanishads, 31, 158, 248,
338

W

wealth, 63, 76, 90, 91, 92,
106, 270, 277, 278, 311
wholeness, 38, 86, 157, 158,
199, 241, 247, 281, 321,
328
wisdom, 17, 18, 19, 28, 36,
37, 39, 44, 53, 55, 56, 58,
61, 63, 65, 66, 68, 91, 101,
102, 115, 118, 131, 141,
158, 160, 164, 175, 199,
200, 206, 215, 236, 258,
265, 268, 275, 283, 285,
294, 295, 297, 303, 308,
320, 322, 325, 326, 328

Y

Your Essential Self, 21, 163,
174, 198, 246, 338

Z

Zen, 63, 66, 90, 139, 146,
184, 197, 283, 294, 313,
338